BERMONDSEY

ITS HISTORIC MEMORIES

AND ASSOCIATIONS

BY

EDWARD T. CLARKE

The cover shows Remains of Bermondsey Abbey
from the churchyard of St. Magdalen, looking southwards

Bermondsey, Its Historic Memories and Associations,
first published in 1900,
is here republished by Michael Wood and FamLoc

FL

A FamLoc Book
Available in Print and eBook Format

Originally published 1900
This FamLoc Edition first published 2015
Copyright © 2015 Michael Wood
All rights reserved.

ISBN-13: 978-1514191194
ISBN-10: 1514191199

CONTENTS

LIST OF ILLUSTRATIONS   Page vii

ORIGINAL 1900 PREFACE   Page ix

PREFACE TO FAMLOC EDITION   Page xi

MONASTIC BERMONDSEY

CHAPTER I   Page 1
Ancient Bermondsey - Remarkable events and famous residents - The Monastery - Power and dignity of the Priors and Abbots

CHAPTER II   Page 9
The Benedictines - Character of mediaeval monasticism - Bermondsey in Domesday Book - Foundation of the Monastery - Arrival of the French monks - Petreius, the first Prior of Bermondsey

CHAPTER III   Page 23
The Cluniacs - Growing importance of the Monastery - Death of Robert of Mortain, Earl of Cornwall - Earl William - The "Rood of Grace" - Dream of Henry the First - The Earl of Mortain becomes a monk of Bermondsey

CHAPTER IV   Page 44
The early Norman Kings and Bermondsey - Bounty of King Stephen - Henry the Second - Prior Henry Swansey - King John - St. Thomas's Hospital - The Monastic School

CHAPTER V   Page 63
Henry the Third - The Crusaders - Edward the First - Sequestration of the Priory by Edward the Second - Attack on the Alien Priories under Edward the Third - The King appoints the first English Prior - Richard the Second - Naturalization of the Priory, and erection into an Abbey

CHAPTER VI   Page 77
The Abbey of St. Saviour - Critical circumstances of the time - Thomas Thetford, third Abbot - His suit against the King - The Monastery under his sway - Avocations of the monks - The Abbey Church

CHAPTER VII   Page 91
Abbot John Bromleigh - Guardian of Katherine of Valois - Compilation of the "Annales de Bermundeseia"

CHAPTER VIII   Page 106
Abbot John de Marlow - Officiates at the funeral of Edward the Fourth, and entertains Elizabeth Woodville - His "indenture" with Henry the Seventh - Robert Wharton or Parfew, last Abbot of Bermondsey - Becomes Bishop of St. Asaph, subsequently of Hereford - Surrender and dissolution of the Monastery

BERMONDSEY HOUSE AND ITS OCCUPANTS

CHAPTER IX   Page 120
The "New Men" of the Tudor regime - Sir Thomas Pope a type of these - His early success - Favour of Henry the Eighth and Sir Thomas More - Clerk of the Briefs in the Star Chamber - Clerk of the Crown - Warden of the Mint - Knighted, and made Privy Councillor - Treasurer of the Court of Augmentations - His share of the monastic spoils - He builds Bermondsey House, and founds Trinity College, Oxford - Guardian of the Princess Elizabeth at Hatfield House - His death

CHAPTER X   Page 140
The Ratcliffes, Earls of Sussex - Earl Henry protects the Princess Elizabeth - Earl Thomas - His devotion to Elizabeth - Appointed Viceroy of Ireland - His difficulties and contest with Shane O'Neill - The Earl urges the marriage of the Queen - Disputes with Leicester - Embassy to Vienna - Lord Sussex makes Bermondsey House his town residence - The Northern rebellion - Sussex invades Scotland - Visit of Queen Elizabeth to Bermondsey House - Death and character of the Earl

MODERN BERMONDSEY

CHAPTER XI   Page 167
Growth of Bermondsey - Leather industry - The seventeenth century - A Cromwellian legend - Pepys - St. Mary Magdalen's Church and the Rectors of Bermondsey - Jamaica Row Chapel and James Janeway - Townsend, Mason, Watson, and the Deaf and Dumb School - Bacon's Free School - Bermondsey Spa - Curtis's botanic garden - Joanna Southcott - Loyal Bermondsey Volunteers - Mr. G. W. Phillips, the historian of Bermondsey, and Mr. Garland Phillips, the Missionary Martyr of Tierra del Fuego

CHAPTER XII   Page 210
Manufacturing Bermondsey - Eminent representatives of the leather trade - Churches, schools, and public institutions - The new Municipality - Importance of cultivating local history

NOTES TO TEXT   Page 236

Edward T. Clarke

LIST OF ILLUSTRATIONS

Remains of Bermondsey Abbey
Bermondsey Abbey
A window in The Gateway
Ancient Window (Bermondsey Abbey)
Head of King John, near The Gateway
Bermondsey Priory, A.D. 1300
Saxon ornaments in the Great Wall, near The Churchyard
Apiary in The Conventual Garden
North Gate, Bermondsey Abbey, taken down in 1805
Remains of Conventual Buildings, demolished in 1805
North Gate-House, from the west
West Gate of Bermondsey Abbey, existing in 1777
Saxon, Norman, and Renaissance remains, piled up in Riley's Park
Facsimile of Indenture, bearing The Great Seal of Bermondsey Abbey
Saxon Cross fixed in the wall adjoining the North Gate
Sir Thomas Pope
Inside one of the rooms under the Hall, Bermondsey House
Outside the Hall
Portion of Hall, Bermondsey House
Inside a room adjoining those under the Hall, Bermondsey House
Thomas Ratcliffe, Earl of Sussex
A ground-plan of Bermondsey Abbey
Jamaica House, from Cherry Garden Street
Jamaica House, garden front
St. Mary Magdalen's, Bermondsey, west front, 1841
St. Mary Magdalen's, 1804
Ancient wall on the east of St. Mary Magdalen's, exhibiting masons' and other marks
St. Mary Magdalen's, from the east, 1810
Jacob's Island
Plan of Jacob's Island and waterside district
Ancient houses in Long Walk
St. James's Church, Bermondsey, 1829

Old toll-house and bridge in Upper Grange Road, 1820
Old stone-fronted house in Grange Walk
Leather Exchange, Bermondsey
Colonel Bevington, J.P.
R. V. Barrow, Esq., late M.P. for Bermondsey
A. Lafone, Esq., M.P.
St. Olave's Grammar School
The Town Hall, Spa Road, Bermondsey
The Free Library
St. Mary's Church, Rotherhithe

PREFACE

Although, in the present day, apparently a prosaic region, and gradually losing more and more of that local colouring which once invested it, it is possible that few districts of London, save Westminster and the City, possess more interesting memorials than Bermondsey, or are surrounded with associations of a more remarkable character.

There is something pathetic in the present aspect of that spot which was once the site of a Royal Palace and a famous Abbey, and around which there still linger traditions of chivalry and romance, of learning and sanctity. Bermondsey Square was once the great court of the Monastery, surrounded on all sides by the conventual buildings.

On its eastern side, a portion of what is now known as Long Walk, and the ground between that passage and Grange Walk on the south, was occupied by the Palace, dating from the time of the last Saxon Kings, which, under the Norman and early Plantagenet Sovereigns, was frequently used as a Royal residence.

Viewing this spot in its desolation and decay, and reflecting upon its ancient glories, one is involuntarily reminded of Byron's lines on Venice, and tempted to quote them with a slight alteration:

"Her long array
Of mighty shadows, whose dim forms despond,
Above the lordless Abbeys vanished sway."

The fact that the "Annals of Bermondsey," "Annales Monasterii de Bermundeseia," compiled by a monk of the fifteenth century, are preserved in the British Museum, amongst the Harleian manuscripts is a distinction in itself. These "Annals" are now included in the Rolls Publications, and a copy will be found in the Bermondsey Public Library.

The story of William of Mortain, Earl of Cornwall, who, after defying all the power of Henry the First, died a monk of Bermondsey, is one of the most striking episodes of the Norman era. The favour of the Kings, the bounty of the many noble benefactors who lavished gifts upon the Monastery, the illustrious personages who paid their devotions in the Abbey Church, all contribute to enhance the interest of this subject.

After the fall of the Monastery, a stately mansion was built on a portion of its site by Sir Thomas Pope, which was called Bermondsey

House, and which at a later period became the residence of the famous Earl of Sussex.

Although the persons and events mentioned in the earlier portion of the narrative are intimately connected with the history of England, the period embraced by Part I, "Monastic Bermondsey" and Section I of the succeeding part, "Bermondsey House and its Occupants" does not exhaust the interest attaching to Bermondsey. Many circumstances recorded in Section II "Modern Bermondsey" possess permanent interest. Even the history of the ancient parish Church of St. Mary Magdalen is, in itself, illustrative of the ecclesiastical history of England.

As a great centre of manufacturing industry, Bermondsey presents features of special interest to all who are concerned in the commercial prosperity of the country. New importance was conferred upon it by its erection into a Parliamentary borough, and it has now attained a commanding position as the seat of one of the greatest Municipalities of South London.

The portion of this book dealing with the Middle Ages is based upon the monastic "Annals," illustrated by references to other mediaeval chroniclers, and works comprising that period of English history, especially Dugdale, and supplemented by details drawn from the invaluable works of local antiquaries, Mr. G. W. Phillips, Dr. Rendle, and Mrs. Boger.

The writer desires to express his gratitude for the great assistance rendered by the esteemed Librarian, Mr. John Frowde, to whose remarkable attainments the following Resolution of the Library Committee, approved by the Vestry, bears a striking testimony:

> December 11, 1899. - Your Committee note with satisfaction the value of the 'Local Collection' of books in the Library, as shown at the recent Inquiry at the Town Hall respecting the boundaries and name of the new borough, and desire to place on record the public acknowledgments of Counsel - Mr. Wheeler, Q.C., at the Bermondsey Inquiry, and Mr. H. C. Richards, Q.C., M.P., at the Newington Inquiry - of the services rendered by Mr. Frowde in supplying them with historical information.

E.T.C.
October, 1900.

PREFACE TO FAMLOC EDITION

This FamLoc Edition of *Bermondsey: Its Historic Memories and Associations* is a republication of Edward T. Clarke's 1900 original.

There have been the inevitable changes to format and punctuation, especially regarding the quotations, but the prose has been faithfully retained, other than changes to one or two typographical errors and the very few instances where clarity was required. Most of the footnotes of the original related to quotation sources, and have been appended to the relevant quote in this edition. The only explanatory footnote has been incorporated into the new *Notes to Text* chapter at the end of the book, along with two FamLoc notes. The annoted text is underlined.

Bermondsey, its Historic Memories and Association has much information on Bermondsey Abbey, Bermondsey House, Queen Elizabeth, and men of influence, but it must be said it has little or no social history. That said, it is a valuable introduction to the history of Bermondsey.

For most of its history Bermondsey lay in the county of Surrey. In 1889 it became part of the expanding County of London. In 1900, along with Rotherhithe and a small part of Deptford, it became the Metropolitan Borough of Bermondsey. In 1965 the borough became part of the London Borough of Southwark, although the district of Bermondsey still exists.

Some antiquated words and contractions used in *Bermondsey, its Historic Memories and Association*:
Viz was used for "namely", "that is to say", and "as follows".
&c. is an older form of "etc."
Esq. is a contraction of Esquire, much used until fairly recently as a polite title appended to a man's name in the absence of any other title. Originally, it denoted a member of the English gentry ranking

below a knight.

Currency: There were twenty shillings (s.) to the Pound, and 12 pence (d.) to the shilling.

FamLoc Website
Those wishing to discover more about the local history and family history of Bermondsey can visit

www.famloc.co.uk

 - and navigate to the relevant Town or Location from the menu, where additional information on the topics included in this book can be can be found, uploaded and exchanged, and debate entered into.

Finally, we would like to give our thanks to Edward T. Clarke, without whom much of the history of Bermondsey would have been very difficult to collate, or indeed have been lost.

Michael Wood, FamLoc, 2015.

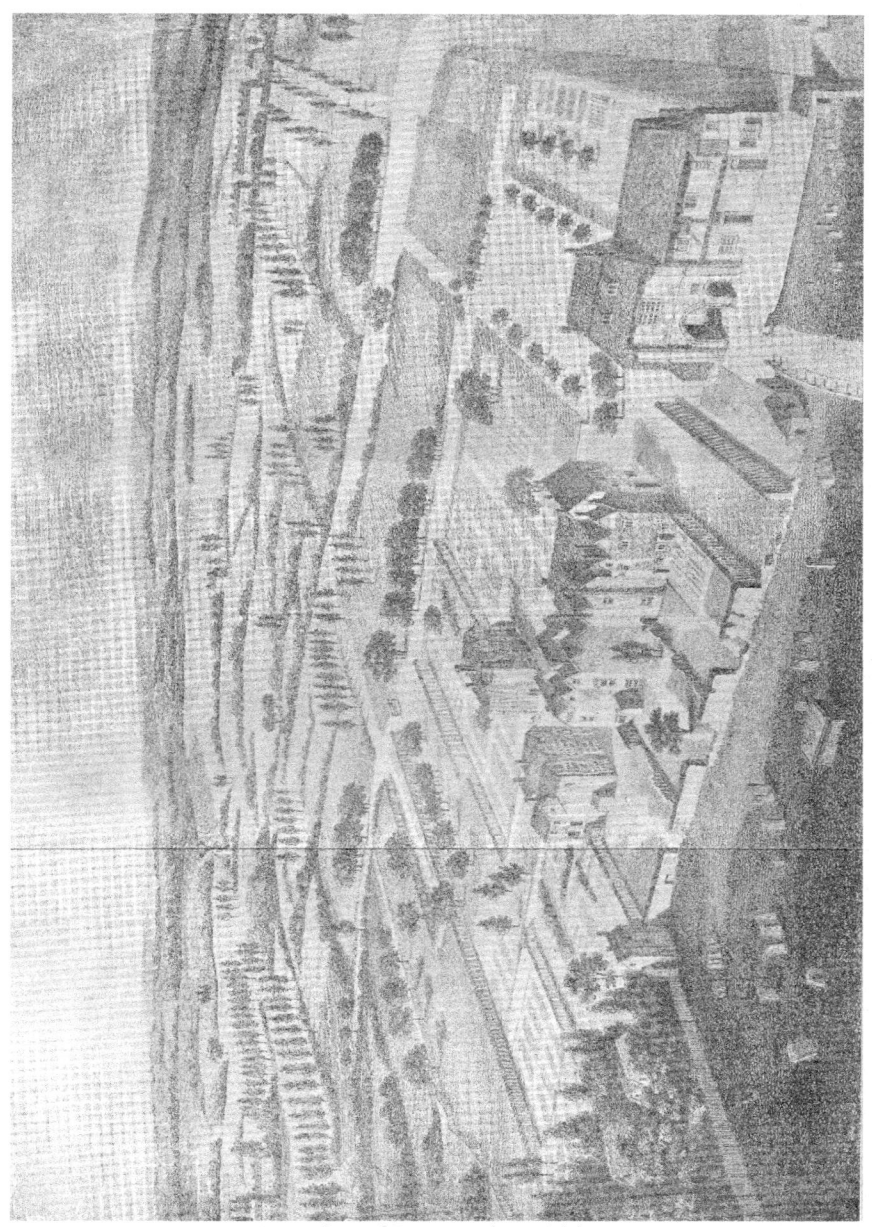

Remains of Bermondsey Abbey
From the Churchyard of St. Mary Magdalen, looking southwards

Edward T. Clarke

CHAPTER I

ANCIENT BERMONDSEY - REMARKABLE EVENTS AND FAMOUS RESIDENTS - THE MONASTERY - POWER AND DIGNITY OF THE PRIORS AND ABBOTS

The pedestrian passing down Tooley Street from London Bridge will speedily reach the entrance to a narrow and crowded thoroughfare, lined with warehouses and shops, once forming the main approach to the Manor of Bermondsey. As "Saint Olave's" Street has, by the ignorant colloquialism of successive generations, been corrupted into "Tooley Street," it is not surprising that the names both of this venerable suburb and its principal thoroughfare should have undergone many transformations: "Beormund's Ey," "Bermundeseye," "Barmsey," even "Barmese," which latter style may possibly have originated with the French monks, to whom their Prior, known to the outer world of Southwark as the "Lord of Barmsey," would have been "Le Seigneur de Barmese." In ancient times Bermondsey Street was known as Barmsie or Barnabie Street, or, as some have said, "Lane," and even in a map of the last century figures as "Barnaby Street." With all its varied appellations, however, it remains one of the most ancient thoroughfares in London, once, no doubt, a mere rural lane leading from the neighbourhood of the river to the Saxon Palace. As in remote times Bermondsey was a portion of the great Southwark Marsh, it is possible that the "Lane" may have been originally a causeway parting the swampy levels on either hand, and providing means of access to the farms which had arisen on the reclaimed ground. Although it is in the pages of Domesday Book that Bermondsey first emerges into the light of history, the reclamation of the land took place in the Saxon times, and the name must have originated at the same period. Its derivation is variously accounted for. Tradition ascribes it to a mysterious Saxon named Beormund, supposed to have been the original proprietor; but this is by some considered mythical, and in a History of Bermondsey published in 1841 by Mr. Phillips, an old resident in the parish, another explanation is offered:

> In the Saxon language beor signifies a nobleman or prince, and mund, peace or security; and when to these is added the termination ea, water, the word 'Bermondsey' may signify the Prince's defence by the river.

This is ingenious, and might be defended on other grounds; but although the utter absence of all contemporary records renders it impossible to affirm positively that such a person as Beormund actually existed, we are inclined to believe that he was not a myth.

We cannot wonder at the obscurity which overhangs the Saxon period, when we know that the century prior to the Norman invasion witnessed the fiercest ravages of the Danes. When Sweyn delivered his ineffectual assault on the City, defended by the strength of its walls and the valour of its sturdy burgesses, though he was repulsed from the north, the hapless dwellers on the southern bank lay defenceless, exposed to all the vindictive fury of his followers. If that had been the period of Beormund's existence, no doubt he and his men were ruthlessly slaughtered, their crops destroyed, their cattle driven off, and their dwellings plundered and burnt. Nothing could have saved them from such a fate, and, as has happened in cases of similar devastation, although the name may have been preserved, no record of the people has been handed down. The bones of the slaughtered husbandmen reposed beneath the ashes of their huts; those who, when peace was restored, came to clear the ground, and to till it anew, were strangers, who naturally desired, not merely to efface the traces, but even the memory, of the catastrophe, hoping only better luck for themselves.

Yet the misty Beormund does not loom more phantom-like in the obscurity of the Past than the subsequent lords of the soil, though many of them were among the greatest in the land. The changes which have occurred in modern times are so complete and absolute that it is difficult indeed for the present generation of residents to realize what Bermondsey was during the Middle Ages.

Who that now walks down Bermondsey Street could form any conception of the scenes which that ancient thoroughfare has witnessed, the passage of royal processions, the progress of mediaeval Knights and Barons on their way to Parliaments that have been held in the abbey, the sumptuous funerals of great personages? Crusaders have passed along Bermondsey Street on their way to the abbey, where they were about to hold solemn council with reference to the preparations for their journey to the Holy Land. It was down Bermondsey Street that, in the beginning of Queen Mary's reign, Sir Thomas Wyatt led his insurrectionary forces to the attack on the City.

All readers of Sir Walter Scott's novel of "Kenilworth" will remember those striking chapters in which the visit of Queen Elizabeth to her loyal soldier and devoted servant, the Earl of Sussex, at Say's Court, near Deptford, is described, and the romantic incidents connected with the young Walter Raleigh, then one of the gentlemen of that lord's household. But few are aware that this famous Earl lived and died in Bermondsey House, built on the site of the ancient monastery, facing Bermondsey Street.

Bermondsey Abbey

The original importance of Bermondsey arose from the fact of its being a royal manor, and an occasional residence of the Sovereigns; and subsequently it became famous as the site of one of the greatest monastic foundations in London, the once-renowned Abbey of St. Saviour. A singular fatality seems to have attended the fortunes of this abbey. Few of the dissolved monasteries, and, we should think, none of equal dignity and importance, have left so few traces in the memory of men, or so completely, as a great writer has said, "dropped out of history." This may, to some extent, be owing to the transference of the name to another foundation. Everyone is familiar with the church near London Bridge which, in former times, was known as St. Mary Overy's, and which did not receive its present appellation until after the dissolution of this monastery. But although St. Saviour's in the Borough is a structure of which Londoners are justly proud, and possesses a remarkable history, there are circumstances connected with our long-vanished abbey which invest it with even greater interest.

Sir Walter Besant has declared that the Abbey of St. Saviour, Bermondsey, was "the Westminster of South London," second only in rank and distinction to the great historic fane on the northern bank. It possessed a shrine the fame of which had spread to distant counties, and which was visited by pilgrims from all quarters. In the conventual church persons of the highest rank were interred: William, Earl of Mortain and Cornwall, nephew of the Norman Conqueror; Mary, daughter of Malcolm the Third, King of Scotland, sister of the consort of Henry the First, and mother of Stephen's Queen; Adeliza de Grantmesnil, wife of Hugh, Seneschal of England; Lady Audley, mother of the leader of the Cornish rebels; Margaret de la Pole, Countess of Suffolk; besides Knights and others of high degree.

Parliaments have been held in the abbey, Councils deliberated on great affairs of State, judges held their courts within its precincts. Princes of the blood and Princes of the Church have lodged in the monastery. Dowager-Queens found in it a last resting-place during life. Yet all this has fallen into oblivion.

The monastery was founded A.D. 1082, and continued as a priory until 1399, when, at the request of Richard the Second, Pope Boniface the Ninth erected it into an abbey. In the present day a

Bishop is far less dignified and imposing than one of the ancient Abbots of Bermondsey. The Abbot, by virtue of his functions, was one of the most eminent personages in London. He was the supreme ruler in his own domain. His Manor of Bermondsey, and the outlying possessions of the abbey in distant shires, were exempt from royal jurisdiction. He was invested with the privileges of a great feudal Baron; he figured in State pageants and public ceremonies. In that gorgeous pageant of the coronation of Anne Boleyn, possibly the most magnificent which the ancient city of London ever witnessed, the Abbot of Bermondsey would not have been the least conspicuous figure amongst those who, wearing mitres and arrayed in rich vestments, rode immediately after the Knights of the Bath, nor his voice the least imposing in that august choir of prelates by whom the psalm was uplifted in the open space before Westminster Abbey.

The high position and the influence enjoyed to the very last by such personages in evidenced by Froude, who tells us in his "History" that the dissolution of the monasteries was viewed with great displeasure by a large body of the laity, because the Abbots were the personal friends of the nobility and gentry, the trustees of their property, and the guardians of their children, and the monks acted in the capacity of family tutors. Their grave character and the importance of their functions invested them with peculiar responsibility; title-deeds and valuable documents were entrusted to their care, as they now are to that of lawyers and bankers.

No better illustration of this spiritual dignity could be afforded than that contained in the description of a writer on "Henry the Eighth and the English Monasteries":

> Abbots formed the bulk of the spiritual peerage, which in those times was both individually more influential and corporately much larger than at present. The position held by them throughout every part of the country gave yet a further weight to their great position as noblemen and local magnates. As such they went pari passu with Baron or Earl of the noblest lineage. On the blazoned Roll of the Lords, the Lord Richard Whiting and the Lord Hugh Farringdon went hand-in-hand with a Howard and a Talbot. This individual ennoblement, indicated by the form of title, is striking. Whiting and Farringdon do not walk merely as the Abbot of Glaston and the Abbot of Reading, but in the Roll of English Peers they still hold

the name by which they were known when playing as children in the country manor- house or poor man's cottage. In the letter-books of Durham Priory, the chiefs of the Cliffords and the Nevilles address the Prior as their equal, in no mere words of empty form. If, on occasion, the layman strikes a higher tone, to which the monk responds in gentleness, it does not affect the ring of trusty and sincere friendship which is caught throughout the entire correspondence. Nor is there anything surprising in this, when the character of the monastic life is realized. The monk of Durham, from his earliest years, combined simplicity of life with surroundings of palatial grandeur, and a state and ceremony equal to that of Courts, and yet more measured. As time passed on, he grew from obedience to command, and naturally, without perceiving it, the peasant's son became the equal of the peer. And all this was done without appeal to principles of democratic levelling.

In some cases the Priors and Abbots of Bermondsey began their career as monks of the same foundation, and, with faculties trained by discipline and study, and experience gained in the fulfilment of conventual offices, they "grew from obedience to command." They were learned men, deep in patristic theology, versed in the revived classic lore, familiar with legal subtleties and refinements, acute logicians, accustomed to the discussion of great questions, both ecclesiastical and political. Their familiarity with persons of the highest rank made them courtly men, and fitted them for the discharge of functions of the utmost delicacy and importance.

John Bromleigh and John de Marlow, to whose guardianship Queens were confided, must have been known as men specially qualified for such a position, possessing that suavity and dignity which would render them agreeable to their royal guests, together with the tact and firmness requisite, in such troublous times, to avoid the pitfalls of intrigue and to maintain the integrity of their trust.

That the Priors and Abbots of Bermondsey were frequently men above the average is proved by the fact that many of them went forth to assume higher dignities and fill more exalted positions, becoming Abbots of even greater foundations, such as Glastonbury, Bishops of Worcester, Hereford, and other sees.

To support this great dignity, the abbey was endowed with

ample possessions: the Manor of Bermondsey was but a portion of the estates which owned the Abbot as lord. Manors in Kent, Surrey, Essex, Hertfordshire, Somerset, were among the grants bestowed upon the monastery at different periods, together with considerable portions of what are now the suburbs of London, parts of Camberwell, Balham, Dulwich, Deptford, and Greenwich. The Old Manor-house, or "Hall Court," at Dulwich is said to have been, until the Dissolution, the summer retreat of the Abbots of Bermondsey. Tithe and rent-charges in many parishes, both in city and country, aided to swell the revenues of the abbey.

The Priors and Abbots of Bermondsey enjoyed extensive patronage, having the presentation to many livings in London and in several of the Midland and Southern counties. In London they appointed the Rectors of St. Andrew's, Holborn, of St. George Botolph, Eastcheap, St. George's, Southwark, and St. Mary, Rotherhithe. The Priory of St. James at Derby was a "cell," or branch establishment, of the great Monastery of Bermondsey.

Heraldry lent its aid to enhance the dignity of these personages:

> The arms of the priory and abbey were borne two different ways: First, party purpale, azure, and gules, within a border argent. The same surcharged with a lion passant gardant, holding in his paw a pastoral staff erect, surmounted with a mitre. Or, within a border argent, semé of B for Bermondsey. This augmentation was probably given on the priory being advanced to an abbey.
> - Phillips' *History of Bermondsey*.

The monastery was dedicated to the Saviour, and the lion in these arms, according to the symbolism of the Middle Ages, was a type of Christ. In Hulme's "Symbolism in Christian Art" we find a passage illustrative of this quoted from "a quaint old manuscript of the twelfth century, written by Philip de Thaun":

> The lion signifies the Son of Mary. He is King of all people without any gainsay. He is powerful by nature over every creature, and fierce in appearance, and with fierce look. He will appear to the Jews when He shall judge them, because they made themselves guilty when they hanged Him on the Cross, and therefore they merited to have no King over them. The square breast shows

strength of the Deity. The shape which He has behind, of very slender make, shows humanity, which He had with the Deity. By the foot, which is cloven, is demonstration of God, Who will clasp the world and hold it in His fist.

So long a period has elapsed since the dissolution of the monasteries, the system of which they were conspicuous features has become so foreign to the life of England, that it is most difficult, living under our present conditions, to realize the time when "the stately monastery, with the good cheer in its refectory and the High Mass in its chapel," was one of the most prominent institutions in the land, when the surface of this island was dotted with convents and chantries, with abbeys and priories. Froude, the historian, says that to most of us the great men prior to the Reformation seem like beings of another world, with whom we have nothing in common.

But if we can carry our minds back to a period so remote and unfamiliar, if we can conceive the conditions under which men lived in the dark ages of English history, if we endeavour to understand the ideas which governed them, we shall be able to appreciate the essential services rendered by the ancient monks to civilization, as well as to literature, history, and even science, in times when they were the only depositaries of learning.

A Window in the Gateway

CHAPTER II

THE BENEDICTINES - CHARACTER OF MEDIAEVAL MONASTICISM - BERMONDSEY IN DOMESDAY BOOK - FOUNDATION OF THE MONASTERY - ARRIVAL OF THE FRENCH MONKS - PETREIUS, THE FIRST PRIOR OF BERMONDSEY

In the days of the Saxon Kings, the Order of St. Benedict had acquired great power and predominance in England, and included within its ranks some of the most illustrious names in early history. The famed Archbishop Dunstan, the Becket of his age, the imperious asserter of ecclesiastical claims, was a member of this fraternity. The Venerable Bede, earliest and most reliable of Saxon chroniclers, belonged to this Order. Benedictines, conspicuous for their talents and learning, had wrested great concessions from the Kings, and in troublous times had even dictated the policy of the State. Nor is this surprising when we consider the character of the Order and the high and varied talents by which it was adorned.

> For the space of 239 years the Benedictines governed the Church in the persons of forty-eight Popes, chosen from their Order, most prominent among whom was Gregory the Great, through whose means the rule was introduced into England. Four of these Pontiffs came from the original monastery of Monte Cassino, and three of them quitted the throne and resumed the monastic life - Constantine the Second, Christopher the First, and Gregory the Twelfth. Two hundred Cardinals had been monks in their cloisters; they produced 7,000 Archbishops, 15,000 Bishops - fifteen of whom took off their mitres, resumed their monk's frock, and died in seclusion - 15,000 Abbots, 4,000 Saints. They established in different countries altogether 37,000 monasteries, which sent out into the world upwards of 15,700 monks, all of whom attained distinction as authors or scientific inventors. Rabanus established the first school in Germany. Alcuin founded the University of Paris, where 30,000 students were educated at one time, and whence issued, to the honour of England, St. Thomas a Becket; Robert of Melun; Robert White, made Cardinal by Celestine the Second; Nicholas Breakspear, the only Englishman ever made Pope, who filled

the chair under the title of Adrian the Fourth; and John of Salisbury, whose writings give the best description of the learning both of the University and the times. Theodore and Adrian, two Benedictine monks, revived the University of Oxford, which Bede, another of the Order, considerably advanced. It was in the seclusion of a Benedictine monastery that the musical scale, or gamut, the very alphabet of the greatest refinement of modern life, was invented, and Guido d'Arezzo, who wrested this secret from the realms of sound, was the first to found a school of music. Sylvester invented the organ.
- Hill's *Monasticism in England*.

The severe training to which the monks of this Order were subjected is thus described by Dean Milman:

> Three virtues constituted the sum of the Benedictine discipline - silence with solitude and seclusion, humility, obedience, which, in the strong language of its laws, extended to impossibilities. All is thus concentrated on self. It was the man isolated from his kind who was to rise to a lonely perfection. All the social, all patriotic virtues were excluded. The mere mechanic observance of the rules of the Brotherhood, or even the corporate spirit, are hardly worthy of notice, though they were the only substitutes for the rejected and proscribed pursuits of active life.
> The three occupations of life were the worship of God, reading, and manual labour.
> For the Divine service the monks awoke at midnight; they retired again, and rose, after a brief repose, for matins. After matins they did not return to their beds, but spent their time in reading, meditation, and the singing of psalms. From prime to noon, and after the brief meal and another period of reading and meditation, was devoted to labour. At particular periods, as at harvest, the labouring brothers did not return home to their religious service; they knelt and performed it in the fields. The Mass was not celebrated on ordinary days, only on Sundays and holidays.
> - *History of Latin Christianity*.

Such a discipline as this would seem to ordinary minds severe enough in its demands on both the mental and physical powers, its denial of needful rest, its imposition of severe labours, its repudiation of natural affections and suppression of tender instincts. But fanaticism was prepared to go farther than this. Devotion and self-sacrifice - or shall we rather say ascetic pride and emulation? - imposed penances and inflicted penalties, the endurance of which would in modern eyes almost seem to deserve the crown of martyrdom. Thus, in process of time, other systems were grafted on the original foundation of St. Benedict, the most austere of which, for a considerable period, was the Cluniac, so called from having been established in the monastery of Cluny, in Burgundy.

Severe, however, as the monastic discipline was, it yet admitted some compensatory advantages. The life of the Benedictine monk was not one of idle contemplation. Instead of being a prey to listlessness and languor, the physical exertion he underwent, coupled with his spare diet, contributed to render his intellect clear and perspicacious. His self-concentration was not so absolute as to prevent the cultivation of habits of observation and reflection. As the essence of the system was that all the faculties of the monk should be employed for the greater glory of God, the Benedictine sedulously cultivated his artistic perceptions, and, adoring the Creator in His works, filled his mind with ideas of beauty. As the servant of God, he sought to diffuse the bounty which the Divine hand has scattered, to clothe a desolate spot with verdure, to convert a dreary waste into a smiling landscape. In his orchards his methods of cultivation and grafting improved the quality of the fruit; in his gardens he combined utility with beauty, cultivating plants of healing virtue as well as flowers of brilliant hue and delicate perfume. In the seclusion of the cloister, when not offering up his soul in prayer, he was "nurturing his mind with great thoughts," pondering on the words of sages and holy men of old, tracing with pen or chisel some image of beauty, some exquisitely symbolical fancy, or, it may be, composing some sweet melodious strain, fitted alike to charm the ear and to melt the heart.

The growth and popularity of the monastic system can excite no surprise when we reflect upon the conditions of life in that age, the barbarity, the ignorance, the grossness of idea, that prevailed. The pious found that to serve God in the world was indeed a matter of supreme difficulty, that seclusion was necessary, not merely in order to pursue their Divine contemplations, but to preserve their purity. The naturally refined and sensitive found in the monastery a refuge from the coarse and brutal association which daily and hourly jarred upon their feelings. The man of lofty and comprehensive views found in the monastery a sphere in which his intellectual powers could silently develop, in which he would be fitted for the prosecution of study and research; the man who combined spiritual with temporal ambition saw, in devotion to the monastic life, a means of elevating himself to a position of high command, of exercising authority in the State, aided by the power of that Church which then ruled over the consciences of men with unquestioned sway. Again, the hardships and privations of the monastic life, the penances and the severe discipline, did not then possess the terrors with which they would now be invested. In that age there was a physical hardihood, a dogged fortitude in the endurance of horrible sufferings, which would now seem almost incredible. The law prescribed mutilation as the punishment for many crimes; the spectacle of men who had undergone judicial maiming and torture was common in every-day life. Humanity, as now understood, had then no existence. Looking back from our present standpoint, the rulers, legislators, and judges of ancient times appear like so many demons, delighting in the infliction of torments. But this cruelty was often met with a spirit of defiance; the victim did not shrink with fearful apprehension from the impending stroke, but nerved himself to meet it with a stoical hardihood that, under other circumstances, would have been deemed heroism.

But although the actual privations and the stern monastic rules might not have appeared so dreadful in those days, it was the continued subjection to this discipline that constituted the great ordeal. The criminal might undergo his mutilation, his scourgings and imprisonments, but when his wounds had healed or his term had expired he might still find some means of living according to his will; but to many monks the cloister has been a scene of daily and hourly conflict. The man of strong passions, impetuous and self-willed, compelled to silence when his pent-up feelings struggled to relieve themselves in a torrent of speech; to self-repression when fierce impulses were throbbing in his veins, when energies, not to be subdued by fasting and maceration, were striving for outward manifestation; to these, and such as these, the conventual discipline must have been the most terrible of all ordeals. To the heedless and unthinking in the outer world, a cloister might seem an abode of peace, of serene and methodical discharge of stated duties; but who could tell what spiritual tragedies were there enacted? In many cases the influence of the system was not powerful enough to modify the original nature, and, as usually happens when men are gathered into communities, jealousies and heart-burnings would arise, breaches of discipline occur, and mutinous tendencies appear, requiring the utmost firmness and discretion on the part of the Superiors. But great was the praise of him who succeeded in bearing the burden of his cross, in acquiring those virtues which may have been foreign to his nature, in persevering, in spite of spiritual dejection, mental weariness, and physical suffering, in the thorny path which had been traced out for him.

And, although our ideas have changed, it is impossible not to regard the efforts of the early cænobites with tender and respectful sympathy. They were striving after a noble ideal. To wean themselves from all fleshly cravings, all carnal delights, to offer up the daily sacrifice of their human passions, their natural yearnings, to render themselves meet for the companionship of exalted spirits, to purify their minds and hearts that they might attain a clearer knowledge of Him who is the essence of purity, so to divest themselves of their earthly trammels that they might be drawn within the focus of His rays and absorbed in the effulgence of His glory, such were the objects which many of the mediaeval monks set before them and pursued with heroic steadfastness and constancy. From such we shall not withhold our praise.

When going forth into the world, they manifested no arrogant assumption of superiority, they exhibited lowliness and meekness, and strove to win the hearts of laymen by acts of beneficence and charity. Amidst the barbarism of the age, they offered a silent protest in favour of the claims of a Sovereign greater than all the mighty ones of the earth.

They were styled "regular," in contradistinction to the "secular" clergy. The secular priest, living amongst his parishioners, partaking of their festivities, and, although unable to form social ties, sharing to some extent in their joys and sorrows, might not be able to free himself from the leaven of worldliness. But the monk, living in a community apart from the world, severed from all secular interests, acknowledging no lay superior, was, by the very nature of his vocation, devoted in an exclusive and especial manner to the service of God and His saints. He was invested with the character of an apostle and the authority of a teacher, and so great were the services rendered to the Church and the world in the early days of Monasticism that, in time, when the fervour of piety had subsided, it was easy for ambitious and unscrupulous men to make the merits of their predecessors a stepping-stone to the acquisition of wealth and privileges, and a means of rendering the cowl of the monk a symbol of greater power than the coronet of the Earl or the mitre of the Bishop.

Their sphere of influence was not, in the Middle Ages, limited to any country. A monk distinguished for his zeal and talents might be selected to negotiate with foreign Sovereigns, to fill a Professor's chair in a foreign University, or, as a missionary, to carry the Cross into distant regions. St. Boniface, the Apostle of Germany, was an English Benedictine. Foreign monks followed in the train of the Norman Conqueror; an Italian Benedictine, Lanfranc of Pavia, became Archbishop of Canterbury; and many others were raised to high preferments. It was natural that William should desire to strengthen his throne by the support of men who had no Saxon leanings; but the incoming of foreign monks was even encouraged by native Englishmen, owing to a revival of religious fervour which marked the early period of the Norman rule. It may have been that, in their simple piety, the Anglo-Saxons regarded the misfortunes which had befallen their race and country as a Divine visitation, that they conceived God to have turned His face from them, and that they sought to propitiate His offended majesty by establishing religious foundations and employing the prayers of holy men from other climes.

Some such motives may have influenced Alwin Child, an eminent and wealthy citizen of London, in founding a monastery for Cluniac monks in Bermondsey, towards the close of the Conqueror's reign. Otherwise it would appear strange that he, a man of Saxon birth, should have set aside the claims of his own countrymen, and given the preference to foreigners. It is true that he had to consult, not merely his own predilections, but also the wishes of the King, for Bermondsey at this time was a royal demesne. In the eyes of William, a monastery filled with Saxon monks would have been likely to prove a hotbed of sedition, and to afford facilities for a dangerous propaganda.

As we have previously said, it is in the pages of Domesday Book that a description of Bermondsey first occurs. Another circumstance worthy of note is that the true signification of the word "Domesday" appears to have been first given in the "Annals of Bermondsey." Mr. W. de Gray Birch, F.S.A., in his learned and interesting account of Domesday Book, devotes a considerable space to the origin of the name, and says:

> The term 'Domesday' has been of some difficulty in respect of its signification. The Anglo-Saxon domas were 'laws,' or 'dooms'; and the 'Dom-boc' of King Alfred was, if it actually existed, a code of laws. . . The term 'Domesday' may, no doubt, owe something to the 'Dom-boc' for the construction of the name, but we must remember that it bears in its colophon the title of 'Description.' . . .
> Some see in the word 'Domesday' a metaphorical 'Dies Judicii,' or 'Judgment Day'; others, a 'Liber Judiciarius,' or 'Book of Judgments,' because it spares no one, as on the great Day of Judgment, and its decision must be final and without controversy.

But although Mr. Birch quotes the Chronicle of Bermondsey as one of the authorities for the date of Domesday Book, and also for the place of its deposit, he makes no allusion to the very distinct statement contained in our monastic annals.

The Monk of Bermondsey, after stating that the King appointed the Survey to be made in 1083, says, under head of the following year, that he directed the volume containing it to be deposited "in thesaurario, quod dicitur Domus Dei." Commenting on this passage, Stow tells us in his quaint language:

> The Boke of Bermondsey saith, this boke was laid up in the King's Treasury, which was in the Church of Winchester or Westminster, in a place called Domus Dei, or God's House; and so ye name of the boke, therefore called Domus Dei, and since, shortly, Domesday.

The following is the account of Bermondsey extracted from that venerable register:

> In Brixistan Hundred the King holds Bermundeseye. Earl Harold held it before. At that time it was rated at 13 hides, now at 12. The arable land is 8 carucates or plough-lands. There is one carucate in demesne, and 25 villani, and 33 bordarii, with 9 carucates. There is a new and

handsome Church. And 20 acres of meadow and woodland for 5 hogs in pasnage-time. In London are 13 burgesses at 44 pence. In the time of King Edward it was valued, as it now is also, at 15 pounds, and the Sheriff hath 20s. The Earl of Mortain holdeth 1 hide, which, in the time of King Edward and afterwards, was in this Manor.

The hundred of which Bermondsey then formed part, "Brixistan," or Brixton, is said to have derived its name from Brixi, a Saxon land-owner in the time of Edward the Confessor. The tenure by "Earl Harold," as the Conqueror, sternly resolved only to recognise the son of Godwin as a usurper, styles his luckless rival, of course means that Harold held it as Crown property during his brief reign. The carucate, or "plough's worth," that is, the area that one plough could till annually, is a word introduced by the Normans. Beamont tersely puts it that the hide was the ploughable land, the carucate that which was actually ploughed.

The "churls" (ceorls) of Edward and Harold had now become "villani," or "villeins regardant," cultivating lands held by them under the lord, and compelled to take their share in tilling his demesne. The "bordarii" formed a class less easily identified. Some had considered them as mere drudges, hewers of wood and drawers of water. Others suppose that they lived as "cottagers on the borders of a village or manor; but in some cases, at least, this cannot be correct, for they are found as dwelling near the 'aula,' or manor-house."

Mr. Hunt, in his work on "Norman Britain," says that the bordarii were men who before the Conquest had been known as "landless churls," and who now occupied dwellings assigned them by the steward, usually forming a cluster round the mansion or tower of the lord.

Phillips, in his "History of Bermondsey," says:

> The lands of the King must have run out considerably some way in having 20 acres of pastures and wood to fat 5 hogs in pasnage-time. This number of 5 would not be worth mentioning in the record, but that they seem to be the share of the lord, paid him yearly out of what the woods produced.

Mr. Birch says:

Woodland was always carefully estimated, because of the important item of beechmast and acorns, a food so indispensable among the Anglo-Saxons that Kentish lands not provided with it within the precincts of the estate conveyed by charter usually had 'dens, dænu, denbæro,' pig-feeding tracts of woodland, far away from the land itself, specially set apart and named as belonging to it. The right of feeding hogs was called pasnage, pannage, or pasnagium.

With reference to the "burgesses in London," Mr. Phillips says:

Thirteen burgage-tenements in London were also holden in this manor at the nominal rent of £11 . . . The reputed annual value of the manor (i.e., of the lordship), in Edward the Confessor's time, as well as at the time of the Survey, was £900 of our present money (1841), out of which the Sheriff was allowed 20s., i.e., £60 of our present currency, for collecting the rents and paying them into the Exchequer.

It will be observed that in the extract from Domesday Book there is no mention of any building except the church, to be presently referred to. In vol. i., p. 34, however, the following statement appears with reference to the Earl of Mortain, mentioned in the preceding extract: "The same Earl has in Bermondsey one hide of the King's land, on which his house (domus ejus) is situated."

This "house" was, of course, a tower or castellated mansion of the usual Norman style. The nobleman in question, whose proper style was Count of Mortain and Earl of Cornwall, was the younger brother of the famous Odo, Bishop of Bayeux, and therefore half-brother of the Conqueror. After the death of Duke Robert, Arletta, or Herleve (for her name is spelt both ways), mother of William, married the Lord of Conteville, in Normandy, by whom she had these two sons and a daughter, Muriel. The Conqueror, both before and after his accession to the English throne, showed great favour to these kinsmen, and bestowed upon the younger the important county of Mortain, in the Cotentin.

Of these brothers Odo possessed the greater talents, and combined within himself the qualities of the warrior, the prelate, and the statesman. But these high faculties were marred by overweening ambition, insatiable rapacity, selfishness, and cruelty. Robert, on the other hand, was loyal and chivalrous, and possessed some generous and affectionate qualities. His talents were chiefly military; he was a renowned warrior, and had displayed his prowess on many fields. At Hastings he had fought at the head of the chivalry of the Cotentin, the Norman province in which his county of Mortain was situated.

In 1069 Robert of Mortain was appointed by the Conqueror, together with the Count d'Eu, to cope with the Danes, who had landed in great force at the mouth of the Humber, and afterwards invested York. The invaders, however, retreated on the approach of the royal forces, and took shelter in the fens. The Norman leaders watched their opportunity, and, on the Danes accepting an invitation to festivities from the disaffected Saxons, attacked and defeated them with great slaughter, pursuing them to their ships. The services of Count Robert were rewarded by immense grants of land; the King created him Earl of Cornwall, and bestowed upon him no less than 793 manors in nineteen counties. As, in those days, the possession of lands granted by the Crown was accompanied with great power and privileges, it is easy to conceive the princely rank enjoyed by this illustrious Earl, who when in the neighbourhood of London resided at his tower in Bermondsey.

We also learn from other sources that a palace then existed, possibly built by Edward the Confessor, who would appear to have been the first royal owner of the Manor of Bermondsey. Leland was of opinion that other "good buildings" existed here before the foundation of the monastery, and it has been said that Alwin Child himself possessed a residence in Bermondsey.

The "new and handsome Church" mentioned in Domesday was evidently that recently built by Alwin Child, and dedicated to the Holy Saviour. Its vaults were destined soon to receive the first of a series of illustrious tenants. Amongst the personal friends and companions-in-arms of Earl Robert of Mortain was Hugh de Grantmesnil, who had also fought with distinction at Hastings, and was subsequently created Viscount (in the Norman sense) of Leicestershire, and Governor of Hampshire. He also received extensive grants of land, and was appointed, in conjunction with Fitz-Osbern and Odo, Bishop of Bayeux, one of the Regents during the absence of King William on the Continent. He also filled the high office of Seneschal of England. Hugh de Grantmesnil was a man of frank and loyal character, with a deep vein of piety underlying his soldierlike qualities. He was one of the founders of the Abbey of St. Evroult, in Normandy. In early life he had married a lady of great beauty, Adeliza, daughter of Ivo, Count of Beaumont-sur-l'Oise, who, dying in 1087, was buried in the Church of St. Saviour, Bermondsey.

As the monastery is stated to have been founded in 1082, it does not at first sight seem clear why seven years should have elapsed before it received any occupants, for we find no mention of monks until 1089. But when we reflect, not merely on the solid character of the structures, but also on the ideas which then influenced those engaged in their erection, we are inclined to believe that, although the foundation may have been laid in 1082, years were probably spent in the construction. All engaged in the building of a church or a monastery were imbued with the feeling that they were employed in a sacred work. From the architect down to the meanest labourer, all were conscious of the importance of their task. The sculptor who, with tender and loving hand, made the lifeless stone the medium for the embodiment of his glowing fancies was not more devoutly painstaking than the workman who lowered the stone into its course. Time was no object to them. Day by day, month by month, year by year, the work went on, slowly but steadily rising into completeness, until at length architects and artificers, masons and labourers, gathered to gaze with exultation on the stately edifice, feeling that the participation in such a work formed a landmark in the lives of all.

The brethren who were to form the nucleus of the new community were Cluniacs. These monks, in the words of Fuller, author of the "Church History," were "Benedictines sifted through a finer search, with some additional invented and imposed upon them by Odo, Abbot of Clugni, in Burgundy, who lived A.D. 913."

The Abbey of Clugni, or Cluny, which had become one of the most famous then existing, was governed at the period of the foundation of our monastery by an Abbot who held office for sixty years, and was subsequently canonized by the name of St. Hugh. Ranke, in his "History of the Popes," says that the position and authority of an Abbot of Cluny were similar to those of a Pope. The pious personage who was now the Head of this Order ruled over no less than 10,000 monks in the numerous "cells" or affiliated convents. Of these the most renowned was the Monastery of La Charité on the Loire, the government of which had been entrusted by Abbot Hugh to his Prior, Girard, who bore the reputation of a saint. Under this Prior, for there was no other Abbot in the Order save he of Cluny, there are said to have been 200 monks at La Charité, and out of this body four were selected to become the first occupants of the Monastery of Bermondsey.

It was in May, 1089, the second year of William Rufus, that these four monks of La Charité arrived in Bermondsey. They were named Petreius, Osbert, Richard, and Umbald. We can figure to ourselves these black-robed strangers from 'Beside the murmuring Loire,' with hollow faces and eyes preternaturally bright, bodies worn with fasting and vigils, but with the signs of a lofty and indomitable purpose manifest on their brows and in the lines of their countenances. We see them as they ascend some rising ground to survey the region in which their lot has been cast. The scene was different indeed to the vine-clad terraces of the Loire, yet the monks may have felt that "their lines had fallen in pleasant places." A green expanse of meadow and pasture lay before them, with cattle grazing and sheep browsing on the herbage; tiny streams, shaded here and there by willows and alders, flowed around, while, further off, some of greater volume supplied water-power to the mills. The cots of husbandmen and the huts of herdsmen and labourers dotted the expanse; woods bounded the horizon, forming a background to the tower of the great Norman lord, Robert, Earl of Mortain and Cornwall, which rose grimly in front of them, a symbol of haughty isolation and dominion. Long-haired churls were toiling in the fields; calls and exclamations in an uncouth and unfamiliar tongue smote upon the ears of the monks. Their eyes may have softened as they gazed upon these sons of the soil, amongst whom their lives were henceforth to be passed. Their experience of feudal tyranny enabled them to conceive the hardships of these men's lot, the exactions to which they were subject, the outrages to which they might be exposed from lawless men-at-arms. The "bordarius," the villein of lower grade, would be regarded as the legitimate victim of every arrogant oppressor. The scorn with which the lords often treated their luckless vassals was exaggerated by their retainers, and rendered more bitter by the malignity of subaltern insolence. Although the monks felt that they were intended to be a spiritual garrison, upholding the sway of the conquering race, still, the consciousness of their Divine mission inspired them with the idea that they were destined to furnish solace and relief to these sorely-tried toilers, and to mitigate the hardships of their lot.

"The monks," says Professor Thorold Rogers, "in the Middle Ages were the physicians, the students of Nature, the founders of schools, teachers of agriculture, fairly indulgent landlords, and advocates of genuine dealing towards the peasantry."

This indicates the lines they would have been likely to follow. Although it is said that the Cluniacs did not follow the field-labours of the Benedictines, yet, in directing the operations of their servants, the latter would have been impressed by their superior knowledge, and listened reverently to the instruction they imparted. The difference of language would have presented little difficulty; monks who were always prepared to go forth into distant lands accustomed themselves to the acquisition of foreign dialects. Nothing was so likely to gain the confidence of the churls as relief afforded to their bodily ailments, and the monk came amongst them as a "leech," learned in symptoms, cunning in herbal remedies, skilled in the rude surgery of the times, the healer at once of the body and the soul. In seasons of difficulty and distress they resorted to him, receiving his counsel as the voice of an oracle; on their beds of death they sought for him to smooth their passage to the grave. It is easy to conceive the immense influence which a being invested with such attributes and endowed with such powers must have acquired over the untutored minds of those by whom he was surrounded.

Men who were thus specially selected to be the first occupants of a new monastery always formed a chosen band. They would have been distinguished among the brethren of their own convent for piety, and for the possession of virtues that would not suffer by transplantation to a foreign soil. Their leader, Petreius, a man of extreme sanctity, was consecrated Prior of Bermondsey by the Superior of his Convent of La Charité, and his subsequent career justified the choice which had been made. The position of the new Prior was no obscure one. Established in the midst of a royal demesne, he was brought into direct communication with the King and the members of the royal family and household. His advice and spiritual consolation were sought by the noble and the wealthy. The number of the monks would have rapidly increased, and among the novices youths of distinguished race would, no doubt, be found.

Setting his brethren an example of purity of life and of obedience to the monastic rules, fervent in prayer, foremost in works of beneficence and charity, the light of Petreius shone before men with all the lustre of the Apostolic virtues. At the period of his arrival there was ample room for the exercise of these pacific qualities. The fermentation caused by the events of the preceding year had scarcely subsided. It was not long since the turbulent Bishop Odo, finding a new justiciary appointed in his stead, entered into a conspiracy to depose Rufus in favour of his elder brother, Robert, Duke of Normandy. Sympathy for the claims of that Prince was strong amongst the Norman lords, many of whom thought that he had been unjustly set aside, and amongst those who joined in an attempt to place him on the throne were Robert of Mortain and Hugh de Grantmesnil. Earl Robert defended Pevensey Castle against the King, but ultimately both he and his friend De Grantmesnil made their submission, and were received into favour. William Rufus, who was politically sagacious, knew that he could rely on the honour of these Barons, both of whom afterwards rendered him eminent services; but Odo was banished without hope of recall.

CHAPTER III

THE CLUNIACS - GROWING IMPORTANCE OF THE MONASTERY - DEATH OF ROBERT OF MORTAIN, EARL OF CORNWALL - EARL WILLIAM - THE "ROOD OF GRACE" - DREAM OF HENRY THE FIRST - THE EARL OF MORTAIN BECOMES A MONK OF BERMONDSEY

Following the course of all human institutions, many of the Benedictine monasteries had deteriorated from the austere virtues which had once distinguished them, illustrating the impossibility of binding men down in perpetuity to the maintenance of hard and fast rules. But in those days there was so much vigour and vitality in the monastic system that any abuses which crept into its practice were not regarded as furnishing reasons for its abolition. Just as the political reformers of 1830 believed that their mission was not to destroy, but to purify the Constitution, so the zealots of the Middle Ages held that reformation of the monastic rules and strict enforcement of a salutary discipline would suffice to avert danger from their cherished institution. "Reform, that you may preserve" became their watchword.

The Order, or Cluniac branch of the Benedictines, was distinguished by stricter observation of silence, greater abstemiousness, more frequent performance of Masses, and extraordinary care in the preparation of the Eucharist. Increased solemnity, more awful mystery, invested every service. Twice daily, in their conventual churches, a solemn Mass was performed, at which two Hosts were offered. The strange doctrine of Transubstantiation, the conversion of the consecrated bread into the body of Christ, the Divine virtue imparted to the elements, was held, in all its mystical significance, by these austere monks. The bread of life, partaken of by the worshipper, was believed to infuse a portion of the Divine essence into his being, to nourish his soul, to impart to him extraordinary powers of resistance. It is not, therefore, surprising that such ceremonies as the following should have been used in the preparation of the Host:

They first chose the wheat grain by grain, and washed it very carefully. Being put into a bag, appointed only for that use, a servant, known to be a just man, carried it to the mill, washed the grindstones, covered them with curtains above and below, and, having put on himself an alb, covered his face with a veil, nothing but his eyes appearing. The same precaution was used with regard to the meal. It was not bolted until it had been well washed; and the warden of the church, if he were either priest or deacon, finished the rest, being assisted by two other religious men, who were in the same Orders, and by a lay brother, particularly appointed for the business. These four monks, when matins were ended, washed their faces and hands; the three first of them did put on albs; one of them washed the meal with pure clean water, and the other two baked the Hosts in the iron moulds, so great was the veneration and respect the monks of Cluny paid to the Holy Eucharist.

The greater part of the Saxon monasteries had been Benedictine, and it was not until after the Conquest that any Cluniac houses were founded in England.

William de Warenne, a Norman favourite of the Conqueror, who gave him his daughter Gundred in marriage, creating him an Earl, and bestowing 300 manors upon him, took a journey to Rome in 1077, accompanied by his wife, and, stopping on their way at the Abbey of Cluny, were most hospitably entertained by the monks. In pursuance of their intention to found a religious house for the welfare of their souls, they resolved, out of gratitude for this hospitality, that it should be a monastery of the Cluniac Order. With the assent of King William, the Earl and Countess applied to the Abbot, who sent over four of his monks, the principal of whom, named Lanzo, became the first Prior of the Monastery of St. Pancras at Lewes, which was founded and endowed by the Earl. Many other Cluniac houses besides those of Lewes and Bermondsey arose within the early Norman period, of which the Prior of Lewes became the chief, exercising the delegated authority of the Head of the Order. In time, when the Prior came up to attend Parliament, or to transact business in London, a residence was provided for him in Tooley Street, a lordly mansion nearly opposite St. Olave's Church.

The noble family just mentioned did not neglect Bermondsey, for Richard Guett, described as the brother of the Countess of Warenne, bestowed the Manor of Cowyk, or Quickbury, on the monks of this priory. Nor had Alwin Child withdrawn his fostering care. In addition to bestowing rents in the city of London on the monastery, he stimulated other persons of wealth and distinction to enrich it with grants of manors and churches. The King, William Rufus, although an open scoffer at religion, and, in general, dealing in the most unscrupulous manner with Church property, retaining for his own use the revenues of vacant abbeys and benefices, yet made the monks of Bermondsey the recipients of his bounty, surrendering his property in the manor to them. His Chancellor also, Robert Bluet, Bishop of Lincoln, conferred upon the priory the Manor of Charlton in Kent. In 1093, "by concession of Geoffrey de Mandeville," the monks received the estate of Hallingbury in Essex. This noble Norman, who had rendered great services at Hastings, was rewarded by extensive grants of land in Essex, the earldom of which was subsequently conferred upon his grandson. Geoffrey de Mandeville was also the first Constable of the Tower.

The sequestered situation of the Monastery of Bermondsey, standing as it did at some distance from the main lines of route, was counterbalanced by circumstances that operated in its favour. It stood in the midst of a royal demesne, in the immediate vicinity of a royal palace, and of a residence belonging to one of the greatest nobles in the land. It would have received visits from the Earl of Warenne, so strongly interested in the flourishing condition of Cluniac houses. The gallant Hugh de Grantmesnil would dismount at the priory gate, reverently enter the church, and, kneeling by the tomb in which the remains of his beauteous and beloved Adeliza were deposited, offer up a silent prayer for the repose of her soul. The great Earl of Cornwall himself would bow his haughty head before the saintly Prior, and crave to be remembered in his prayers.

As we see that men of all classes, from the King downwards, vied with one another in showering benefactions on the monastery, and paying honour to its occupants, we may conclude that the original monks eschewed politics, and confined themselves to the discharge of their legitimate functions. Avoiding intrigues, and repudiating every element of disturbance, their pure and useful lives commanded the respect of all who witnessed them. Vicious as the courtiers of Rufus too often were, they yet could not withhold their admiration for such bright examples, for men who, compared with themselves, seemed to belong to another order of being. The ignorant and uncultured felt an instinctive reverence for the "clerkly scholar"; the coarse and brutal, from whose lips torrents of blasphemy and ribaldry poured, were quelled in the presence of men to whom impurity was abhorrent; the fierce and violent man, accustomed to terrorize and intimidate, found himself confronted with a moral courage proof against threats, and an intrepidity that no fury could appal. Such a man as the Prior Petreius, upholding the cause of an oppressed peasant, would speak with the authority of a Hebrew prophet, denouncing God's judgments upon evil-doers. Strong in his Divine assurance, the lowly monk would stand forth as the champion of righteousness, unmoved by the charge of insolence and presumption, and undismayed by the penalties that might await his hardihood.

But this boldness had its reward. The feudal lord, whose will had never before been challenged, who had been accustomed to see nothing around him but the "dark deference of fear and slavery," found himself arraigned in the name of a mightier Sovereign than the Conqueror, and under the provisions of a code more rigorous than the justice of the land.

At first amazed and indignant, his better sense ultimately prevailed, the beams of justice penetrated the clouds with which pride and self-indulgence had obscured his understanding, and he came to respect and admire the man who had checked him in the full career of his iniquity. Thus, in the days of their purity, monasteries were asylums for the oppressed, and sources from whence a stream of bounty flowed, for the comfort of the lowly and the suffering.

In April, 1094, died the pious founder of the monastery, Alwin Child. The "Annals" merely record the circumstance of his death, without informing us whether he was buried, as usually happened in such cases, in the church of his foundation. Although only twelve years had passed, he had lived to see it a great and flourishing institution, the object of royal favour, and of the bounty of many noble personages, dignified, above all, by the saintly virtues of its Prior.

Although Dugdale, in his "Baronage of England," declares that he has been unable to ascertain either the place or the time of

Robert of Mortain's death, there is reason to believe that he was slain in battle in Northumberland. This chivalrous Earl is supposed to have obeyed the summons of the King, and to have joined in the expedition against Robert Mowbray, Earl of Northumberland, who had unfurled the standard of rebellion. This noble, a man of gigantic stature and formidable aspect, is said to have been one of those haughty and imperious personages to whom it is equally repugnant to admit equality or to acknowledge superiority. Scornful of his brother nobles, and unwilling to submit to the dominion of the King, he entered into a conspiracy for the dethronement of Rufus. Timely measures, however, succeeded in quelling the rebellion; the Earl of Northumberland was captured, and consigned to a dungeon, where he languished for more than thirty years.

Earl Robert was succeeded in his titles and vast estates by his only son William, for his remaining children were daughters, one of whom had been on the point of marrying a son of her father's friend, Hugh de Grantmesnil; but this union did not take place.

William of Mortain, Earl of Cornwall, was a man of different temper to his predecessor. Brave as his sire, he yet lacked the loyalty and unselfish devotion of Robert, but manifested more of the ambition and turbulence of his uncle Odo. The standard of St. Michael, the great banner of his house, under which the chivalry of the Cotentin had rallied in the war with King Henry of France, which had shone conspicuous in the foremost ranks on the field of Hastings, which in the Northumbrian battle had been borne to victory by the followers of the fallen chieftain, was, under Earl William, more frequently unfurled as the symbol of rebellion. Brought up under the influence of Bishop Odo, who had bequeathed to him his possessions in England, the new Earl appeared to have imbibed the restless ambition of that prelate. He would almost appear to have been intoxicated with his elevation, but had it been so we can hardly feel surprised, when we reflect on the grandeur of his position. In these days of titular nobility it is difficult to realize what was meant by an earldom in the Middle Ages. An Earl in the present day is indeed a great social personage, enjoying precedence and a degree of respectful observance; but he is invested with no authority by virtue of his rank, and is outvied in wealth and splendour by many commoners. But the great feudal lords who bore that title in olden times were something more than mere landed proprietors, whose power is limited to the granting of leases, and whose principal function is the receipt of rents. Holding their lands by feudal tenure under the Crown, administering their property with the delegated authority of the King, their tenants held of them under like conditions, and were bound to appear in arms at their summons and follow them to the field. In days when there was no standing army, an Earl was the King's General, commanding the levies of his province or district, and holding his castles as fortresses for the Sovereign. The estates which had been granted to Robert of Mortain in England and Wales, not to mention his Norman fiefs, made the Earl of Cornwall one of the greatest and most powerful personages in the realm. Lord of many castles and strongholds, his ample revenues and the number of his vassals constituted elements of danger, and made him peculiarly formidable as a conspirator. The bounty which the Conqueror had lavished on his kinsmen had not extinguished jealousy, and though in the case of Robert there was little evidence of this feeling, it rankled constantly in the breast of the Bishop of Bayeux. That prelate, hated by the English people for his tyranny and exactions, not content with his position as Earl of Kent and Justiciary of England, aimed at the Papal tiara and the spiritual sovereignty of Christendom. Fortunately, no doubt, for Europe, the Conqueror arrested his brother as he was preparing to set forth with a great retinue to prosecute his intrigues at Rome, and threw him into prison, where he remained until shortly before the death of William. After prolonged resistance to the entreaties of those who surrounded him, foremost among whom was Robert of Mortain, whose affection for his brother Odo was great, the King reluctantly consented to release the Bishop, although warning them of the evils likely to result from his liberation. We have already seen that Earl Robert had reason to remember this.

    Foiled in his Roman attempt, defeated in his rebellion against Rufus, deprived of his high office and his great earldom, Odo retired to his Norman see, there to feed his resentment and to foster intrigues against the King who had banished him. It is easy to conceive how this proud, malignant, and vindictive prelate laboured to instil the subtle poison of his hatred into the mind of his nephew, William of Mortain. In making him the heir of his forfeited possessions, which could not be obtained without a reversal of the royal judgment, he was sowing the seeds of rebellion in the mind of the young Earl. Magnifying his services and enumerating his wrongs, the Bishop constituted Earl William his avenger, and fostered the hatred which that young lord had entertained from childhood towards Henry the First. The strange story related of Earl William in connection with the death of William Rufus, absurd as it is, would yet to some extent show the result of the Bishop's teaching.

> At the very hour the King was killed, the Earl of Cornwall being hunting in a wood at some distance, and left alone by his attendants, was met by a huge black goat, bearing Rufus, all black and naked, with a wound in his breast. The Earl adjured the goat by the Holy Trinity to tell him whom it was he carried, and was answered: 'I am carrying your King to judgment - yea, that tyrant William Rufus: for I am an evil spirit, and the avenger of his malice which he bore to the Church of God, and it was I that did cause his slaughter, the protomartyr of England, St. Alban, commanding me so to do, who complained to God of him for his grievous oppressions in this Isle of Britain' - all which the Earl related soon after to his followers.

Such is the circumstantial account given by the chronicler, Matthew Paris. Grotesque and ridiculous as it is, such a tale would have found ready credence in an age which implicitly accepted marvels of all kinds. If the whole were not a monkish invention, it is possible that the Earl might have availed himself of the superstition of the times to embody, in this guise, an expression of his own hatred towards the ruling house. There is no reason to suppose that William of Mortain was more superstitious than most of his contemporaries. He is described by William of Malmesbury as "a man of character, consummate in counsel, and energetic," evidently, therefore, possessing intellectual force and vigour of understanding. The aversion he entertained towards Henry the First, which finally brought them into collision and precipitated the ruin of the Earl of Cornwall, is intelligible enough. It is impossible to read the history of that subtle and crafty Prince, frigidly despotic and deliberately cruel, without feeling that many of his qualities were eminently fitted to excite the abhorrence of a frank and generous nature.

Accomplished according to the ideas of the time, politic and sagacious, endowed with some of the essential qualities of a great ruler, the "clerkly King" yet manifested a cunning and duplicity altogether unworthy of his high office, and which in some respects recall the conduct of Louis the Eleventh of France. Although brave enough and not devoid of military skill, he sought more frequently to achieve great results by tortuous ways and cunningly devised methods than by force of arms. The manner in which he played upon the weaknesses of his brother Robert, and craftily availed himself of his heedlessness and unsuspicion, exhibits him rather in the light of a pettifogger than a great Sovereign. He forbore to plunder the Church, and showed favour to monks, who have therefore drawn his portrait in strong contrast to that of his brother Rufus; but we cannot contemplate his career without feeling detestation of his cruelty and dissimulation.

William Rufus had been profuse and extravagant; his Court had presented a scene of licentious indulgence. He tolerated the lawless conduct of many of his followers, and sought to retain the disaffected by crafty policy and abundant largesses. Henry, on the other hand, was disposed to hold the reins of authority with a firmer hand, to repress lawlessness and curb insubordination, to enforce respect for the kingly office and functions. Sedition was always seething amongst the Norman lords, though repressed by the vigorous hand of the Conqueror, and held in check by William Rufus by means of gifts and connivance, sometimes, indeed, by main force; for Rufus, though a profligate, possessed all the courage of his race. At the period of Henry's accession the elements of disturbance were gathering to a head, and it was not long before the storm burst forth. In 1101 Duke Robert, urged by many of the Norman Barons, landed in England, and prepared to assert his claim to the Crown; but, with his usual indolence and procrastination, he wasted valuable time, and allowed himself to be again overcome by the wiles of his brother. He finally withdrew, with the delusive promise of an annual payment to be made by the King, and left the latter free to deal with his disaffected Barons.

One of the fiercest and most turbulent of these was the maternal uncle of William of Mortain, Robert de Belesme, of the House of Montgomery, Earl of Shrewsbury and Count of Ponthieu, possessor of great estates in England, Normandy, and Maine. His character, equally treacherous and violent, made Henry resolve to deal with him first of all. Causing the Earl of Shrewsbury to be narrowly watched, the King discovered many proofs of his treasonable practices, and he was summoned to appear before the legal tribunal and clear himself from the charges brought against him. The Earl came, attended by many partisans; but feeling the impossibility of making a successful defence, he fled, and hastened to rally his adherents and fortify his castles against the King. His three principal strongholds were Arundel, Bridgnorth, and Shrewsbury. King Henry assembled a great army, and laid siege to Arundel, which after holding out for three months capitulated; then, marching northward, he secured the submission of Bridgnorth, and invested Shrewsbury, which was defended by the Earl himself, who is said to have displayed great engineering skill. The overwhelming forces of the King, however, rendered the fortress untenable, and De Belesme, coming forth, laid the keys at Henry's feet. Although Robert de Belesme was a double-dyed traitor, and had also deserved death for many acts of cruelty and oppression, the politic King was unwilling to proceed to extremities. The connections of this felon Earl were so numerous and powerful that his execution might have caused many of Henry's supporters to fall away. The King therefore contented himself with confiscating the Earl's possessions and banishing him the realm. As the Chronicle of Bermondsey briefly states, under the year 1102: "And this year King Henry exiled Robert de Belesme, Earl of Shrewsbury."

We are not told whether William of Mortain took any part in the revolt of his uncle or had joined in the invitation to Robert of Normandy. There is, however, reason to believe that, although his sympathies were with the Norman Duke and the Earl of Shrewsbury, he had hitherto remained quiescent, contenting himself with filling with dignity his position as a great English Baron, and occupying himself with important buildings and the endowment of religious foundations. Dugdale tells us:

> This Earl William built the Castle of Mountacute in Somersetshire, and called it by that name from the sharpness of the hill on which he did set it (Mons acutus, Mont aigu). And likewise founded a priory near thereunto, which he amply endowed, annexing it as a cell to the Abbey

of Cluny in Burgundy.
He also gave to the Abbey of Bec, in Normandy, his lordship of Preston, in the Rape of Pevensey, in Sussex.

On St. Michael's Mount, in his earldom of Cornwall, are still to be seen the ruins of William of Mortain's chapel.

But the arrival of Duke Robert is said to have unsettled the mind of the Earl of Cornwall, and the subsequent revolt of Robert de Belesme, and the banishment of that near kinsman, increased his discontent with the existing regime. He had never relinquished the hope of securing the estates of his uncle Odo, and would appear to have actually taken possession of some portions of that property. He now resolved to make his formal demand for investiture with the title and possessions of the Earl of Kent, and urged his claim, not with the moderation of a man whose plea is doubtful, but with the vehemence of one whose rights are unjustly with-held, fiercely declaring that "he would not put on his cloak till he could procure the inheritance derived to him from his uncle."

The King met the impetuosity of the Earl with calmness and self-possession, above all with his habitual dissimulation. This scene must have been one peculiarly impressive to a student of character - the essential contrasts between these two great personages: the Earl bold, frank, impetuous, and haughty: the King grave, impenetrable, smoothly dissembling, secretly discerning in this an opportunity of humbling another great vassal. His reception of this demand cannot be better described than in the words of Dugdale:

> Unto which demand the King, at first considering his own unsettled condition, gave a subtle and dilatory answer. But when he discerned that those clouds from whence he doubted a storm were over, he not only denied his request, but began to question him for whatsoever he possessed unrightfully, yet, that he might not seem to oppose what was just, modestly yielding that he should have a lawful trial for the same.

While the litigation was pending, we may readily imagine that the tower in Bermondsey must have presented an animated scene: The arrival of the Earl with his train of vassals and dependents, his Knights and retainers, both from his English and Norman estates; messengers riding hither and thither; the coming of other seditious

Barons, applauding his spirit and encouraging him in his resistance; banquets in the hall, where the Earl, seated in state at the head of his board, looks exultingly around, whilst amid the draining of goblets and unsheathing of swords his guests anticipate the verdict of the courts, acclaiming him as Earl of Kent, Cornwall, and Mortain.

Who can say what visions of grandeur and dominion filled the imagination of the young Earl in the excitement of such a moment? Lord of the fairest domains in England, possessor of many of the strongest places in the country, with easy access from his earldom of Kent to the Norman coast, he might, at a favourable moment, emulate the Conqueror, bring over his Norman vassals, unite them with his English retainers, and, assailing King Henry with overwhelming forces, depose him in favour of Duke Robert. Under the easy and indolent sway of that Prince, Earl William would have become more powerful than Godwin, and have ruled as Mayor of the Palace, with authority as unquestioned as Pepin d'Héristal's. The sounds of revelry, and the shouts of acclamation, taken up and re-echoed by the vassals in the courtyard and the precincts, would have been borne to the adjacent monastery, where a holy man was kneeling in prayer for the imprudent Earl. The pious heart of the Prior Petreius was grieved at the danger his friend and neighbour was incurring. He had known and respected the loyal virtues of the father, and saw with pain how that hero's death had left the passions seething in the breast of the son without control. Hugh de Grantmesnil was dead, and there seemed to be none whose influence could curb petulance and check rebellious tendencies. But even had there been such, their admonitions would probably, in this instance, have been as fruitless as those of the aged counsellors of Rehoboam. If we believe William of Malmesbury, the Earl of Cornwall needed no incitement, but was himself the fomenter of sedition and the moving spirit in the revolt that was impending. The Prior of Bermondsey might inculcate patience and exhaust every persuasive argument, but the Earl would listen with ill-suppressed irritation, and pursue his course heedless of remonstrance.

The King was fully sensible of the danger. He had no intention of allowing an already too powerful subject to be aggrandized by the possession of the earldom of Kent. Aware of Earl William's aversion to himself, and secretly incensed at his arrogance, he had resolved, sheltering himself under the forms of law, to strike a decisive blow at that lord's power. The Earl found his claim to the succession of Bishop Odo for ever set aside, and the condition of England was not now such as to inspire hopes of a successful rising. King Henry had consolidated his authority; he was supported by able chieftains and sagacious counsellors. The fate of the great Earl of Shrewsbury had cowed the spirit of rebellion, and led most of the Anglo-Norman lords to range themselves under the King's standard. Furious with rage and disappointment, Earl William crossed the Channel and plunged headlong into rebellion. It is possible that he little thought, when thus precipitately abandoning them, that he had looked for the last time on his fair domains, that henceforth no rood of English land would call him lord. He may have thought that the King would hardly venture to dispossess him, or that whatever might be confiscated would be regained by a successful rebellion. Normandy, nominally governed by Duke Robert, was really in a state of chronic anarchy; the Duke, although physically brave, was the personification of moral weakness, and had earned the contempt both of his subjects and his enemies. Powerful Barons like William of Mortain and his uncle, Robert de Belesme, despised the authority of their chief, and waged war at their pleasure. Earl William, at the head of his vassals and of all the turbulent and rapacious warriors who flocked to his standard, allured by the prospect of plunder, made a number of fierce but unsuccessful attacks on the King's castles in Normandy. Failing in his attempts to reduce these, he next turned his arms against the King's partisans, and ravaged the estates of Richard, Earl of Chester, who was then a minor and under the guardianship of Henry. In this career of devastation he was ably seconded by the ferocious Robert de Belesme. The King appealed to his brother to check these disorders; but the Duke, although at first feebly remonstrating with the rebels, ultimately allowed himself to be involved in their conspiracy. The King now confiscated all Earl William's possessions in England, and razed his castles to the ground. He then invaded Normandy, where many of the inhabitants, weary of the laxity of Duke Robert and of the lawlessness and rapacity of the nobles, welcomed his arrival. The Duke, however, and his rebellious Barons were not to be overcome without a struggle. After an interval of sieges and casual combats, the decisive battle was fought on September 28, 1106. King Henry had laid siege to Tenchebray, a fortified town belonging to the Earl of Mortain.

> In engineering formula, entrenching over against De Mortain's stronghold, he built his fort 'Malvoisin,' and to check sallies set horse and foot therein, William (De Mortain) munitioning freely the while, and, with admired skill, convoying forage and all necessaries to the gates.
> And when the royal force augmented, drew closer, and prepared to attack, De Mortain, under the eventualities incident to homage, claimed his suzerain's aid, and called Robert de Belesme, as a kinsman, to the rescue.
> - Cobbe's *Norman Kings of England*.

The Duke responded to his feudatory's call, and on Saturday, the vigil of St. Michael, the armies of the King and his brother prepared to close in mortal conflict. The ducal force advanced in three divisions - Robert in the main battle, with William de Mortain in front and Robert de Belesme behind - weaker in Knights, but with foot soldiers in fuller ranks.

> The Princes and others on either part dismounted, in proof of purpose. Shrill trumpets sounded, and, on the instant, the vans of each host, charging the other, locked weapons. Robert's trained Crusaders, in a fierce onset, repulsed the royal bands, and De Mortain, attacking from point to point, thrust their thronging masses into rout. Cries and shouts announced a crisis, when Hélie (Count of Maine) with his horsemen bore down on the flank, and, shock on shock, brake up the Norman corps. In the mêlée De Belesme fled, but the Duke fell into the hands of Gaudri, the King's chaplain, and William de Mortain surrendered to the Breton knights.
> - Cobbe's *Norman Kings of England*.

Thus fell the proud and turbulent Baron who had deemed himself the rival of a King. He may have imagined that this day, being the vigil of his patron saint, would be propitious; but fortune had for ever forsaken him. On that fatal day the standard of St. Michael was trampled in the dust, and the Lord of St. Michael's Mount had tasted for the last time the pride of leadership. He had borne himself in a manner worthy of his father, displaying to the full courage, conduct, and energy. The close of that disastrous day beheld the great Earl of Mortain and Cornwall a landless captive, stripped of all his vast possessions, his followers slain or dispersed, the very castle he had hastened to relieve in the possession of his enemies.

What a theme for the Prior of Bermondsey! What a fruitful subject for a homily on the vanity of human aspirations and the fleeting character of earthly possessions! Alas! "how are the mighty fallen!"

Brought to England with the other captives, Earl William was consigned to the Tower, where he is said to have been fettered and deprived of sight. The practices of Henry the First render this only too probable, and the writer of the History of the Norman Kings, previously quoted, cites among the witnesses of that monarch's cruelty "The sombre form of blinded Mortain."

We have now to relate an incident which, though seemingly trivial, yet had a most important bearing, both on the subsequent fortunes of the captive Earl and those of the Monastery of Bermondsey. We are told that in the year 1117 a crucifix was found near the Thames, which afterwards became famous as the "Rood of Grace," or Holy Cross of Bermondsey. Some have represented it as having been fished out of the river, but the words of the chronicle are "prope Thamisiam" (near the Thames). At what exact spot it was found, or by whom discovered, we have no more information than of how it came to be deposited there. Some servant of the monastery, it may be, some "villein" or "borderer," passing along the river's bank, came suddenly upon this object, all counterparts of which were at that time regarded with superstitious awe. Filled with terror and amazement, not daring to touch the sacred emblem, which, to his untutored mind, would seem to have dropped from the clouds, he flew to the monastery to relate his marvellous discovery. The monks would have gone in procession to the spot, caused the precious relic to be reverently raised, and borne with all solemnity to the priory church, there to be enshrined. The church was dedicated to the Saviour; this miraculous discovery of His image may have seemed a pledge of Divine favour, a visible token of the Lord's grace, a sign that the soil on which the effigy of the Redeemer had been deposited was thereby hallowed, that the monastery and its possessions were taken under His special protection.

The holy Petreius was a man after God's own heart; he "walked with the Lord." It is more than probable that, in one of those moments in which the best of men have yearned for some tangible recognition, Petreius may have besought God to vouchsafe some sign, some visible token of His favour. The discovery of the cross would have appeared to come as the answer to his prayer. We might be disposed to smile with contemptuous pity at the superstitions of that benighted age, but have we not in the present day the miracles of Lourdes? Have not many images of the Virgin and of saints been "miraculously" discovered, had chapels built for their reception, and been adorned with the gifts of the faithful? When we have such examples before our eyes at this close of the nineteenth century, we cannot wonder that the unquestioning devotion of the twelfth believed that the cross of Bermondsey had fallen from heaven. We may conceive the joy and exultation that filled the heart of the Prior, with what a fervour of gratitude he would have poured forth his thanks prostrate before the altar. The fame of the miracle spread; the great and the lowly hastened to see the object so strangely discovered, and to bend in adoration before it.

A legend gradually grew up around the cross, favoured, as usually happened in such cases, by accident and coincidence; stories of miraculous recoveries, of marvellous escapes from peril, as the result of petitions offered up before it, were widely disseminated, and increased the multitude of worshippers. For centuries the "Rood of Grace" continued to be the pride and glory of St. Saviour's, Bermondsey, and was visited by pilgrims from all quarters.

In the following year, the supposed virtue of the Holy Rood was signally manifested. We read in the chronicle: "And in the same year, by the miraculous power of the Holy Cross, William, Earl of Mortain, was liberated from the Tower of London."

It is not clear how this is to be understood, whether it is meant that the Earl escaped or was released. We may form a conjecture from the context. The passage immediately following says: "And King Henry, in a dream, was saved from lions, through the sanctity of the first Prior, Petreius, who appeared unto him, and who, whilst living, was endowed with Divine virtue."

Possibly the King, softened by this singular vision, and unable to refuse any request of the saint, may at his entreaty have consented to release his captive. Twelve years had elapsed since the fatal battle of Tenchebray, the Earl's castles and strongholds had been demolished, his lands bestowed on others, even his county of Mortain conferred upon Count Stephen of Blois, afterwards King of England.

Whether Earl William had or had not been deprived of sight, his long captivity might have caused him to be forgotten by his former adherents, and the loss of all his possessions would have rendered him no longer formidable. We shall hear of the Earl again in the reign of Stephen, but the chronicle is silent with reference to his life during the seventeen years which preceded the accession of that monarch.

The ancient chroniclers tell us that Henry the First was habitually troubled by frightful dreams, by images of horror and despair. In his uneasy slumbers, the "mimic Fancy" woke, and lent her powerful aid to sharpen the stings of conscience. Stow says:

> In the year 1130 the King complained to Grimbald, his Saxon physician, that he was sore disquieted of nights, and that he seemed to see a great number of husbandmen with their rustical tools stand about him, threatening him for wrongs done against them. Sometimes he appeared to see his Knights and soldiers threatening him, which sight so feared him in his sleep that oft-times he rose undressed out of his bed, took weapon in hand, and sought to kill them he could not find. Grimbald, his physician, being a notably wise man, expounded his dreams by true conjecture, and willed him to reform himself by alms and prayer, as Nebuchadnezzar did by the counsel of Daniel.

King Henry's dream of the lions appears to have so powerfully impressed him that, both before and after the death of Petreius, he lavished benefits on the monastery. The Manor of Bermondsey had been secured to the monks by a charter of William Rufus, solemnly confirmed by Henry; but in addition to this the King bestowed upon them part of his demesne of Rotherhithe, Dulwich, a hide of land in Southwark, and Whaddon, near Croydon, besides the advowsons of churches in Kent.

The King's example, and possibly the fame of the Holy Rood,

had drawn further benefactions from great personages. In 1118 Robert, Earl of Leicester, gave the Manor of Wideford to the monks of Bermondsey. This nobleman, Count Of Meulent in Normandy, created Earl of Leicester by Henry the First, was now advanced in life. He was a distinguished warrior, and had loyally served the two generations of Norman Kings. He was one of the royal hunting-party in the New Forest on the occasion when Rufus received his death-wound, after which catastrophe he hastened with Prince Henry to Winchester to secure the royal treasure, as well as the succession to the Crown of England. In 1106 the Earl of Leicester commanded the King's forces in Normandy, and it was to his talents and military skill that Henry owed his victory at Tenchebray. Both William of Malmesbury and Henry of Huntingdon are in accord when treating the character of this noble warrior. The former chronicler says:

> Conducted gradually by budding hope towards fame in the time of the former Kings, he attained to its full bloom in Henry's days, and his advice was regarded as though the oracle of God had been consulted; indeed, he was deservedly esteemed to have obtained it, as he was of ripe age to counsel, the persuader of peace, the dissuader of strife, and capable of very speedily bringing about whatever he desired from the powers of his eloquence.

Amongst the benefactors of the monastery at this period we find a name which has been embalmed in immortal verse, that of Marmion. Sir Walter Scott's Marmion was purely a fictitious personage, although his creator endowed him with the titles which the lord of whom we are about to speak actually bore. Robert Marmion, who lived in the time of Henry the First, was really

> Lord of Fontenay,
> Of Lutterward and Scrivelbaye,
> Of Tamworth Tower and town.

His Norman castle was Fontenay-le-Marmion, near Caen. He was hereditary Champion of England, his ancestors having acted in the same capacity towards the Norman Dukes, and it was through one of his female descendants that the family of Dymoke inherited the Championship. Lord Marmion bestowed upon the monks of

Bermondsey a hide of land at Widefleet, together with a mill and "other things pertaining." This land, we are told, was in Southwark, on the borders of Lambeth. It was not surprising that the holy brethren should have imagined their monastery to be specially favoured by Providence, for this was another instance in which a man who had no love for monks in general showed liberality in dealing with those of Bermondsey. We have already stated that William Rufus made them a present of the manor. How little reverence Lord Marmion entertained for monks as a body is evidenced by the following account of the circumstances preceding his death:

> Being a great adversary of the Earl of Chester, who had a noble seat at Coventry in the eighth of Stephen, he entered the priory there, which was but a little distance from that Earl's castle, and, expelling the monks, fortified it, digging in the fields adjacent divers deep ditches covered over with earth, to the intent that such as made approaches thereto should be entrapped, whereupon it so happened that, as he rode out himself to reconnoitre the Earl of Chester's forces that began to draw near, he fell into one of them and broke his thigh, so that a common soldier, presently seizing on him, cut off his head.
> - Dugdale's *Baronage*.

This is certainly less heroic than the death scene portrayed by Scott. One of the grants which would seem, from the frequent references to it in the "Annals," to have been specially valued by the monks was the Manor of Kynwardestone, or Kingweston, in Somersetshire. This estate was bestowed upon them by the Princess Mary, daughter of Malcolm the Third, King of Scotland. This royal lady, distinguished for her piety and virtues, was sister of Henry the First's Queen, and married to Eustace, Count de Boulogne, her daughter by whom, Matilda, became the wife of Stephen, the succeeding King of England. The Princess Mary, Countess of Boulogne, while on a visit to England, died in the Priory of Bermondsey in 1115, and was buried in the Church of St. Saviour. Her husband, Eustace, solemnly confirmed the gift of Kingweston "for the benefit of his wife's soul."
In June, 1119, died Petreius, Prior of Bermondsey, "in the odour of sanctity." That this venerable personage had genuine claims to be regarded as a saint there can be no doubt, but a mediaeval

reputation for sanctity was sometimes founded on very contradictory qualities. The monastic discipline reacted differently on dissimilar natures. The man of naturally harsh and gloomy temper, pursuing his course of mortification and self-torment, often became hardened into barbarity; the Christian virtues of sympathy and compassion, if he ever possessed them, were deadened and altogether effaced; he came to look upon it as meritorious to kill the body in order to save the soul. A spirit breathed beneath his monk's frock as fierce as that which glowed in the breasts of the warriors of Odin. Such a man would feed his pride by exaggerating the conventual discipline by self-imposed inflictions; he would go to the stake in the spirit of a North American Indian to show with what supreme fortitude he could endure torments.

When Hugo of Avalon, afterwards Bishop of Lincoln, sought admission as a youth to the Monastery of the Grande Chartreuse, a stern old monk said to him: "Young man, the men who inhabit these rocks are as hard as the rocks themselves. They have no mercy on their own bodies and none on others."

But marvellous contrasts were witnessed. The system which produced a Dominic also produced a St. Hugh and a St. Francis. The discipline which hardened the heart of one and made him a demon of cruelty, exalted the spirit and developed the virtues of the other. The true saint felt that by mortifying his flesh he was doing that which his Master had done before him, that he was educating himself in the practice of patience and long-suffering. If as a missionary to some barbarous nation he was subjected to torments and bound to the stake, he underwent his ordeal fortified by the Divine example, and exhaled his spirit, rejoicing that he died as a witness for the truth and of love for the Saviour. Not scorn but sympathy, not cruelty but beneficence, not persecution but love of justice, marked the distinction between the stern ascetic, the monastic Pharisee, and the lowly follower of Christ. Yet men of both types have been canonized as saints! Strange calendar, in which the ruthless upholder of some dogma and enforcer of ecclesiastical claims is placed on a level with those whose virtues shine as the brightness of the firmament, and whose lives were marked by beneficence, compassion, helpfulness, by efforts to assuage the sufferings and ameliorate the condition of their fellow-men. Of this latter class, we doubt not, was Petreius, the first Prior of Bermondsey.

The position of the monastery was now assured as one of the greatest religious foundations in England, and it sustained no diminution of favour by the death of Henry the First.

A passage in the "Annals," under the date 1140, states: "This year, William, Earl of Mortain, came to Bermondsey and assumed the monastic habit."

Where he had found shelter, or what had been the course of his wanderings, during the long interval which had elapsed between his deliverance from the Tower and his arrival in Bermondsey, we have no information to show. A cell in the priory was destined to witness the close of that remarkable career. It might be asked why the Earl did not seek to end his days in the monastery which he had himself founded, the Priory of Montacute, in Somersetshire. It is most probable that he was influenced by a grateful remembrance of the saintly Petreius, who we conceive to have interceded for him, and procured his release from captivity. Although in 1140 no monk may have been left who could remember the Earl in the days of his grandeur, all had heard the story of his vicissitudes, and must have been moved by the spectacle of so much greatness in decay; those sightless eyes, which had once gazed so proudly on the face of a King; that withered countenance, once so mobile and expressive; that stately crest, so conspicuous amidst his gallant array of knights and men-at-arms, now bowed with age and suffering, and veiled beneath a cowl. His vast possessions had dwindled to the monastic cell, his rich armour and his gorgeous robes were replaced by the black frock of the monk. How long the Earl survived in his monastic retreat we are not informed; Dugdale could no more verify the date of William of Mortain's death than he could that of his father Robert. All we learn is that he died in the monastery and was buried in the priory church.

In Mr. Cobbe's History of the Norman Kings, we find this gloomy reference to the deprivation of sight, although no date is given: "When William de Mortain, Monk of Bermondsey, lay upon the bier, men saw with horror that he had been blinded by his royal cousin."

We cannot help regarding the career of this Earl of Mortain as peculiarly illustrative of the character of the Norman era. We see in him the turbulence, the arrogance, the desire for aggrandizement, which so strongly marked the conquering race; the litigious spirit of the Normans, together with their intrepid bravery and military skill. In him, as in the rest, indomitable resolution, peculiar keenness in temporal affairs, sagacity and shrewdness, were combined with a strong tinge of superstition and devotional fervour. The Norman lords signalized themselves as much by their endowment of religious foundations and their bounty to churches and monasteries as by their valour in the field and their oppressions in civil life.

Ancient Window (Bermondsey Abbey)

CHAPTER IV

THE EARLY NORMAN KINGS AND BERMONDSEY - BOUNTY OF KING STEPHEN - HENRY THE SECOND - PRIOR HENRY SWANSEY - KING JOHN - ST. THOMAS'S HOSPITAL - THE MONASTIC SCHOOL

We have seen in the preceding chapter remarkable instances of the favour in which the Cluniac Priory of Bermondsey was held by the Kings of the Norman line. We know not that William the First did more than grant the site for the foundation of the new monastery, but his son, William Rufus, although, as we have said, a scoffer and a debauchee, yet deliberately relinquished his property in the manor and solemnly conferred it upon the monks. By what motives could he have been influenced in the bestowal of this grant?

It is not improbable that that secret respect for religion which often lingers in the breasts of the seemingly most hardened and impenitent, that dread of the Unseen Judge, may have prompted his action. Such feelings contributed to strengthen the monastic institution, and to root it more firmly in the land. In that age of rapine and violence, when even well-meaning men were often hurried, through the exigencies of their position, into desperate courses, and impelled to crime; when deeds were perpetrated, and spectacles exhibited, that might have led the despairing beholder to believe that God had relinquished the government of the world, and abandoned men to their own devices, there still remained one hopeful sign, one visible proof that the last link between earth and heaven was not destroyed. Amidst devastated provinces, amidst the blazing ruins of cities, amidst heaps of slain, the monastery still stood, inviolate and inviolable, like the ark of the Lord, riding the storm. Even as the cities of refuge in ancient Israel, its gates opened to admit the panting fugitive, and the shelter of its sanctuary afforded the security of a citadel. It is true that this was not always so, that instances occurred in which monasteries were burnt and razed to the ground, and monks ruthlessly put to the sword. But in general the fiercest warrior shrank from the commission of such impious deeds, and his arm dropped powerless when confronted with the peaceful monk. He felt that these, men, consecrated to the service of God, were too precious to be sacrificed, that the time would come when he himself would be glad to purchase the benefit of their prayers, when those of his household would willingly resign manors to secure the performance of Masses for the repose of his soul.

It is probable enough that such influences may have operated on the mind of William Rufus, impelling him to the exercise of a species of generosity of which his career affords but few examples.

Another circumstance requires to be borne in mind, explanatory of the favour of the Kings, as we have the authority of a great writer for asserting that Bermondsey in ancient times was the "Westminster of South London." The palace, believed to have been built by one of the last Saxon Kings, no doubt afforded a welcome means of rest and refreshment to the Conqueror and his sons when returning from the southern coast or from some hunting excursion. We may imagine a Norman King banqueting in the halls of Edward and Harold, a Norman minstrel singing of heroic "gestes," whilst Ivo de Grantmesnil pauses, goblet in hand, to listen to the metrical narrative of the exploits of his father, the Seneschal, and Marmion, Lord of Fontenay, hearkens, with glistening eye, to the record of his grandsire's prowess: "De Marmion le vieil Roger."

We hear the winding of the horns and see the glare of the torches as Rufus and his jovial train, weary with chasing the deer or the boar, ride into the courtyard, prepared, with the proverbial appetites of hunters, to do execution upon the viands spread within. We hear the revelry prolonged far into the night, startling the monks in the cells of the adjacent priory, and mingling a discordant note with their early orisons. But no such unhallowed sounds disturbed their devotions during the residence of Henry the First. That stern ruler, before whose frown the proudest nobles quailed, listened with bowed head and reverent ear to the spiritual counsels of the Prior Petreius. In imitation of their Sovereign, and eager to show their veneration for him whom the King delighted to honour, the courtiers would have sought absolution from the hands of the saintly monk, and the noblest in the land would have been seen kneeling at the shrine of the "Rood of Grace." Amongst the monuments of the illustrious dead, the tomb of Mary of Scotland, Countess of Boulogne, was an object of reverence to all, whether noble or simple. The Saxon would gaze with peculiar interest and respect upon the resting-place of one who belonged to his ancient royal house, for the Princess Mary was grand-niece of Edward the Confessor. Some Scottish lord, coming on embassy to the King of England, would deem it a pious duty to visit St. Saviour's Church and offer up a prayer by the tomb of King David's sister. The princely Eustace of Boulogne, kinsman of the renowned Godfrey and of Baldwin, King of Jerusalem, would come to view the sacred spot, and beseech the monks not to be remiss in the performance of their Masses for the dead. Nor would Sir Ivo de Grantmesnil, himself a Crusader, fail to pay his devotions at the tomb of his mother, the Lady Adeliza. The Manor of Broxbourne, in Hertfordshire, part of that lady's inheritance, was bestowed by Sir Ivo on the monks of Bermondsey "for the good of his parents' souls."

As we have previously said, Petreius, Prior of Bermondsey, died in 1119, and there then followed, as we sometimes find in the course of the "Annals," a rapid succession of Priors. His immediate successor was Herebran, who did not enjoy his elevation long, for, dying in the course of the ensuing year, he was succeeded by Peter, whose tenure was of even briefer duration, being followed in the same year, 1120, by Walter. Prior Walter must either have been younger or of stronger constitution than his predecessors, for he survived until 1134.

One of the most remarkable features in the "Annals" is the mention of repeated confirmations by successive monarchs of the grants bestowed upon the monastery. It is highly indicative of the unsettled state of the nation and the uncertain tenure by which all property seemed to be held. The Princess Mary bestowed her Manor of Kingweston on the monks of Bermondsey, and the gift was solemnly confirmed by her husband, Count Eustace; but neither this nor the sanction of King Henry the First was sufficient to secure the possession. We find in the succeeding reigns that it was necessary to obtain the confirmation of Stephen and Henry the Second, and this was the case with respect to every grant conferred. Nay, even the royal bounty, the gift of the Manor of

Bermondsey itself by William Rufus, had to be confirmed by his successor. Possession would not appear in those days to have constituted "nine points of the law." It may be that the purely spiritual character of these owners exposed them to encroachment from powerful and unscrupulous neighbours. Whatever respect feudal lords may have entertained for the character of monks, and however unwilling they might be in general to commit outrages upon their persons, they were withheld by few scruples in dealing with the property of those reverend personages. The instance of Lord Marmion is a proof of this; he, though a benefactor to the monks of Bermondsey, acted with violence towards those of Coventry, converting their priory into a fortress and digging pitfalls in their fields.

In the year preceding the death of Henry the First, Walter, Prior of Bermondsey, was succeeded by Prior Clarembald, of whom we shall presently hear more.

We have now come to the reign of that gallant and debonair Prince, who possessed more amiable qualities than any of his predecessors, but whose ambition was the cause of the greatest misfortunes both to himself and the country which he claimed to rule.

Grandson of the Conqueror by his daughter Adela, Count Stephen of Blois was early received into favour by his uncle Henry, and had been for many years one of the most distinguished ornaments of the English Court. Brave, chivalrous, generous and high-spirited, handsome and of imposing aspect, he would appear to have possessed all the qualities of a preux chevalier, all the elements of that character which was supposed to constitute the "mirror of knighthood." In that rugged age, when martial ferocity and arrogant haughtiness were more common than suavity and politeness, Stephen was conspicuous for his bland and courteous demeanour. It was, therefore, not surprising that this brilliant and amiable personage should have won the hearts of the people, and created a strong party in his favour. Nor, although but the younger son of a French feudal lord, was he destitute of means to support his great position. King Henry had endowed him with ample possessions, conferring upon him the county of Mortain, forfeited by the rebellion of the Earl of Cornwall, and also the great estate forfeited by Robert Mallet in England. The King further negotiated a marriage between Stephen and Matilda, daughter of Eustace, Count de Boulogne, and the Princess Mary of Scotland, therefore niece by marriage of Henry himself. This princely alliance was rendered more valuable by the fact that the Countess Matilda was the heiress of her father's possessions, and thus brought Stephen not merely the reversion of the county of Boulogne, but also great estates in England, which had been conferred by the Conqueror upon the father of Count Eustace. Henry the First appears to have had no suspicion that Stephen was aiming at the Crown, which he had bequeathed to his daughter Matilda, or, as she is more commonly called, the Empress Maud, and he may well have been thrown off his guard by the apparent zeal manifested by Stephen, who, when the Barons swore fealty to the Empress, contended with the King's natural son, Robert, Earl of Gloucester, who should be the first to give her that pledge. On the death of King Henry, Stephen threw off the mask, and, aided by his partisans, seized the vacant throne. His brother Henry was Bishop of Winchester, and he had many warm supporters among the clergy. The Pope, Innocent the Second, also sent a letter to Stephen congratulating him on his accession, and fortified by this the new King sought to conciliate the clergy and to rely on their support rather than on that of the Barons, who were greatly divided, and whose adhesion was of very doubtful firmness. The Empress, aided by her brother, the Earl of Gloucester, was not slow in asserting the justice of her claim, and subsequent events, besides favouring the cause of that Princess, embroiled Stephen both with his clerical and lay supporters. It is, however, no part of our purpose to trace the events of this monarch's reign, except in so far as they bear relation to the monks of Bermondsey.

 These monks became the objects of King Stephen's bounty at an early period of his reign, and continued to be through all the vicissitudes of his later life. In his third year he bestowed upon them rents in Southwark, and confirmed to them the Princess Mary's gift of Kingweston. In his sixth year the King confirmed the donation by "Waltheof the son of Swein" of the Church of St. James at Derby. This was something more than the mere gift of an advowson; the church in question was attached to a small priory, which continued until the Dissolution to be a "cell" or branch establishment of the Bermondsey monastery. In the seventh year of his reign the King granted a charter of privileges to the monks, in which he declared them and their belongings free from all tolls, dues, claims, or exactions, empowering them to hold their own court, and investing them with absolute authority both in their Manor of Bermondsey and in all the outlying possessions of the priory. The following year King Stephen bestowed the Manor of Grave upon the monks, and in his ninth year made them a gift of the Church of Writtle. Nor were favours confined to the King alone. We read in the same year that William d'Ypres, the leader of his mercenaries, remitted a payment which the monks were accustomed to make annually to the Lord of Dartford, the said remission being confirmed by the King and by "Henry, Duke of Normandy."

William, Viscount d'Ypres, whom Stephen created Earl of Kent, was a man of sinister reputation. Natural son of Philip, the second son of Robert, Count of Flanders, he had after the death of his cousin, Baldwin the Seventh, laid claim to that principality. This claim, however, was repudiated, and another kinsman, Charles, a chivalrous and humane personage, received the vacant countship. This Count, styled Charles the Good, and who signalized himself by protesting, on a memorable occasion, against Henry the First's barbarous practice of blinding, was murdered in the Church of Bruges whilst hearing Mass. Although William d'Ypres besieged the castle in which the assassins took refuge, he was strongly suspected of having instigated the deed. He was afterwards imprisoned by the King of France, Suzerain of Flanders; but as it was then no easy matter to bring great culprits to justice, the Viscount managed to extricate himself from this difficulty, and, as leader of a band of Flemish mercenaries, entered the service of Stephen. Although high in favour with the King and at times rendering him important services, this Fleming was especially obnoxious to the English nobles. His remission of the payment formerly made by the monks of Bermondsey was an act of grace that he knew would be agreeable to the King, with whose benevolence towards those recluses he was well acquainted.

In 1145 we are told that "Walkelin Maminot" bestowed half Greenwich on the monks. This Norman magnate, head of a family holding large possessions in Kent, was probably a connection of Gilbert Maminot, Bishop of Lisieux, one of the prelates in attendance on the Conqueror during his last illness, who was "specially skilled in physic." In 1138 Walkelin Maminot had held Dover for the Empress Maud, but was prevailed on by Robert Ferrers, Earl of Derby, one of the heroes of the Battle of the Standard, to surrender it to Stephen.

If the monks of this priory still continued to hold aloof from politics, the occasional residence of Stephen at the Palace of Bermondsey must have been like an oasis in the desert of his troubled existence. Removed alike from the turmoil of the city and the turbulence of the provinces, the calm seclusion of Bermondsey would have appeared as a haven of rest. The mild intercourse of the monks would have presented a refreshing contrast to the fierce assertion of rival claims, the denunciations of prelates, and the hoarse shouts of infuriated combatants. In Bermondsey the repose of the harassed King was disturbed by no jarring elements, no strife or discord, the toll of the priory bell, the chant of the monks, with the ordinary sounds of rural life, the lowing of cattle, and the calls of field-labourers, alone breaking the silence. From the precincts dedicated to the Saviour the voice of Jesus appeared to sound: "Come unto Me, all ye that labour and are heavy laden, and I will give you rest."

Stephen's Queen is believed to have received her education in Bermondsey; she knew the veneration which both her mother, the Princess Mary, and her uncle, King Henry, had entertained for the holy Petreius; she was filled with personal and traditional respect for the monks of this priory. The idea is supposed to have originated with the Queen of founding a royal abbey in some equally peaceful spot, in which the voices of friendly monks would offer up prayers for herself and the husband to whom she was devoted. And who so fit to perform these pious functions as the monks of St. Saviour's, with the purity of whose lives she was well acquainted? Who so meet to fill the high position of Abbot as Clarembald, the worthy successor of Petreius? This project was warmly approved by the King, and Faversham in Kent was selected as the site of the new foundation. William d'Ypres, to whom this manor belonged, received in exchange one of the Queen's; and here Stephen and Matilda laid the foundation of the future abbey, destined to become one of great importance, and which, like the Priory of Bermondsey, was dedicated to the

Saviour. In 1148 Prior Clarembald and twelve of his monks quitted Bermondsey to become the first occupants of the Abbey of Faversham. No long period was destined to elapse before this sanctuary received the ashes of its founders. In 1151 Queen Matilda was laid to rest; in 1153 Eustace, her eldest son, was interred; and in October, 1154, the abbey received the remains of Stephen himself. Even in the grave misfortune pursued him. Stow, in his chronicle, says:

> His body rested here in quietness till the dissolution, when, for the trifling gain of the lead in which it was lapped, it was taken up, uncoffined, and plunged into the river, so uncertain is Man, yea, the greatest Prince, of any rest in this world, even in the matter of burial.

Clarembald had been succeeded as Prior by Robert of Blois, who would appear, from this cognomen, to have been a born subject of Stephen's house. This Prior resigned in the year following the death of the King, and was succeeded by Prior Roger. The stream of bounty still continued to flow; noble and commoner vied with one another in heaping benefactions on the monastery.

1154. "William, Earl of Gloucester, gave to the monks of Bermondsey the Church of Camberwell."

1154. "William, the son of Henry of Eltham, gave to the monks of Bermondsey the tithes of Wicklondes, in the parish of Woolwich; and Theobald, Archbishop of Canterbury, confirmed the same."

1156. "Osbert, son of William Ottdener, gave to the monks of Bermondsey the estate of Timberwood." The same year "the advowson of the Rectory of Bengeho, in the county of Hertford, was given by Reginald de Tani."

It is stated that Henry the Second, immediately after his coronation in 1154, held his first Parliament in the monastery of Bermondsey, by which we are, of course, to understand the assembly of Barons and Prelates which then formed a counterpart to that body. It was, no doubt, on this occasion that he confirmed all the before-mentioned donations, and also granted a charter of larger scope, and more minute in its specifications, than that of his predecessor Stephen.

In Miss Strickland's "Life of Eleonora of Aquitaine," we read:

> The Christmas festivities were celebrated that year (1154) with great pomp at Westminster; but directly the coronation was over the King conducted his Queen to the Palace of Bermondsey, where, after remaining some weeks in retirement, she gave birth to her second son, the last day of February, 1155.

The Prince thus born in Bermondsey was subsequently crowned King during the lifetime of his father, and reigned conjointly with him, as Henry the Third; but he is not so styled in the line of English monarchs, as his death occurred prior to that of Henry the Second.

Miss Strickland's description of Bermondsey at this period is so idyllic that we cannot refrain from transcribing it:

> Bermondsey, the first place of Eleonora's residence in England, was, as delineated in its ancient plans, a pastoral village nearly opposite to London, of a character decidedly Flemish. Rich in well-cultivated gardens and wealthy velvet meads, it possessed likewise an ancient Saxon palace and a priory then newly (?) built. Assuredly the metropolis must have presented itself to the view of its foreign Queen, from the Palace of Bermondsey, with much more picturesque grandeur than it does at present, when its unwieldy size and smoky atmosphere prevent an entire coup d'œil.

In 1157 Roger, Prior of Bermondsey, resigned his functions on being appointed Abbot of St. Ouen, and was succeeded by Prior Adam. In 1161 Adam was elected Abbot of Evesham, and resigned the monastery into the hands of Prior Geoffrey, who after two years' occupancy resigned, and was succeeded by Peter. The resignation of Priors from unexplained causes seemed now to have become frequent, for in 1166 Peter laid down his office, and was followed by Raynald. This Prior, "with consent of the convent," leased Widefleet, the gift of Lord Marmion, to the Knights Templars.

Marmion and the Templars! What romantic ideas such a

collocation of names evokes!

The resignation of Prior Raynald followed in 1167, he being succeeded by a second Roger. Next year Walkelin Maminot the younger bestowed upon the priory a charge on the lordship of Chippenham Dillehurst, and also the Church of Birling, "with all thereto pertaining." A royal grant of warren, and numerous gifts of tithes, churches and estates by persons of note, signalized the reign of Henry the Second. In 1175 Prior Roger resigned, on being created Abbot of Abingdon, a high preferment, as that abbey was both a great and ancient foundation. Robert de Bethlehem, Werric, Bertrand, and Constantius, succeeded one another as Priors within a few years, and, on the death of the last in 1186, a Prior assumed office whose name has given rise to considerable confusion. Henry de "Soliac," i.e., de Soilly, probably belonged to the noble family of that name in France, and his high rank may have caused him to be confounded with the Prior of whom we are about to speak. We are told in the "Annals" that Henry de Soliac, becoming Prior in 1186, died the same year; that Adam, succeeding, also died after a short interval, being followed by a second Henry - three Priors in one year. Some later monastic historians, possibly considering that an error may have crept into the Bermondsey Chronicle, have ignored the second Prior Henry, and represented Henry de Soliac as playing the remarkable part really enacted by his successor. A note in Dugdale, however, informs us that Henry de Soliac really died in 1186, and that Henry, the successor of Adam, so often confounded with his namesake, has been ascertained to be Henry Swansey, nearly allied to the reigning House of Plantagenet. This lordly Prior of Bermondsey was in 1189 elevated to the high dignity of Abbot of Glastonbury. This abbey had until recently been the first in England, but in 1154 Pope Adrian the Fourth, the only Englishman who ever filled, the Papal chair, and who had been educated at St. Alban's, gave precedence to the latter institution. Nevertheless, the Abbots of Glastonbury continued until the Dissolution to be among the greatest spiritual peers, maintaining a princely establishment, and being attended by a great retinue when coming to Parliament or making any official progress.

Two circumstances connected with the subsequent career of Henry Swansey are of such historic interest that we cannot refrain from relating them, and feel some pride in the fact that a quondam Prior of Bermondsey should have had a share in such remarkable events.

Henry the Second when in Wales had been informed by some of the bards of the existence of a tradition amongst them that Arthur and his Queen Guinevere were buried in Glastonbury Abbey, in the neighbourhood of certain pyramids which then stood within its precincts. On his return to England the King acquainted Abbot Henry Swansey of this circumstance, and requested him to make a search amongst these pyramids for the remains of King Arthur. The Welsh bards had also told him that Arthur would be found buried, not in a stone chest, as was supposed, but in a hollowed oak. Acting upon this information, the Abbot appointed a day for the search to be instituted in the presence of the whole convent. Giraldus Cambrensis was one of those privileged to be present, and it is from him we glean the particulars of the examination. The monks dug for some time all round the pyramids, and at last they came to a large leaden cross lying upon a stone. It was brought up, and found to bear the following inscription:

> Hic jacet sepultus inclytus
> Rex Arthurus in insula Avaloniæ,
> cum Guinevera uxore sua secunda.

The Isle of Avalon was the ancient name of Glastonbury.

> The slab was then removed, and a stone coffin discovered, which, being opened, was found to contain the bones of the Queen. Her rich golden hair still lay about the remains, but, touched by one of the monks, it fell into dust. They continued to dig lower until they had reached about sixteen feet below the surface, when they came across a huge oak, just as the Welsh bards had predicted. This was opened, and in it they found the bones of the King, which were of an enormous size. Giraldus tells us that one of the shinbones was taken out and placed against the leg of the tallest man present, and it reached above his knee by three finger-lengths. The skull, he says, was of a colossal size, and they could count ten or more wounds upon it, all of which, except one mortal wound, had cicatrized over.
> The Abbot then ordered the monks to gather the remains together, and they were conveyed with great solemnity to the church, where a mausoleum was afterwards erected for them, with two divisions, the

whole splendidly carved. At the head of this mausoleum they placed the King's remains, and at the foot those of Guinevere.
- Hill's *Monasticism in England*.

Thus the legendary British champion, the hero of romance and song, was proved not to have been the mere figment of a poet's brain.

Whilst Richard Coeur-de-Lion was detained in captivity by the rapacious German Emperor, Henry the Sixth, a relative of the latter, named Savaric, who was also Chancellor, coveted an English benefice, aspiring to the bishopric of Bath and Wells, to which he and his imperial kinsman felt that the Abbey of Glastonbury would be a superb addition. They brought pressure to bear upon Richard, who was willing to agree to anything in order to regain his freedom. Further representations were made to the Pope, who was assured that the dissensions between the abbey and the bishopric had long been a great scandal to the Church, and the. Pontiff's consent to the union was thereby secured. Neither the Abbot nor his monks as yet knew anything of the matter, but a private message was sent to Abbot Henry, requesting him to come over to the King at once. The Abbot obeyed, but his utmost haste did not keep pace with Richard's impatience for his arrival. As soon as he reached the place of detention he was welcomed by the King, who said:

> Dear Cousin, if you had come sooner I had been sooner released; the Emperor presses me to give Savaric the Abbey of Glastonbury as an addition to the bishopric of Bath and Wells, and you shall be promoted to the bishopric of Worcester, now vacant.

It is not stated whether Abbot Henry Swansey needed much persuasion to induce him to consent to this. We may charitably suppose that he was finally led to acquiesce, less by the glittering bait of the episcopal mitre than by a desire to secure the liberation of his King; and returning to Glastonbury, he resumed his functions without imparting anything to his brethren. He was suddenly called away to London, and very soon after his departure Savaric, who had now arrived and taken up his bishopric, sent for Harold, the Prior of Glastonbury, to confer with him on matters connected with the monastery. The Prior set out, taking two other monks with him, anticipating some new difficulties and contentions; but when they arrived Savaric asked them where their Abbot was. They replied that he was gone to London. "Then," said Savaric, "you are discharged of him, for I am your Abbot!"

Whilst this conference was being held, Savaric's agents were on their way to Glastonbury. The interview was only a trick to get the Prior, who had charge of the monastery in the absence of the Abbot, out of the way, that they might the more easily effect their purpose. Abbot Henry was invested with the bishopric of Worcester, where he died in 1195. His lordly rank and the remarkable incidents of his career make him a conspicuous personage in the line of Priors of Bermondsey, but his conduct indicates the change which had taken place since the days of Petreius and Clarembald. On this change we shall have occasion to dwell more fully in the next chapter.

As might have been expected, the monks of Glastonbury were indignant at the manner in which they had been juggled out of their rights, and handed over, like a flock of sheep, to a rapacious foreigner. Although compelled for the time to yield obedience to Savaric, they did not rest until they had induced Richard, now at liberty, and no longer disposed to support the German pretensions, to revoke the grant and disunite the abbey from the bishopric.

We observe no signs of royal favour conferred upon the Monastery of Bermondsey during the reigns of Richard the First and John. The absorption of the first-named monarch in foreign enterprises left him little leisure for domestic affairs, and the rapacity of John, and the straits to which his struggles, both with the Papacy and his own subjects, reduced him, made him more inclined to fill his coffers with the spoils of monastic treasuries than to enrich those institutions with further grants.

Probably, in the long line of English Kings, no ruler of so few merits has gained such lasting fame, or perhaps it would be more correct to say that he is immortalized by his very infamy. The association of all other Sovereigns with Bermondsey is forgotten, but the tradition of "King John's palace" still lingers amongst the inhabitants, and some persons living on the site believe that they can still discern vestiges of that structure. A portion of Long Walk, to the east of Bermondsey Square, was formerly known as King

John's Court, and it is probable enough that this may have been the courtyard of the ancient palace.

We learn little with reference to the dealings of King John with the monks of the priory, but Mr. Phillips states that the advowson of the Church of Writtle, in Essex, granted to the monks by Stephen,

> was taken from them again by King John, and by him given, anno 1203, to the hospital at the Church of St. Mary in Saxia, at Rome (commonly called the Hospital of the Holy Ghost), to which it was confirmed by King Edward the Third.

John is also believed to have sequestrated the priory and expelled the monks, but at whatever time this may have taken place, they were again in peaceable possession towards the close of his reign: for we find that in 1213 Prior Richard erected an almonry or hospital on the "Cellarer's Ground," adjoining the priory, "for the benefit of indigent children and necessitous converts."

We have now come to a matter which has been much disputed, viz., whether the great Hospital of St. Thomas had its origin in Bermondsey. The hospital just mentioned, founded by Richard, Prior of Bermondsey, was by him dedicated to St. Thomas of Canterbury, and known as St. Thomas's Hospital.

Mr. Phillips, in the painstaking and meritorious "History of Bermondsey" we have so often quoted, the compilation of which reflects the greatest credit on his industry and research, says:

> This house, on account of its being dedicated to St. Thomas, and founded about the same time, hath been confounded by Stow and others with the present hospital of that name, which originally joined to, or was a part of, the Priory of St. Mary Overie, and was removed, 1228, to the place on which it now stands [i.e., in 1841], on the eastern side of the borough.

But in the section of his work immediately following Mr. Phillips says, under head of "St. Saviour's Hospital":

> Agnes, the sister of Thomas a Becket, Archbishop of Canterbury, and widow of Thomas Fitz-Theobald de Heili, gave to the Hospital of St.

Saviour, in Bermondsey, ten shillings of annual rent issuing out of her estate in London, in the parish of Stanying Cherche, at Blanche Apulture, in the tenure of William Cook, which Theobald, her son, confirmed to them. Bishop Tanner hath inferred from the words of this donation that there was another hospital in Bermondsey dedicated to our Saviour; but as there are no records which give any account of such a foundation, and the hospital last mentioned, though dedicated to St. Thomas, might, with great propriety, be called St. Saviour's, as belonging to the priory of that name, and built within its precincts, we may reasonably suppose they were one and the same, and that the sister was moved to this act of charity by a pious regard to the memory of her brother, the patron thereof.

One passage in this illustrates the strange transformations which the names of some City localities have undergone: "Stanying Cherche," of course, refers to the ancient Church of Allhallows, Staining, but "Blanche Apulture" means the Manor of Blanche Appleton, within the precincts of the City, to which Edward the First allowed the privilege of a market, and hence "Mart Lane," now corrupted into "Mark."

The utter destruction of all the monastic buildings, and the disappearance of all registers and records, has involved the early history of these foundations in obscurity; but enough has been ascertained to prove that Stow was not mistaken in assigning at least a share in the foundation of St. Thomas's to the monks of Bermondsey. We learn that after the burning of St. Mary Overy's Church and Convent in 1212 the monks erected a temporary building for their accommodation, and after the rebuilding of their monastery this was used as a "hospitium," or place of rest.

> Sometimes it received the retainers of some great man whose suite was too large for the priory, but it became gradually more and more a home and rest for the sick, the weary, and the poor; and in the reign of Henry the Third, Peter des Roches, Bishop of Winchester, incorporated it with an almonry founded by Prior Richard of Bermondsey. The united foundation was dedicated in the name of St. Thomas à Becket, it being called by Peter des Roches 'The Spital of St. Thomas, the Martyr of Canterbury.'
> - *Southwark and its Story.*

This description gives a very pleasing idea of the functions discharged by the mediaeval monks. A monastery was then a "house of hospitality," where the weary might find rest and refreshment. The bequests so liberally bestowed upon these institutions were intended not merely for the maintenance of the monks, but for the relief of the poor, and the exercise, within the walls of the monastery, of hospitality towards all who might claim it. There were then no work-houses; no system of Poor Law relief existed; the functions now performed by guardians and relieving officers were then chiefly discharged by monks. The term "hospital" in those times did not mean an establishment exclusively devoted to the treatment of disease, but although it included such treatment, it also meant an asylum for the aged and infirm, for the orphaned and the helpless.

It would appear that the old St. Thomas's Hospital long continued to be under the supreme control of the Bermondsey Superiors, as it is stated that in 1482,

> the hospital was ceded by the Abbot of Bermondsey to a president, master, and brethren. There were then in the hospital a master and brethren, and three lay sisters residing in the hospital. Forty beds were made up for infirm and impotent folk, all of whom had victuals and firing allowed them.

We shall now see the monks of Bermondsey figuring in a scarcely less sacred capacity, that of instructors of youth. The Monastic School of Bermondsey was a seminary of great importance, being, as we shall see from the following extracts, one of the three great public schools in London. Stow in his "Survey of London" says:

> In the reign of King Stephen and of Henry the Second there were in London three principal churches which had famous schools, either by privilege and ancient dignity or by favour of some particular person, as of doctors which were accounted notable and renowned for knowledge in philosophy. The three principal churches which had these famous schools by privilege must needs be the Cathedral Church of St. Paul for one, seeing that by a General Council holden in the year of Christ 1176 at Rome, in the patriarchy of Lateran, it was decreed that every cathedral church should have its schoolmaster to teach poor scholars

and others as had been accustomed, and that no man should take any reward for license to teach.

The second, as most ancient, may seem to have been the Monastery of St. Peter at Westminster.

The third school seemeth to have been in the Monastery of St. Saviour at Bermondsey, in Southwark, for other priories, as of St. John by Smithfield, St. Bartholomew in Smithfield, St. Mary Overie in Southwark, and that of the Holy Trinity by Aldgate, were all of later foundation, and the friaries, colleges, and hospitals were raised since then in the reigns of Henry the Third, Edward the First, Second, Third, etc., all which houses had their schools, though not so famous as those first named.

The very dubious language used by Stow: "may seem," "seemeth to have been," etc., arises from the fact that the monk Fitz-Stephen, who wrote a description of London in the reign of Henry the Second, does not specify the churches by name, no doubt because they were so well known to his contemporaries. His account is as follows:

> The three principal churches possess, by privilege and ancient dignity, celebrated schools, yet often by the favour of some person of note, or of some learned man, eminently distinguished for their philosophy; other schools are permitted upon sufferance. Upon festival days the masters made solemn meetings in the churches, where their scholars disputed logically and demonstratively; some disputed for show, others to find out the truth. Rhetoricians spake aptly to persuade, observing the precepts of art, and omitting nothing that might serve their purposes; the boys of divers schools did cap or pot verses, and contended for the principles of grammar. There were some which on the other side, with epigrams and rhymes, nipping and quipping their fellows and the faults of others, though suppressing their names, moved thereby much laughter among their auditors.

And these were the Dark Ages!

This description, even if we had no other accounts to guide us, would enable us to form an idea of the course of study pursued in the higher monastic schools. In all these logic was of paramount importance, cultivated by the monks, many of whom were skilled dialecticians, and instilled into their scholars as the only means of threading the mazes of scholastic philosophy. Under this training they grew accustomed to precision of statement, to clearness of definition, and acquired ability to detect sophistry in argument. Rhetoric was held in high honour, as "giving greater command of the beauties of language," furnishing the aspirant with a choice repertory of tropes and figures necessary for the panegyrics in which they so liberally indulged, and enabling them to embellish their writings and discourses with swelling periods and ornate flourishes. In the higher schools, Cicero and Quintilian, the great masters of this art, were sedulously studied. The concentration of mind upon a few subjects caused these to be mastered with a thoroughness that would put to shame many modern students. The writings of William of Malmesbury furnish us with an example of the amount of classical learning imbibed by a mediaeval monk, and although it is not to be supposed that monks in general were as erudite as he, still, those who devoted themselves to study acquired a minute and accurate knowledge of their subject. Those only who were specially qualified for the task were appointed as teachers, and under their instruction their pupils became expert grammarians and skilled arithmeticians. Music was one of the special subjects of tuition. Moreover, although many are disposed to believe that the Bible was a sealed book in the Dark Ages, sacred history and portions of Scripture were required to be learnt by the pupils of the monks. We know nothing now either of the teachers or the taught; the records of the Monastic School of Bermondsey perished at the Dissolution, like the registers of the monastery itself. But there can be little doubt that when the school was at the height of its reputation, and when the Court abode at the adjacent palace, many youths of noble race were placed under the tuition of the monks, and the Church of St. Saviour's Priory must have echoed with disputations such as those described by Fitz-Stephen.

No better illustration of the oblivion into which so much that was existing prior to the Reformation fell could be afforded than the inability of Stow, who belonged to the next generation, to give any account from personal knowledge or information of those once famous establishments so recently extinct, or, rather, suspended.

The author of a "History of Westminster School," lately published, says that it appears to be the successor of an ancient monastic school, but of this he has no information whatever.

The Monastic School of Bermondsey, however, was flourishing immediately prior to the Dissolution, for Leland in his

"Cantio Cygni," published in 1530, in which he describes famous buildings on or near the river's bank as the "Swans of Thames," thus commemorates it:

> And hail, thou too, O House of Charity, the nurse
> Of many students, helped by Gifford's purse!
> Thou happy, snowy Swan, hast thy serene abode,
> Where Barmsey of her well-known isles is proud;
> Well-known indeed, for there we see the shrine,
> Where her priests labour in the work Divine.

This school, dissolved with the monastery in 1537, was subsequently revived in the newly-named parish of St. Saviour's, Southwark, and exists to this day as St. Saviour's Grammar School.

Head of King John, near the Gateway

CHAPTER V

HENRY THE THIRD - THE CRUSADERS - EDWARD THE FIRST - SEQUESTRATION OF THE PRIORY BY EDWARD THE SECOND - ATTACK ON THE ALIEN PRIORIES UNDER EDWARD THE THIRD - THE KING APPOINTS THE FIRST ENGLISH PRIOR - RICHARD THE SECOND - NATURALIZATION OF THE PRIORY, AND ERECTION INTO AN ABBEY.

The long and turbulent reign of Henry the Third is only marked in the annals of Bermondsey, over and above those events which belong to general history, by the King's permission to the Prior and convent to hold a weekly market on Mondays, and a fair on the eve and morrow of the Holy Trinity in their Manor of Charlton. This, be it observed, was not the famous "Horn Fair."

The period embraced by the King's reign was also signalized by the succession of no less than twenty-five Priors, amongst whom an extraordinary mortality seems to have prevailed, as on more than one occasion three are recorded as having died within a year.

Some passages in the "Annals" give a terrible idea of the sufferings endured by the people in that age of lawless violence. In 1261, the forty-sixth year of Henry the Third, wheat was sold "in London and over all England" at the enormous price of twenty-four shillings the quarter, equivalent to nearly forty pounds of the present currency.

"And therefore the poor of the kingdom ate nettles, and anything else growing on the land, from failure of food." It seems unnecessary to add after this, "And hence many thousands died."

One incident, however, connected with the reign possesses great interest as relating to Bermondsey. We find frequent allusions to the Crusades, and under date 1270: "This year, Edward, first-born son of King Henry the Third, with his mother Eleanor, went to the Holy Land."

On one of the occasions mentioned, many of the noblest in the kingdom, who had taken the Cross upon them, assembled in the Monastery of Bermondsey to arrange the preliminaries of their journey. It is impossible to reflect upon such an incident as this without a thrill of emotion: The Knights of the Cross, on their way to rescue the Holy Sepulchre from the profaning grasp of the infidels, meeting in the priory dedicated to the Saviour, and kneeling before the Holy Cross of Bermondsey to implore the Divine favour for their undertaking. Does it not remind us of that sublime scene in Melrose Abbey, portrayed by Scott with all the power of poetry, when -

> Above the suppliant chieftains wave
> The banners of departed brave;

and

> From many a garnished niche around
> Stern saints and tortured martyrs frowned.
>
> And slow up the dim aisle afar,
> With sable cowl and scapular,
> And snow-white stoles, in order due,
> The holy Fathers, two and two,
> In long procession came;
> Taper, and host, and book they bare,
> And holy banner flourished fair
> With the Redeemer's name.
>
> Above the prostrate pilgrim band
> The mitred Abbot stretched his hand,
> And blessed them as they kneeled;
> With holy Cross he signed them all,
> And prayed they might be sage in hall,
> And fortunate in field

However weaned from the world, however indifferent their cloistered seclusion and their unvarying routine had rendered them to human interests, none of the monks could have gazed upon a scene like this without an unwonted fire gleaming in their eyes, and their breasts being agitated by feelings to which they had long been strangers. Although, even in the early Crusades, the holy professions and the noble sentiments with which the adventurers set forth speedily gave way to sordid rivalry, to evil and malignant passions, still, those enterprises will be surrounded to all time with a halo of imperishable interest. They were the first great examples of "making war for an idea." Amidst all the rapacity and self-seeking, the ferocity and licentiousness, by which the conduct of the Crusades was disgraced, there were some who to the very last retained the purity of the original idea, and who fought with pious zeal to save Christendom from the reproach of allowing the Sepulchre of the Lord, and the scene of His labours and His sufferings, to remain in the possession of unbelievers.

Many of this noble company, with the cross embroidered on their mantles, who now thronged the Monastery of Bermondsey, were, no doubt, about to set forth in pursuance of some pious vow, some solemn pledge, long previously given, and now, at length to be redeemed. The fervour and the spirit of self-sacrifice which had led many to mortgage, or even to sell, their possessions in order to procure the means of equipping themselves for this arduous undertaking, of providing stores and means of transport, glowed in the breasts of those who gathered in the priory church. Many a gallant Knight, swelling with hope and confident of success, had set forth at the head of his retainers, and after enduring incredible sufferings and privations, tortures and imprisonment, had returned alone, halting and enfeebled, his costly armour exchanged for a pilgrim's gown, and nought but a pilgrim's staff to guide his steps.

The monks must have sighed as they reflected how few of the noble band before them would probably return to their native land.

Another circumstance worth noting is that in the twenty-fifth year of Henry the Third "William de Eborum, and his fellow justices-itinerant, held their assize on the 6th of May," in the Priory of Bermondsey.

The reign of Edward the First was marked by some extraordinary proceedings with reference to the clergy. The King's necessities, and the heavy expenditure incident to the wars waged by him, induced him to levy contributions both on the regular and secular clergy. These persons might have submitted, however unwillingly, to the exactions, had it not been that the reigning Pope, Boniface the Eighth, issued a Bull, in which he prohibited all Princes from levying, without his consent, any taxes upon the clergy, and all clergymen from submitting to such impositions, and threatened both with the penalty of excommunication in case of disobedience. The result of this was that the King, meeting with determined resistance to his demands, resolved, so as to guard himself from the penalty incurred by direct violence, to deprive them of the protection of law. All restraint upon rapacity being thus removed, priests were despoiled and plundered with impunity, whilst the King and his functionaries looked on with affected indifference. To such an extent was spoliation carried that the Archbishop of Canterbury himself was attacked on the highway, stripped of his equipage and "furniture," and at last reduced to board himself with a single servant in the house of a country priest. Finally, driven to despair, and regardless of the Pope's denunciations, most of the clergy submitted, and made a compromise with the King in order to receive once more the customary protection of citizens.

How the monks of Bermondsey fared during this period of rapine we are not informed, but we can hardly suppose that they were exempted from sharing the fate of their brethren. The only mention of the King's dealings with them occurs in the eighteenth year of his reign.

> King Edward the First granted to the monks of Bermondsey the manors of Hallingbury, Wideford, Cowyk, Upton, and Richmond, which had fallen into the hands of the said King through the felony of Adam de Stratton.

We have previously adverted to the uncertain tenure by which the monastic possessions appeared to be held, as the numerous bequests and donations, ostensibly granted in perpetuity, seem in many cases to have been but temporarily enjoyed. The foregoing statement affords the most striking instance of this. Out of the five manors mentioned, Hallingbury had been granted to the monks of Bermondsey by Geoffrey de Mandeville, in the time of William Rufus; Cowyk (or Quickbury) in the same King's reign, by Richard Guett, described as the brother of the Countess of Warenne; and Wideford, by Robert de Beaumont, Earl of Leicester, General of Henry the First.

There appear, however, to have been frequent exchanges and transfers of property. It is stated that the Manor of Wideford, with those of Upton, Bengeho, Cowick, and part of Monksbury, the convent demised in the reign of Edward the First to Adam de Stratton, but from his negligence and misconduct they were twice forfeited to the King, who restored them each time to the convent.
- Wilkinson's *Londina Illustrata*.

In the reign of Edward the Second we find further allusions to those terrible calamities which appear to have been of frequent occurrence, for Professor Thorold Rogers says, in his "Economic Interpretation of History," that famines in the early Middle Ages occurred in England every seven years.

A famine is stated in the "Annals" to have afflicted the land in 1316, the incidents of which call up images of unspeakable horror. Wheat is said to have been sold on this occasion throughout England at forty shillings the quarter. The poor were reduced to allay the pangs of hunger with substances of the most loathsome description, and, horrible to relate, even to cannibalism! As a culmination of horrors, it is related that the dying were unheeded and the dead left unburied. Such was life in mediaeval England.

In 1321 we are told, "This year Thomas, Earl of Lancaster, was beheaded at his own castle of Pontefract." In connection with this it is stated in Phillips' "History of Bermondsey,"

> In 17th Edward the Second, A.D. 1324, the King issued his letters patent for arresting the Prior and certain monks of this house for entertaining certain rebels therein. These rebels were probably some of the adherents of Thomas, Earl of Lancaster, who after his defeat about two years before had taken sanctuary in this convent.

The Earl of Lancaster, who was a Prince of the blood, being first cousin of the King, had been the leader of the Barons in their opposition to the King's favourites. After exercising great power and influence and gaining many successes, he was defeated and captured at Boroughbridge. Hume thus describes him:

> His public conduct sufficiently discovers the violence and turbulence of his character; his private deportment appears not to have been more innocent, and his hypocritical devotion, by which he gained the favour of the monks and populace, will rather be regarded as an aggravation

than an alleviation of his guilt.

If the monks were really so much influenced by the practice of those arts, no doubt they welcomed these adherents of their fallen favourite, and readily granted them the privilege of sanctuary. As usual, we look in vain for details of these transactions, which possess such interest. With what pleasure a narrative of these incidents would now be read! We should be glad to know who were the persons thus seeking sanctuary. From such a strong measure being resorted to as the arrest of the Prior and monks, it is clear that they could have been no common fugitives. As most of the nobility and gentry in England were implicated in Lancaster's rebellion, it is extremely probable that they were persons of high rank and distinction, whose attainder would further aggrandize the favourites of the King. We can imagine these poor hunted fugitives, footsore and weary, possibly lying till nightfall hidden amidst the woods and bushes on the borders of Bermondsey; then, when the welcome shades had fallen, stealing fearfully across the fields to the gate of the monastery. Holding their breath and starting at every sound, real or imaginary, they felt, when the gate closed behind them, like men rescued from drowning, or who had received a reprieve on the scaffold.

The Prior whose hospitality occasioned his arrest was named John de Cusancia. He does not appear to have suffered from his imprisonment, for his tenure of office was the longest in the history of the priory, and terminated in 1359, not by death, but resignation, after being Prior for thirty-six years. We have no means of accounting for the great mortality which at times prevailed amongst the Priors, except by surmising that some were aged and sickly men, who may either late in life have acquired sufficient interest to secure their appointment, or that some of them may have been nominated as "warming-pans" to hold the seat for someone who was not yet prepared to fill it. As they were always foreigners, their transplantation to another clime may have been detrimental, and it is not improbable that unaccustomed fare may have abridged their span of life. These were no longer the days when a Prior was expected to set an example of self-denial and mortification to his monks. Elevation to the dignity of a Superior presented opportunities for indulgence, and a foreign Prior, indemnifying himself for long abstinence, might have found the good cheer of England a dangerous luxury.

After all that we have seen of the grandeur and importance of this great monastery, it seems remarkable that, except in cases of preferment to still higher dignity, any man should willingly have resigned the Priory of Bermondsey. The holy men who first held that office had regarded it as a sacred trust; they had considered themselves as soldiers of the Lord, commanding a garrison of His followers, holding it as a fortress in His name. Zealous in the fulfilment of their duties, steadfast in the maintenance of their post, they never dreamt of relinquishing it until death came as "Kind Nature's signal for retreat."

But the spiritual fervour and devout earnestness which had characterized the first monks had long decayed.

Bermondsey Priory, A.D. 1300

We have now to consider some remarkable circumstances connected with the monastery which may serve to explain much that is obscure. The Monastery of Bermondsey was an "alien priory," one of a numerous class that had arisen after the Conquest. Many of the foreign Barons who had been so liberally endowed with English land were connected with the founders of the great foreign abbeys, or more or less attached to them by predilection; therefore they sought to make these institutions participators in the royal bounty. They either themselves endowed, or secured grants of land in England to, many of the foreign houses. Robert of Mortain made the Monastery of St. Michael's Mount, in his earldom of Cornwall, dependent on that of St. Michael-in-Peril-of-the-Sea, in Normandy. Hugh de Grantmesnil was one of the founders of the Norman Abbey of St. Evroult. When the estates granted were extensive or important, it became customary to erect a monastery on the spot, a "cell" or branch of the parent foundation. All the Cluniac monasteries in England were cells of the great French Abbey of Cluny. Thus, the Priors of Bermondsey, although enjoying great privileges and being invested with the power of feudal lords, were the dependents and tributaries of a foreign Superior. Their revenues were taxed for his behoof. Under such conditions their very state must have seemed an empty pageant, the imposing titles with which they were dignified a hollow mockery.

Just as the Benedictines lapsed from their Apostolic purity, so the Cluniacs degenerated from the austere renunciation and the pious zeal which had distinguished them. The Abbey of Cluny itself, corrupted by the influence of increasing wealth, had fallen into laxity, and the Abbots, instead of being solicitous for the welfare of its branches, regarded them in no other light than as sources of revenue. When this was the case with the parent foundation, it was no wonder that the alien Priors should have become spiritually indifferent and neglectful of their duties. In the middle of the fourteenth century the Cluniac houses are said to have remitted annually the great sum of £2,000 to the French abbey. This sum, according to the relative value of money, would represent about £60,000 of our present currency.

> Whilst England and France remained at peace, this transmission of wealth out of the country was tolerated by the English rulers. War, however, brought the subject prominently before them, and led to various acts of suppression and confiscation. King John is said to have seized the priories dependent on the foreign houses (of different Orders) and applied their revenues to the relief of his own necessities.

These, numbering eighty-one, were compelled to pay into the royal treasury the sum hitherto sent abroad.

Nor was this draining of the resources of the country for the benefit of foreigners the only evil complained of. As most of the monks in these houses were Frenchmen, they in many cases acted as spies, and imparted information to the enemy.

- Henry the Eighth and the Dissolution of the Monasteries.

The matter came to a crisis in the early part of Edward the Third's reign.

In the Cluniac houses there had long been a feeling of discontent on the part of those English subjects who had there embraced the religious life. In the fourth year of this King's reign they laid their grievances before Parliament, in the shape of a petition. They stated that, in the opinion of many, the houses were not governed properly; that, in some priories, such as Montacute and Bermondsey, which ought to have had from thirty to forty members, there were not a third of that number; that all the revenue thus saved was being sent out of the country; that there was no election allowed them; that not twenty were professed in the province; and that some of the English members were kept forty years before being allowed to take their vows, whilst others were never permitted to do so. The petitioners begged that Parliament would insist on someone in England having powers to settle the question of profession, and they suggested that the Prior of Lewes would be a fitting person. Finally, they pointed out that the great evil (magnum malum) was that the French monks, however few, were always the masters, and that English subjects were habitually treated as inferiors. It was difficult, if not impossible, they urged, for them to live together in this way. To this remonstrance the King replied ordering the matters complained of to be looked to, 'lest he should have reason to act in a more severe manner.'

- Henry the Eighth and the Dissolution of the Monasteries.

It was not, however, until the death of Prior Peter de Tenolio, in December, 1372, that the question was finally decided with reference to Bermondsey. On January 18, 1373, Edward the Third appointed the first English Prior, Richard Dunton. From this time until the dissolution of the monastery no foreigner held sway in Bermondsey. The long line of alien Priors had come to an end; the outlandish names which figure in the "Annals" of Bermondsey disappeared for ever. Clarembald and Bertrand, Imbert and Hugo,

Henri de Soilly and Geoffrey de Deliviz, John de Cusancia and Peter de Tenolio, pass from the pages of our chronicle.

Richard Dunton! The very name is significant of the English victory. We involuntarily figure to ourselves a sturdy Anglo-Saxon, bold and self-reliant, solidly built, "Black-browed and bluff, like Homer's Jupiter."

No doubt he was one of those whose public spirit had not been quenched by the monastic routine, and who had long chafed at the humiliating subjection in which the community had been maintained. But, although the appointment of this Prior was the initial step, the monastery was not yet severed from all dependence on the Abbey of Cluny. The final triumph, however, was not destined to be long postponed, but before describing it we cannot refrain from relating an incident which gave rise to great rejoicing.

The Abbots of Battle, in Sussex, were among the greatest in that lordly company. Possessing a princely establishment at Battle Abbey, they also had a stately mansion in London, the "Abbot of Battle's Inn," in Tooley Street. The Conqueror had exempted them from all episcopal jurisdiction, and they steadfastly and successfully resisted the claim of the Bishops of Chichester to exercise authority over them. They further possessed the remarkable privilege, should they, in any part of England, encounter a condemned criminal, of pardoning and releasing him. In the latter part of Edward the Third's reign, this great position was filled by Hamo de Offington, a bold and high-spirited man, with martial instincts.

> In 1377 the French, having taken the Isle of Wight and carried off the Prior of Lewes, coasted towards Winchelsea; and Hamo, raising his vassals, hastened to the defence of the town, and successfully resisted a vigorous and prolonged assault.

For this exploit the warlike Abbot is styled by Fuller "the saviour of Sussex and all England"; and the popular admiration was embodied in the local proverb: 'Ware the Abbot of Battel when the Prior of Lewes is taken prisoner.'

When next the Lord Hamo came up to attend Parliament, we may imagine the chorus of congratulation that awaited him, and the number of noble and gallant personages that would have thronged the "Inn" in Tooley Street. With what exultation Prior Richard Dunton would have hastened to greet his brother, feeling that the victory of that reverend champion was a prognostication of his own impending triumph!

It came in 1380, and we will now set forth the charter of emancipation, the most important ever conferred upon the monks of Bermondsey:

> Richard (2nd), by the Grace of God, King of England and France, and Lord of Ireland, to all to whom these presents shall come, greeting. Know ye, that of our special grace, and in consideration that the Priory of Bermondsey, which is the foundation of our progenitors, and of our patronage, has been very much burthened with corrodies, through the undue government and negligence of the Alien Priors, who were before these times, and, by many other ways, dilapidated; as well in the decay of the buildings as the decrease of the revenues belonging to that Priory, till the time when our beloved in Christ, Brother Richard Dunton, an Englishman, who is Prior there at present, had the government thereof, the which Brother Richard, in his time, very much retrieved the state of the aforesaid Priory, with the advice of our Council, and for the fine of 200 marks, which the said Brother Richard paid to us in the Hanaper of our Chancery, have granted for us and our heirs, as much as in us is, to the said Brother Richard, that he and his successors for ever be Denizens, and in all respects as Denizens, and not reputed and treated as Aliens: and that they shall freely have the said Priory, with all the Lands and Tenements, Revenues and Possessions, Knights' Fees, and Advowsons of Churches, appertaining to the said Priory, without paying anything to us or our heirs for the said Priory, or for any possessions belonging to the same, on account of any war commenced, or to be commenced between us and our Adversary of France, and the heirs of the said Adversary, at any time whatsoever hereafter, as long as the Prior and Convent of the aforesaid Priory, or the Prior and the major part of the Convent, shall be English, of English extraction; always provided that if, from henceforward, it shall happen that the aforesaid Prior, or the greatest part of the Convent aforesaid, during the aforesaid war, shall be Alien, then, during that time, the said Priory, with the Lands, Tenements, Revenues, Possessions, Fees, and Advowsons of Churches, shall be again taken into the hands of us or our successors, and the Prior there shall be burthened to pay to us and our heirs during the said war, such rent as used to be paid to us by way of farm for the said Priory before the present grant.

This saving clause made provision for a contingency that never occurred. With what gratification must the monks, assembled in full convent, have listened to the reading of this charter! And with what exultation would the heart of Prior Dunton have swelled when, mounting to the highest point of the monastery, he surveyed the goodly prospect of his manor, with its orchards and gardens, its woods and pastures, and felt that he was the first real "Lord of Barmsey"! Absolute master of the estates of the priory, released from all dependence on a foreign Superior, burdened by no exactions, he could henceforth employ the monastic revenues for their legitimate purposes, for the repair and embellishment of the sacred edifice, for the maintenance of the proper number of monks, and in the practice of that charity and hospitality which were among the most important functions of such institutions. He devoted himself at once to the task of re-edification. The same year he rebuilt the cloister and refectory. In 1387 he covered the nave of the church with lead, put new windows in the presbytery, with gilt tables for the high altar and the morning altar. This worthy Prior resigned his office in 1390, and was succeeded by John Attleborough, who was destined to ascend to high preferment.

During the priorate of this incumbent, the Church of St. Saviour received for a time the remains of a Prince, whose tragic fate was one of the causes of Richard the Second's downfall.

Thomas of Woodstock, Duke of Gloucester, one of the uncles of King Richard, a man of bold and resolute character, was regarded by many of the people, and especially by the citizens of London, as a pillar of justice, and an upholder of sound policy, on account of his advocacy of English interests and his aversion to the favourites of the King. He had been instrumental in securing the overthrow of these, and also in bringing peculators to justice. There is no evidence of his having engaged in any treasonable practices, but the King was led to believe that the Duke of Gloucester intended to depose him, and finally made up his mind to destroy his uncle. With this view, having carefully laid his plans, he suddenly appeared, with a few attendants, at the Duke's castle, as if paying a friendly visit. Froissart tells us:

The Duke of Gloucester had already supped, for he was very temperate in his diet, and never sat long, either at dinner or supper; he immediately went out to meet the King, and paid him all the respect due to a Sovereign, as did his Duchess and her children. When the King entered the hall, the table was again laid out for him, and he ate some little; but he had before said to the Duke, 'Good uncle, have five or six horses saddled, for you must accompany me to London, as I am to have a meeting to-morrow with the citizens; we shall surely see my uncles of Lancaster and York, but I shall advise with you what answer to make to the Londoners' demands. Tell your house-steward to follow us with your servants to London, where they will find you.'

The Duke, suspecting nothing wrong, too easily consented; everything being ready, the King took leave of the Duchess and her children, mounted his horse, and the Duke did the same, attended by only three squires and four varlets. They took their way to Bondelay, to avoid the highroad to London and Brentwood, with the other towns through which it passes. They rode hard, for the King pretended impatience to get to London, and conversed all the way with the Duke of Gloucester. On their arrival at Stratford, near the Thames, where an ambuscade had been laid, the King galloped forwards, leaving his uncle behind; on which the Earl-Marshal went to the rear of the Duke with a large body of men, and said, 'I arrest you in the King's name.'

Thus treacherously seized, the Duke of Gloucester was smuggled over to Calais, then in the possession of England, and done to death in the following manner:

> ... that on the point of his sitting down to dinner, when the tables were laid, and he was about to wash his hands, four men rushed out from an adjoining chamber, and, throwing a towel round his neck, strangled him by two drawing one end, and two the other.

Another account, said to be founded on the confession of one of the accomplices, alleges that the Duke was smothered with pillows, and not strangled. In any case he was foully murdered. The corpse of the unfortunate Prince was brought back to England, and is said to have lain in the Church of St. Saviour, Bermondsey, before being conveyed to its last resting-place.

In the last year of his reign, Richard the Second entreated Pope Boniface the Ninth to erect the Priory of St. Saviour's into an abbey, and the Pope complying, Prior John Attleborough became the first Abbot of Bermondsey. The same year, 1399, Abbot John resigned on being created Bishop of "Athelfeld." The name is so given in the "Annals," but the learned editor of the Rolls Publications declares that he has been unable to identify this see, and suggests that possibly the Irish diocese of Ardfert may be intended.

Saxon ornaments in the Great Wall, near the Churchyard

CHAPTER VI

THE ABBEY OF ST. SAVIOUR - CRITICAL CIRCUMSTANCES OF THE TIME - THOMAS THETFORD, THIRD ABBOTY - HIS SUIT AGAINST THE KING - THE MONASTERY UNDER HIS SWAY - AVOCATIONS OF THE MONKS - THE ABBEY CHURCH.

The Monastery of St, Saviour, Bermondsey, had now attained the zenith of its greatness. Its connection with the proud Abbey of Cluny was permanently severed; the King's charter had freed it from all dependence; its principals were no longer nominated by a foreign Superior, but elected by the chapter of monks, sanctioned by the King, and confirmed by the Primate of England. It was now indeed "the Westminster of South London." Declared "denizen," henceforth purely an English foundation, the monastery came to be regarded, not as a Cluniac, but a Benedictine abbey, and its chiefs stood on an equal footing with the great Abbot of Westminster himself. We shall see them hereafter officiating in conjunction as prelates of equal dignity.

The conditions, however, at the opening of the fifteenth century were widely different to those under which the monastery was first founded. The Church still remained dominant, in the enjoyment of its authority and privileges, in possession of its ecclesiastical property, but monks had long ceased to be regarded with the reverence which had attended them in the earlier ages. Often abandoned to sloth and indulgence, performing their functions with mechanical indifference, they no longer set examples of industry and devotion, of sobriety and self-restraint. Bitter satirists had sprung up even in their own body, who lashed the vices of their brethren with unsparing severity. More perilous still, a spirit of inquiry had been aroused amongst the people, partly through the preaching of Wickliffe and his followers, partly owing to altered political conditions and social relations. Circumstances had enabled the English to assert their natural independence; they had long emerged from the thraldom in which they had been maintained under the Norman Kings. Magna Charta had produced its natural result in the development of Parliamentary institutions; even the rising of Wat Tyler had enabled the commons, in some instances, to wrest concessions from their feudal lords. They no longer received the teaching of the Church with unquestioning reverence; they no longer accepted the monkish legends, the multiplied fables, and the pseudo-miracles, with infantine credulity. Persecutions for heresy, as usual, only served to confirm the opinions that were sought to be suppressed, and, although more than a century was destined to elapse before the power of the Romish Church was broken, on the part of many, obedience to the laws which secured its privileges was accompanied with a sullen resentment and a deep though repressed indignation. The state of the alien priories must have had a great deal to do with fostering the growth of this feeling. Foreign monks, haughty and contemptuous, lording it over Englishmen, with no sympathy with the natives, or attachment for the land in which they were domiciled, pitilessly exacting payment of tithes and dues from the hard-living peasants, would have excited aversion towards their Order in general. But these foundations were doomed. During the reign of Richard the Second most of their estates remained in the King's hands, and negotiations were entered into with many of the foreign abbeys for the disposal of their property. Richard's successor, Henry the Fourth, began by showing favour to the alien priories. In the first year of his reign, 1399, he restored the conventual houses to the number of thirty-three, reserving in time of war for himself the subsidy they paid during peace to their foreign abbeys. A few years afterwards, on the advice of his Privy Council, he again suspended them, taking certain of their revenues for the support of his own household. In the Parliament of 1402 it had been arranged that all these priories should be again suppressed, and the Privy Council had discussed the question, who were the founders of these houses? In 1408, Henry, by the advice of his Council, took for his household expenses all the revenues of alien priories and the income of all vacant bishoprics and abbeys.

 We thus see that an organized attack on monastic property had now commenced, but, although dealing so unscrupulously with the revenues of aliens, Henry the Fourth solemnly confirmed the charter of independence granted to the monks of Bermondsey by his predecessor Richard. The King had his personal reasons for sparing this abbey. He was afflicted with leprosy, and it is recorded that on several occasions, when attacked with this virulent disease, Henry took up his abode at an old stone mansion then existing on the borders of Rotherhithe, where he was treated by the Prior of Bermondsey, who was eminent for his skill in physic.

Moreover, whatever laxity may have crept into the administration of the monastery under the later alien Priors, we are not to suppose that it continued to be marked by such defects.

All that we are told of the proceedings of Richard Dunton, the first English Prior, is sufficient to assure us that he was the man to carry out a complete reformation and reorganization. Conscious that the very existence of his monastery was at stake, that the mere emancipation from foreign control was not sufficient to ensure its continuance, he applied himself vigorously to the re-establishment of order and regularity, to tighten the bonds of discipline, and to infuse respect for the monastic character and functions. Honour to Prior Richard is due, for there is no doubt that he was a powerful instrument in saving the monastery from sharing the fate of so many similar institutions.

Abbot John Attleborough had been succeeded by Henry Tomstone, who held office for about thirteen years, but of whom we have no special mention. At the death of this Abbot, on May 19, 1413, a successor was elected whose career possesses more than ordinary interest.

Thomas Thetford, third Lord Abbot of Bermondsey, appears, from the very meagre items of information we are able to glean about him, to have been a man fitted alike to discharge the functions of his high office with dignity and to deal successfully with the difficulties arising from the circumstances of the time. The position he had attained was one the grandeur of which it is now scarcely possible to conceive. He was at once the high-priest of a great religious foundation, the principal of a college, and a temporal lord of greater power and authority than any now existing. The Abbot was the supreme ruler of the monks, their spiritual father, the judge from whose decisions no appeal was possible. To him it belonged to direct their studies and assign their occupations. The vow of obedience they were required to take placed them unreservedly at his disposal. He was himself required to set them an example of obedience, to be the embodiment of the Rule in practice. In many cases, even to the last, Abbots showed themselves worthy of their position, and exerted themselves to govern their communities with discretion and firmness. As during the Dark Ages monasteries had been receptacles of learning, where the efforts of monks preserved the lamp of science from extinction, they formed in many cases counterparts of the colleges of Oxford and Cambridge, the brethren representing Fellows, and the Abbots heads of houses. The education of the young was mainly in their hands; they officiated both as teachers in monastic schools and tutors in private families. At the Universities, monks were tutors and professors. The records of the ancient chroniclers abound with examples of monastic learning. Familiarity with masterpieces of classical literature was combined with theological lore; and the Benedictines, above all, were renowned for their cultivation and profound knowledge of history.

The charters of the ancient Kings had conferred great privileges on the heads of the Bermondsey monastery, and invested them with high authority. They were empowered to hold their own court, and to do justice on those who committed offences within their domain. These charters had been confirmed by Richard the Second and Henry the Fourth, who had expressly renounced all authority, and left the Abbots free to exercise their independent jurisdiction. They are said to have had the power of life and death.

The Abbot had now no great competitor in his immediate neighbourhood; he was no longer overshadowed by the majesty of the King, in his adjacent palace, or by the martial pomp of a great feudal Baron, like the Earl of Mortain and Cornwall. Lordly neighbours in adjoining districts were many. There was the Abbot of Battle, at his stately "Inn" in Tooley Street; the Prior of Lewes, opposite St. Olave's Church; the Abbot of St. Augustine's, Canterbury, at his town residence in the Borough; the great Cardinal Beaufort himself, at Winchester House, near the Priory-of St. Mary Overy's. Last, though not least, the famous General of the French wars, Sir John Fastolfe, frequently abode at his spacious mansion of Fastolfe House, on the north side of Tooley Street, from whence, "looking southwards, half a mile, over fields and meadows," he could see "the towers and walls of St. Saviour's

Abbey." Visits of ceremony and exchange of civilities took place between the Lord of St. Saviour's and his dignified compeers. The Cardinal, though his diocesan, exercised no authority over him, but it is presumable that certain arrangements entered into during the time of the alien priory were still in force.

> The Bishops of Winchester did formerly claim of this Convent an annual procuration or entertainment for one day, when they held their visitations in this part of their diocese; but, on a revival of this claim, A.D. 1276, by Nicholas de Ely, then Bishop, the Convent pleaded an exemption. The Bishop contested it, and, at length, a compromise took place on the following conditions, viz.: That the Prior and Convent, and their successors, on the first coming of every Bishop of Winchester to Bermondsey after his installation, should, in token of their regard for him as their Diocesan, meet him in procession, and, in lieu of a procuration or entertainment, should pay unto him and his successors five marks of silver, at his house in Southwark, and, in every succeeding year, two marks and a half at Michaelmas. Moreover, that, whenever it should happen that the Bishop should go beyond sea, the said Prior and Convent should receive him in procession on his return.
> - Phillips' *History of Bermondsey*.

The Bishop's visitation would have brought him close to the abbey gates, as it included the secular Church of St. Mary Magdalene's, on or about the site of the present parish church of that name. This church, which is often supposed to have been the abbey church, is, however, a distinct foundation, though originally built by the monks, and devoted to the use of the servants and tenants of the monastery. In time it became recognised as the parish church of the manor, the advowson of which was vested in the convent. The parish priest was even in those times styled Rector of Bermondsey, and was evidently a personage of no mean consequence amongst the clergy of South London.

Yet this Rector, coming to the abbey on business, and "craving speech of My Lord," would, on being ushered into the Abbot's presence, approach him with as much reverence as if he were the Archbishop of Canterbury himself.

The respect which secular priests were accustomed to pay to the monastic dignitaries is exemplified in a letter addressed to the Lord Chancellor Audeley by the Rector of a parish in

Somersetshire, about the time of the Dissolution. The Rector in question had been desired by the Lord Chancellor to call upon the Abbot of Athelney, one of the minor abbeys dependent on Glastonbury, and consequently not so eminent a personage as "My Lord of Barmsey," and to sound him with reference to the proposed change.

> I met the said Abbot coming from Mass in the church, about ten o'clock, and delivered unto him, as reverently as i could, your lordship's letter. Then said the Abbot: 'Come with me to my chamber, and I will tell you my mind.'

In the dialogue which ensued, the Rector represents himself as bearing his part with the most submissive deference, prefacing every reply or observation with "My Lord."

A magnate like the Abbot of Bermondsey was accustomed to correspond with great personages both at home and abroad, and to entertain men of the highest rank. When appearing at Court or entering an illustrious assembly, the Abbot would receive the respectful salutations of Dukes and Earls.

The household of a great Abbot usually consisted of many persons, both lay and clerical. The Abbot of Glastonbury was attended by a retinue of a hundred persons when appearing in public, and his establishment included many more.

In Tewkesbury Abbey, at the time of the Dissolution, there were "a hundred and forty-four liveried servants."

Although we do not suppose that the establishment of the Abbot of St. Saviour's was maintained on such a princely scale, there is no doubt that it was suitable to the dignity and importance of his position. Men of good family were often found among the dependents of those lordly ecclesiastics. A gentleman of ancient lineage but small estate, anxious to place a younger son well, would be glad to secure his admission into the household of the Abbot of Bermondsey.

It was not long before the mettle of this new Abbot was put to the test. Stow tells us that in 1417,

> Thomas Thetford, Abbot of Bermondsey, held a plea in Chancery against the King for the Manors of Preston, Bermondsey, and Stone, in

the county of Somerset, in the which suit the Abbot prevailed and recovered against the King.

The particulars of this suit are not given, but, as the alien priories had been absolutely suppressed in 1414, we are led to conjecture that the Crown may have claimed these manors as having been originally granted on conditions that had not been fulfilled. In all the vicissitudes through which it had passed, the foreign Priors of this monastery appeared to have meekly bowed to the storm, and to have borne the invasion of their chartered rights without an effort to maintain them. It may have been the remembrance of this, or a desire to test the forbearance of the Abbot, that led the officers of the Crown to endeavour to wrest these estates from him; but if so, they had found more than their match - a strong man, determined to guard the rights and privileges of the community which he had been appointed to rule, to permit no encroachment even on the part of the Sovereign, to firmly hold all property secured to the monastery by law, and to hand down its possessions unimpaired to his successor. And we have also in this case a striking instance of the altered conditions of the realm and of the force which law had now acquired. These were no longer the times when powerful and unscrupulous individuals could override judicial decisions and treat charters as waste paper. Even the powerful Henry the Fifth, flushed with his victory at Agincourt, found himself unable to extort the surrender of vested rights, and was compelled to bow to the decision of his own Judges. That independence which has so long been the honourable characteristic of the English Bench was here signally manifested.

This is not the only instance we have of Abbot Thetford's vigour in enforcing claims. The negligence or indolence of former Superiors had, as usual, encouraged encroachment and tolerated non-compliance with legal obligations. In 1419 the Abbot compelled the Rector of Beddington to pay the annual pension due from him to the convent, and in 1426 he gained a suit at the Ilchester Assizes against "John Mayes and Thomasia his wife," who appear to have been in unlawful possession of "a messuage, dovecot, nine acres of land and twelve of pasture, with all pertaining," forming part of the Manor of Kingweston, the memorable bequest of the Princess Mary of Scotland.

A man who was thus zealous in asserting his own rights and enforcing the claims of his community would have displayed no less firmness in the government of his monks and the superintendence of the great institution committed to his care.

The Abbey of St. Saviour was a structure of considerable magnitude, comprising an extensive range of cloisters, monastic offices, state apartments, and quarters for the reception of those who claimed its hospitality. The present Bermondsey Square was the main court of the monastery, surrounded by cloisters, and on the north occupying part of the present Long Walk, and the portion of Abbey Street between that passage and the wall of St. Mary Magdalene's Churchyard was the conventual church, the "Ecclesia Major Sancti Salvatoris de Bermundeseye." This was a large edifice, built in the Norman style, with little external decoration, but, as in many other cases, the grandeur was reserved for the interior.

One of the most important of the monastic offices was the Chapter-house, which, being much the same in all monasteries, is thus generally described in Stanhope's "Monastic London":

> This room or hall generally had three rows of stone seats one above the other, a reading-desk and settle, a place enclosed called the 'judgment' in the centre, a seat for the Abbot or Prior higher than the benches, and a large crucifix directly behind the desk. At 9 a.m. the monks assembled here, and, being seated, the proceedings were commenced by a short religious service. Then followed the reading of the sentence of the Rule from the desk, after which the Table was read, and anyone who had omitted a prescribed office solicited pardon. Then the Commemoration for the Dead - the Martyrology and Obituary - was recited, and always brought to a close by the 'Requiescat in pace.' To this succeeded the voluntary confessions, and after that came the accusation, or 'Clamatio,' of offenders.
>
> The monastic courts, taking cognizance of everything within the precincts of the conventual property, were held here. The sway of these courts reached the tenants of the monks and all those seculars who were in any way subservient to them, together with those strangers who committed crimes upon the lands pertaining to the monastery.

The jurisdiction in secular matters, Mr. Stanhope says, was usually exercised by the Seneschal of the abbey, who was "often a layman of rank."

As we are told that the Abbots of Bermondsey possessed the power of life and death, we must infer that in certain cases capital punishment was inflicted. If we accept the assertion of some authorities, the term "Neckinger" applied to a stream which formerly flowed on the east of Bermondsey Abbey, and the name of which is still retained by the district, would appear to have a sinister signification.

A local antiquary, Dr. Rendle, who wrote a very interesting and valuable book on "Old Southwark and its People" thus descants upon the much-disputed etymology of this word:

> Gerarde will, I think, help us to the original meaning of the name. He says of the wild willow herb that it is to be found nigh the place of execution at St. Thomas a Watering (near where now is the Green Man) and by a stile by the Thames' bank, near to the 'Devil's Neckerchief,' on the way to Redriffe (Rotherhithe). The 'Devil's Neckerchief' would seem to be euphemistic or slang for the gallows, or rope, or the 'hempen collar.' In Atkinson's 'Glossary,' 'neckinger' is a neckerchief, as 'muckinger' is a dirtied handkerchief. The variations of old English words are common enough, as 'kercher,' 'handkercher.' In short, the 'Neckinger' is nothing more than neckerchief, but implies, I think, its proximity to a place of execution, the 'Devil's Neckerchief,' on the way to Redriffe.

If this could be substantiated, it would be natural to suppose that the place of execution in question was the Abbot's gallows; but in the absence of any precise information we cannot undertake to fix the site. We have, of course, no record of any of the proceedings in the monastic court of Bermondsey, or of any of the cases tried therein, and can only hope that if death-sentences were passed they were few and far between. To return to less lugubrious subjects, the Almonry or almshouse was

> an important appendage to all monasteries, which were, indeed, throughout the Middle Ages the great fountains of charitable aid. It was usually a large stone building erected near the church, wherein all kinds of relief were freely and amply granted to the suffering and indigent poor. The alms were, for the most part, distributed on fixed days, but no one was ever sent empty away. The tenth part of all monastic revenues was set apart for this department.
> - *Monastic London.*

"The monks," says Professor Thorold Rogers, "were the relieving-officers of the period."

Apiary in the Conventual Garden

We may conceive that in the days of Abbot Thetford the same severe abstinence was not practised as in those of the saintly Petreius, and no doubt the "Kitchener" and "Refectioner" were as important members of his household as of that of Abbot Boniface at Melrose. Passages in the "Annals" referring to the high price of certain spices and condiments would seem to indicate that these had now become indispensable requisites. But although Well-filled larders and amply-stocked cellars are always pleasant to contemplate, the parts of this establishment which would possess paramount interest in modern eyes were the library and scriptorium.

> The books, being mostly manuscripts, were rolled and placed in painted presses or almeries. Many of these were of the most bizarre kind, but prominent among them always stood the family narrative of the monastery, edited by their classical Actuarius, or historiographer.

> Among them were, however, invariably good copies of the old Greek and Latin masters . . .
>
> The Scriptorium. - This was sometimes called the Domus Antiquariorum, but was simply the writing-room. The Abbot, Prior, Sub-Prior, and Precentor only were admitted into this treasury of beautiful missals, and other [manuscript] books of Divine offices of the early Church. A certain selected number of the brotherhood, surnamed the Antiquarii, were here continually employed in copying, or writing up the monastic daily history. Under these Antiquarii, who were men of superior stamp and education, worked the Scriptores or Librarii, copyists. The writing was generally good and clear. The character of the lettering nearly approached the present Roman. The first painters of the age were frequently engaged in illuminating the MSS. Gold and azure were the principal and favourite colours employed. Under these painters performed their pupils, or limners.
>
> - *Monastic London.*

The loving care bestowed both upon the writing and illuminating of these manuscripts often rendered them absolute works of art, models of calligraphy as well as colouring. The ingenuity of the monastic scribes was exercised in embellishing their performances with fanciful devices, scrolls, foliage, floral decorations. Moreover, it is easy to understand how a scribe, concentrating his faculties upon the transcription of a classical or sacred author, studying the text, incessantly comparing the copy with the original, labouring with devotional fervour, would become imbued with the very spirit of the writer, able to discern hidden significance, and to penetrate the very soul of genius. As Raphael said, "To comprehend is to equal."

One of the most interesting and authentic accounts of the learned labours of monks, as well as of the benefits accruing from monasteries, is furnished by a dignitary of the Church of England. Dr. Tanner, Bishop of St. Asaph in the reign of George the Second, wrote a work of great learning and research, entitled "Notitia Monastica," which remains a standard authority on the history of monasticism in England. When describing the labours in the scriptorium, the Bishop says:

> John Whethamsted, Abbot of St. Alban's, caused above eighty books to be thus transcribed (there was then no printing) during his abbacy. Fifty-eight were transcribed by the care of one Abbot of Glastonbury;

and so zealous were the monks in general for this work that they often got lands given and churches appropriated for the carrying of it on. In all the greater abbeys there were also persons appointed to take notice of the principal occurrences of the kingdom, and at the end of every year to digest them into annals. In these records they particularly preserved the memoirs of their founders and benefactors, the years and days of their births and deaths, their marriages, children, and successors; so that recourse was sometimes had to them for proving persons' ages and genealogies, though it is to be feared that some of these pedigrees were drawn up from tradition only, and that in most of their accounts they were favourable to their friends and severe upon their enemies. The constitutions of the clergy in their national and provincial synods, and (after the Conquest) even Acts of Parliament, were sent to the abbeys to be recorded, which leads me to mention the use and advantage of these religious houses. For, first, the choicest records and treasures in the kingdom were preserved in them. An exemplification of the charters of liberties granted by King Henry the First was sent to some abbey in every county to be preserved. Charters and inquisitions relating to the County of Cornwall were deposited in the Priory of Bodmin; a great many rolls were lodged in the Abbey of Leicester and Priory of Kenilworth, till taken from thence by King Henry the Third. King Edward the First sent to the religious houses to search for his title to the kingdom of Scotland, in their leigers and chronicles, as the most authentic records for proof of his right to that Crown. When his sovereignty was acknowledged in Scotland, he sent letters to have it inserted in the chronicles of the Abbey of Winchcombe and the Priory of Norwich, and probably of many other such places; and when he decided the controversy relating to the Crown of Scotland between Robert Bruce and John Baliol, he wrote to the Dean and Chapter of St. Paul's, London, requiring them to enter into their chronicles the exemplifications therewith sent of that decision. The learned Mr. Selden hath his greatest evidences for the dominion of the narrow seas, belonging to the King of Great Britain, from monastic records. The evidences and money of private families were oftentimes sent to these houses to be preserved. The seals of noblemen were deposited there upon their deaths; and even the King's money was sometimes lodged in them. Secondly, they were schools of learning and education, for every convent had one person or more appointed for this purpose, and all the neighbours that desired it might have their children taught grammar and Church music without any expense to them. In the nunneries, also, young women were taught to work and read English, and sometimes Latin also; so that not only the lower rank of people who could not pay for their learning, but most of the noblemen's and gentlemen's daughters, were educated in these places. Thirdly, all the monasteries were in effect great hospitals, and were most of them obliged to relieve many poor people every day; they were likewise houses of entertainment for almost all travellers. Even the nobility and gentry, when they were upon the road, lodged at one religious house and dined at another, and seldom or never went to inns; in short, their hospitality was such that, in the Priory of Norwich, 1,500 quarters of malt and above 800 quarters of wheat, and all other things in proportion, were generally spent every year. Fourthly, the nobility and gentry provided not only for their old servants in these houses by corrodies, but for their younger children and impoverished friends, by making them, first, monks and nuns, and in time Priors and Prioresses, Abbots and Abbesses. Fifthly, they were of considerable advantage to the Crown: (1) By the profits received from the death of one Abbot or Prior to the election, or rather confirmation, of another; (2) by great fines paid for the confirmation of their liberties; (3) by many corrodies granted to old servants of the Crown, and pensions to the King's clerks and chaplains, till they got preferment. Sixthly, they were likewise of considerable advantage to the places where they had their sites and estates: (I) By causing great resort to them, and getting grants of fairs and markets for them; (2) by freeing them from the forest laws; (3) by letting their land at easy rates. Lastly, they were great ornaments to the country; many of them were really noble buildings, and though not actually so grand and neat, yet perhaps as much admired in their times as Chelsea and Greenwich Hospitals are now. Many of the abbey churches were equal, if not superior, to our present cathedrals, and they must have been as much an ornament to the country, and employed as many workmen in building and keeping them in repair, as noblemen's and gentlemen's seats now do.

Before closing this chapter, let us take a glance at the abbey church. This it was that formed the principal link between the community and the outer world. Here knightly and noble personages paid their devotions; here pilgrims resorted to bend in adoration at the shrine, and offer up their petitions before the "Rood of Grace," which still, after the lapse of three centuries, retained its high renown. We can see them, under the influence of gratitude for some imputed favour or protection, gazing with adoration on the cross, and hanging upon the adjacent wall their "votive offerings," rude or costly. We see the crosses multiplied, fixed at regular intervals in the walls, figured in the pavement, everywhere, the symbol of the Redeemer's sufferings, the holy emblem of the patron of the abbey. As the sunbeams stream through the lofty stained windows, we see evidences of how closely chivalry and religion were associated in the Middle Ages. The banners of Knights whose ashes lie beneath the nave hang drooping from the walls; the armour and the swords of the departed warriors are, like them, mouldering to decay. A famous company lie buried in the church, many of noble, some of princely rank, and their sculptured effigies, in attitudes of prayer, add to the solemnity of the scene. Gorgeous and impressive ceremonies dazzle the eyes and overpower the senses of beholders.

> When the monks, clad in their white robes and black hoods, which formed the costume of their devotions, passed in pompous procession, chanting solemnly psalms of dole, the fragrant incense in the silver thuribles percolating its innocuous essences around the blazoned altar, brightly illuminated by the flames of many tall candles, and the full, broad, swelling harmony of the great organ filling the vast interior, the effect, it can well be imagined, was above all things grand.
> - *Monastic London.*

CHAPTER VII

ABBOT JOHN BROMLEIGH - GUARDIAN OF KATHERINE OF VALOIS - COMPILATION OR THE "ANNALES DE BERMUNDESEIA."

On the death of Abbot Thetford in 1432, John Say or Bromleigh, as Dugdale says he is styled in the charter, was appointed as successor. Many instances of these double names occur in ecclesiastical history; the unfortunate Abbot of Reading was known as Hugh Cook or Farringdon.

A later Abbot of Bermondsey was styled Robert Wharton or Parfew. A custom frequently prevailed in those days of designating a man both by his patronymic and the name of his birthplace. As, however, the new Abbot is styled Bromleigh in the "Annals," we shall retain that appellation.

He was destined to occupy a peculiarly onerous and delicate position, that of guardian of a Queen. Although many illustrious persons had been entertained in the monastery, we have no record of one of such exalted rank having been hitherto received as an inmate.

On a certain day in the summer of 1436, the Abbot having been previously notified of the impending arrival of Queen Katherine of Valois, a stroke on the great bell, twice repeated, summoned the monks from all parts of the monastery to the church, where they robed themselves, and prepared everything for the reception of their royal guest. Upon the near approach of the Queen being signalled, two of the great bells rang out a peal of welcome, and the Abbot, advancing at the head of his monks, saluted her with his benediction, and aspersed her.

> The procession then entered the church, and made a stand before the crucifix, where the visitor prayed.
> Service in honour of the Saviour as the patron saint followed, the singing-boys in the choir sang, the organ played, and at the termination of the whole, the Queen would find the best accommodation the abbey

could furnish provided for her use.

No further mention of the ancient palace occurs, and, as it is stated that Henry the First gave a portion of it for the enlargement of the cloister, it would be natural to suppose that the gradual extension of the abbey buildings had absorbed the former royal residence. It may be that the state apartments appointed for the reception of personages of exalted rank were situated in the remaining portion of the palace.

The Queen, who now became an honoured inmate of Bermondsey Abbey, came thither under very singular circumstances. She is usually represented as having been sent to Bermondsey either by Humphrey, Duke of Gloucester, then Protector of the realm, or at the instance of Cardinal Beaufort, who, as Bishop of Winchester, desired that the Queen should be secluded in his diocese. However this may have been, it is evident that Queen Katherine came to the abbey in a sort of disgrace, from the fact that her wedded husband, Owen Tudor, was at the same time committed to Newgate as a criminal for the sole offence of having married her, and that she was powerless to prevent this indignity.

Katherine of Valois, left a widow after a brief enjoyment of nuptial glories, found herself, whilst still young, established in a foreign land, amidst harsh and unfriendly people, and between herself and the leading magnates of the realm, Humphrey, Duke of Gloucester, and Cardinal Beaufort, there was little, if any, sympathy. What more natural than that her heart, yearning for sympathy and affection, should have opened to the influence of the handsome Welshman, Master of her Wardrobe? He, like herself, was an alien, serving a King not of his own race, yet with the memories of ancestral glories, the pride of ancient lineage - above all, the sense of national injuries - to bring them into unison, and to link them together by an indissoluble bond. There can be no doubt that the affection which arose between the royal lady and her aspiring servant was genuine, and that the stolen joys which the hapless Queen was enabled to snatch were sweeter than the utmost transports of her former union. The grandeur of the first match may have dazzled her imagination; the figure of the conqueror, albeit the destroyer of her own kindred, may have been irresistibly imposing to her girlish eyes; the pride of being united to the victorious monarch and sharing the glory of his throne may have dulled the sense of natural resentment at the injuries inflicted on her country and the calamities of her house. But, though pride and admiration may have impelled her to accept the union with the royal warrior, it is doubtful whether her heart was really touched, and whether she felt any genuine love for Henry.

The loves of Queen Katherine and Owen Tudor must have inspired great sympathy amongst retainers and dependents, for the secret appears to have been singularly well kept, and the Queen had borne three sons before the Duke of Gloucester appeared to have any inkling of the matter. These sons were Edmund of Hadham, subsequently created Earl of Richmond, and who became father of Henry the Seventh; Jasper of Hatfield, afterwards raised to the earldom of Pembroke; and Owen, who was born at a very inconvenient time, when the Queen was compelled to appear in the Palace of Westminster, and who, being hastily conveyed to the monastery, was brought up by the monks, and finally died a monk of Westminster.

Even this untoward circumstance did not appear to have reached the ears of the Protector, for it was not until long afterwards, when the Queen was again pregnant, or, as some say, after she had actually given birth to a daughter, that the secret of her marriage was discovered. At first there was merely a suspicion in the mind of Duke Humphrey that a marriage was contemplated, and, acting upon this idea, he issued a proclamation denouncing pains and penalties against anyone who should presume to marry a Queen-Dowager, and the actual discovery of the marriage appeared to rouse him to fury. The Duke immediately gave orders for the arrest and imprisonment of Owen Tudor, together with a priest who attended him, and his servant, and the Queen was despatched to Bermondsey. The Cardinal and Protector, who agreed in nothing else, appear to have been at one on this point. It is satisfactory to learn that the bolts and bars of Newgate proved insufficient to retain the hardy Welshman in captivity, and that he and his companions escaped.

There is something peculiarly touching and impressive in the reception of the sad daughter of the Valois by the monks of Bermondsey. Smarting under this humiliation and indignity, afflicted by the incarceration of her lawful husband and the separation from her children, the Queen was also suffering in body, and felt the stroke of death impending. On entering the precincts of the monastery she might have addressed Abbot Bromleigh in the words of Wolsey: "Father Abbot, I come to lay my bones amongst you!"

But what a soothing influence must have fallen on the wounded spirit of this royal lady when, entering the holy fane of St. Saviour's, she received the blessing of the Abbot and the respectful salutations of the monks! The "Father Abbot" received her as a father, and the monks as brethren in the Lord. When kneeling before the "Rood of Grace," and pouring forth her supplications for her captive husband, her children, now practically motherless, and herself, a Divine peace must have been infused into her soul, and when the sweet strains of the hymn to the Saviour rose around her, mingling with the solemn tones of the organ, it would have appeared like the answering Voice, breathing the promise of joys eternal.

Let us consider the significance of Queen Katherine's reception by the monks of Bermondsey. In her then condition she had no manors to bestow upon them, no princely gifts with which to reward their hospitality, no influence to use in their behalf, yet they received her with as much honour as if she had come amongst them as the bride of the Victor of Agincourt. It is pleasing to contemplate the many instances occurring in English history in which those who had fallen from their high estate, subject to the wrath of Sovereigns, and exposed to the contumely of the multitude, even in peril of their lives, found a tender and respectful welcome in a monastery. We have seen that, in the time of the alien priory, John de Cusancia risked imprisonment and the sequestration of his priory by sheltering the fugitive adherents of Lancaster. When the King who had destroyed Lancaster, Edward the Second, was himself brutally murdered, and his ferocious Queen had vowed deadly vengeance against anyone who should remove his body from Berkeley Castle for burial, it was an Abbot who opposed the majesty of Heaven to the threats of the female tyrant, and undertook the task from which Knights and nobles recoiled.

> At last the Abbot of Gloucester boldly entered the blood-stained halls of Berkeley with uplifted crosier, followed by his brethren, and, throwing a pall emblazoned with his own arms and those of the Church over the bier, bade his people, 'in the name of God and St. Peter, take up their dead Lord and bear him to his burial in the church, to which he had given so many pious gifts'; and so commenced the 'Dirige.' No one ventured to interrupt, much less to withstand, the Churchmen in performing the offices for the dead.
> - *Lives of the Queens of England.*

The dying Wolsey, stripped of all his honours and dignities, fallen and disgraced, sank into the fraternal arms of the Abbot of Leicester.

No doubt Abbot Bromleigh shared that sympathy which appeared to have been aroused in the breasts of all except the rulers of the State for the hapless Queen who was now committed to his charge. It is pleasing to find evidences that the conditions of these men's lives did not always blunt their sensibilities, nor prevent them from feeling tenderness and compassion for human frailties and sufferings. The monks of Westminster, who received the infant Owen, not merely sheltered the babe, but shielded the mother, for her secret had evidently remained safe with them.

Though, no doubt, tended with all solicitude, Queen Katherine's health continued to decline, and, after languishing for six months, she died in the abbey on January 3, 1437.

> Her body was removed to the church of her patroness, St. Katherine by the Tower, where it lay in state February 18th, 1437; it then rested at St. Paul's, and was finally honourably buried in Our Lady's Chapel at Westminster Abbey.

In the course of the same year the mortal remains of another royal personage were brought to rest, for a time, in Bermondsey Abbey.

Joanna of Navarre, Queen of Henry the Fourth, died on July 9, 1437, at her jointure house, Havering-Bower, in Essex. This country palace had long been a favourite retreat for both male and female Sovereigns. It was here that Edward the Third secluded himself during the last years of his life, and Isabella of Valois, the child-Queen of Richard the Second, occupied it as a temporary residence. This Queen-Dowager Joanna had known many strange vicissitudes and alternations of fortune. Daughter of Charles the Bad, King of Navarre, she was married in early life to John the Valiant, Duke of Brittany, who was many years her senior, and as his consort she exercised the most beneficial influence in mitigating the violence of her husband, and on more than one occasion prevented great calamities to which his country was exposed by the Duke's rashness and impetuosity. Henry the Fourth when Duke of Hereford, having been banished by Richard the Second, sought the hospitality of the Duke of Brittany, who assisted him to assert his rights to the estates withheld from him by Richard; and during the residence of Henry at the Breton Court he became enamoured of the Duchess. John the Valiant died the same year, 1399, and two years later Henry, now King of England, espoused the widowed Joanna. This marriage was followed by no progeny, although the King had had several children by his first wife, and the Queen had borne four sons and three daughters to the Duke of Brittany.

Queen Joanna did not gain as much favour in the eyes of the English as in those of the subjects of her former lord, but offended them by her avarice, and their dislike was further increased by the rapacity of her foreign followers. Moreover, as usually happens with stepmothers, she was not on good terms with some of the King's family, especially John, Duke of Bedford, with whom she was subsequently associated as Regent of the kingdom, during the campaign of Agincourt. In 1418 the Queen was suddenly arrested on a charge of witchcraft, and of conspiring against the life of Henry the Fifth. As has been shrewdly observed, the first accusation was in those days a convenient pretext for seizing the property of an intended victim, and no serious attempt was made to substantiate the second, although these suspicions caused the Queen four years' imprisonment. Whether the mere accusation became legendary, or whether Joanna may, like Eleanor Cobham, have dabbled in the "occult art," she continued to be known as the "Witch Queen," and her residence at Havering-Bower was regarded with superstitious awe by the peasantry, as the abode of a sorceress.

We are not, however, told that the monks of Bermondsey made any scruple of receiving a Princess of such sinister reputation within their precincts, or that they experienced any unusual trepidation during the watches of the night. From St. Saviour's Abbey the corpse of Queen Joanna was conveyed to Canterbury, where she was buried by the side of her husband, Henry the Fourth.

Possibly, however, the most important event which signalized Abbot Bromleigh's administration was the compilation of those monastic "Annals" which we have so often quoted, the "Annales Monasterii de Bermundeseia."

They are said to have been written by a monk named Robert Preston, no doubt a man of learning, and well qualified for the task; but, as no such work could be undertaken without the permission of superiors, it is probable that they were compiled by the direction of the Lord Abbot. The original manuscript (Harleian MS. 231) is still to be seen in the British Museum, and is described as

> a small quarto on vellum, containing seventy-one leaves, exclusive of blanks, written throughout in the same hand, a clear one, of about the middle of the fifteenth century.

We have reason to be grateful to Abbot Bromleigh and his monk for this epitome of the monastic history, and also to those who preserved it from sharing the fate of so many valuable records which appear to be hopelessly lost. The "Annals" are stated to have been in the possession of the "Howard family" before forming part of the Harleian Collection. Were it not for the existence of this chronicle, scarcely anything would now be known with reference to the ancient abbey, for Dugdale's account is based upon it.

The "Annals" commence in 1042, and end with the death of Abbot Thetford and the election of Abbot Bromleigh, in 1432, thus embracing a period of nearly four centuries. It does not at first sight seem clear why the so-called "Monastic Annals" should commence forty years before the foundation of the monastery; but 1042 was the date of the accession of Edward the Confessor, and may also have been the period at which the palace was built that, when the monk was writing his chronicle, had become a portion of the abbey.

As a genuine specimen of an ancient monkish chronicle, this

work possesses great interest; but although the annalist gives a full list of the Priors and Abbots down to 1432, and minute details of the grants bestowed upon the monastery at different periods, together with such incidental matters as the consecration of altars and enlargement or embellishment of the edifice, he is silent with reference to that which would now possess paramount interest, viz., the internal life of the abbey, and excludes all personal details relating to the Priors, Abbots, or distinguished monks. On the subject of this reticence, the observations of Father Gasquet, an eminent Benedictine of the present day, are worth quoting. That learned monk says:

> In the chronicles and memorials of the various abbeys we still possess, very little information can be gleaned about the interior and domestic life of the inmates. The reason for this is obvious. To the chronicler, as he wrote his volume in the cloister of his monastery, the daily course of the monastic life was so even, uneventful, and well known, that it must have appeared useless and unnecessary to enter any description of it in his pages.
> - *Henry the Eighth and the Dissolution of the Monasteries*.

So even, uneventful, and well known! This description might apply to an abbey in some remote and secluded spot, where nothing occurred from one year's end to another to break the monotony of humdrum existence. But could life at Glastonbury or St. Alban's, at Westminster or Bermondsey, have been uneventful? Besides, is not one irresistibly led to speculate on all that must have lain hidden beneath this superficial calm? Of those who were congregated within the walls of a monastery, ostensibly united by subjection to common laws, how many had acquired that Divine serenity, that calm contentment, which such institutions were supposed to foster? Men of the most dissimilar characters, the torpid and the energetic, the daring and the timid, the amiable and the morose, the pious and the dissembling, gathered under the same roof and brought into daily and hourly contact. Many men, without any vocation or inclination for the monastic life, have been in a manner forced to embrace it, possibly from family arrangements, with a view to resettlement of property, or in some other way coerced. To such the monastery would have provided no happiness. At most it could only be expected that their feelings would in time become blunted, and that conformity to rules, which might at first have been repugnant, would ultimately acquire the force of habit. Again, some of the chronicles and memorials we still possess furnish a very graphic sketch of the course of life in monasteries, and abound with interesting details with reference to the dealings of monks with laymen, together with facts that enable us to understand the character of the Superiors, as well as members of the community who were in any way conspicuous. Take, for instance, the chronicles of St. Alban's and St. Edmund's Bury, together with that valuable record which is included in the same volume of the Rolls Publications as the Annals of Bermondsey, the Chronicle of Dunstable. What a graphic description does the monastic scribe of Dunstable give of the tumult in the town, the multitude swarming around the priory, and the perplexity of "Dominus Prior" when compelled to comply with the demands of the burgesses! It is impossible to read this as well as the account of other incidents occurring in the Dunstable Chronicle without lamenting that circumstances connected with our abbey, which in detail would possess permanent interest, are either passed over in silence by the monk of Bermondsey or barely stated in as few words as possible. This may be partially accounted for by the fact that these are not contemporary annals, but a summary or digest compiled from registers which it was the special duty of certain monks to keep. These records have disappeared, as Mr. Phillips says, "in the general wreck of the abbey's fortunes"; and, as many of the dissolved monasteries have left no materials whatever for their history, we must be thankful for small mercies, and congratulate ourselves on the possession of this meagre narrative, which enables us to form at least a faint idea of the once great Abbey of St. Saviour. It must have been with a special object in view that Abbot Bromleigh directed the monk Preston to make this abstract, possibly in order to leave to his successors a concise account of the bequests and grants conferred upon the monastery, that might at any time be readily consulted without the trouble of wading through a number of volumes.

 The Chronicle of Bermondsey is sufficiently discursive, and embraces a wide area. The exploits of English monarchs, their wars with the French, the Scots, and the Welsh; the struggle between Popes and Emperors, the Crusades, schisms in the

Church, (Ecumenical Councils, the rise of monastic Orders, the canonization of saints - all these high matters fill the pages of our "Annals." But interesting as they are, they are, with few exceptions, culled from the writings of William of Malmesbury, Henry of Huntingdon, Roger de Hoveden, etc., and it is not without vexation that we find such details usurping the place of local history. From first to last, from the Prior Petreius to Abbot Thetford, we are told nothing of the origin or family of any of the Superiors, nor is any attempt made to sketch the character of men who must, we feel, have been remarkable.

The pages of the chronicle are strongly flavoured with mediaeval superstition; they teem with signs and wonders - fiery crosses seen in the sky, two moons visible at once, the sun and moon turned into blood, streams flowing blood, the frequent appearance of comets, betokening disaster. We hear of earthquakes, floods, terrific storms, one of which, that burst over Bermondsey, not only appalled the monks, but led "divers who were then here from Normandy, Burgundy, and the uttermost parts of Gaul," to declare that they had never heard such formidable and tremendous peals. It is edifying to observe the pious horror with which a catastrophe that occurred in the church at Winchcombe is related. In October, 1091, a thunderbolt fell, making a hole in the roof through which a man might pass, shivering a great beam to fragments, and strewing the church with them, shattering the crucifix and throwing down the image of the Virgin. This was followed by "a frightful odour, insupportable to human nostrils." At length, however, the monks of the abbey succeeded, by a deluge of holy water, in discomfiting the "enemy."

The love of the marvellous displayed by the monks may be readily explained by the circumstances of their lives. They believed themselves to be engaged in a spiritual conflict, waging war against the powers of the air, which was teeming with invisible agencies. The Enemy and his satellites were ever on the alert; the slightest accident that occurred was supposed to be due to his machinations. A monk in his cloister was often a counterpart of the Manchegan Knight, combating evil spirits as the Don conceived himself to be contending with enchanters and genii.

In spite of this, however, we should be inclined to regard the monk of Bermondsey as less superstitious than most of his brethren. The circumstances he relates are copied from the other mediæval chroniclers, and he probably considered them as articles of faith, to which no monk could refuse to subscribe; but beyond the incident of the storm and the miracle-working power of the "Holy Rood" he does not, as many of his brethren unquestionably would have done, represent Bermondsey as the scene of any marvels. He was writing at a much later period and under altered conditions. There is a certain dignity in his narrative; he states circumstances which he is bound to mention, without dwelling upon or unduly magnifying them.

It should, however, be borne in mind that this love of the marvellous was by no means confined to Romish chroniclers, as the famous Sir Richard Baker, in his chronicle, written in the seventeenth century, freely indulges in the same vein, and many Puritans were notoriously superstitious.

North Gate, Bermondsey Abbey, taken down in 1805

Remains of Conventual Buildings, demolished in 1805

An incident that occurred during the sway of Abbot Bromleigh would serve to show that the "Rood of Grace" was regarded as being favourable to hymeneal aspirations. In one of those famous "Paston Letters," which afford such glimpses of life in the fifteenth century, John Paston wrote to his mother, who was then in the Metropolis:

> Go visit the Rood of North Door and St. Saviour in Bermondsey, among while ye abide in London, and let my sister Margery go with you to pray to them that she may have a good husband ere she return home.

This was in 1465.

The expressions used in this letter have given rise to great confusion in later times, for the following reasons: John Paston, it will be observed, speaks of the "Rood of North Door." In a topographical work containing a description of Bermondsey, it is stated:

> In front of the buildings attached to the chief, or north gate of the abbey was a rude representation of a small cross, with some zigzag ornamentation; the whole had the appearance of being something

placed upon or let into the wall, and not a part of the original building; and there it remained till the comparatively recent destruction of the last remnant of the monastic pile. In a drawing made of the remains of the abbey in 1679, which was afterwards engraved by Wilkinson in his 'Londina Illustrata,' the same cross appears in the same situation; from this it has been conjectured, apart from the corroborative evidence of tradition, that this was the old Saxon cross found near the Thames.

North Gate-house, from the West

This, however, was not the case. The "Rood of Grace" was preserved in the abbey church, and the words of John Paston are very explicit. He speaks of the "Rood of North Door" and "St. Saviour in Bermondsey," and further on recommends his sister to pray to them, thus showing that he referred to separate and distinct objects. It is not, however, surprising that the cross fixed in the wall beside the north gate should have been confounded with the "Rood of Grace," as it survived the destruction of that more famous relic by several centuries, and on the demolition of the last remains of the abbey at the beginning of the present century, the following attempt was made to preserve it.

> In the grounds that belonged to the late James Riley, Esq. (situated at the end of the present churchyard), a pyramid was erected for the purpose of receiving the Saxon cross and one-half of the diagonals

belonging to the line of wall of the abbey. A small square Roman tablet was also placed above the cross, with the following notice: 'This obelisk was erected by James Riley, A.D. 1806, with stones of the ancient Abbey of Bermondsey, to perpetuate the ornaments used therein.'
- Phillips' *History of Bermondsey*.

West Gate of Bermondsey Abbey, existing in 1777

    This praiseworthy effort to preserve at least one memorial of the ancient abbey, so long the glory of Bermondsey, does not seem to have been appreciated as it deserved by the successors of that estimable gentleman. The cross and obelisk were removed many years ago, on the grounds being converted into building land, and it is not now known what became of them. The fate of the "Rood of Grace" will be related in the second part of this work.

    The Abbots of Cluny still continued to cast longing eyes upon the rich foundation that had so long been their dependency. Although nearly eighty years had elapsed since the Priory of Bermondsey was withdrawn from their control, the Abbot of Cluny in 1457 despatched three of his monks to England to lay before the King his "indisputable" claim to the Monastery of Bermondsey. The time was singularly ill-chosen. It is difficult to understand how the Abbot could have believed that the English, after their disasters and losses in France, would have been willing to resign one of their most important monasteries to the government of a French abbey. His emissaries prosecuted the suit with zeal, but their arguments and representations were heard with indifference by the King and his Council. After many months spent in fruitless solicitations, they departed as they came, and one of them penned a doleful epistle to the Abbot of St. Alban's, bewailing their inability to obtain "justice," and stating that his brother, the "Archdeacon," had died of vexation at the ill-success of the mission.

These efforts must have occasioned Abbot Bromleigh as much amusement as contempt.

Saxon, Norman, and Renaissance remains, piled up in Riley's Park

CHAPTER VIII

ABBOT JOHN DE MARLOW - OFFICIATES AT THE FUNERAL OF EDWARD THE FOURTH, AND ENTERTAINS ELIZABETH WOODVILLE - HIS "INDENTURE" WITH HENRY THE SEVENTH - ROBERT WHARTON OR PARFEW, LAST ABBOT OF BERMONDSEY - BECOMES BISHOP OF ST. ASAPH, SUBSEQUENTLY OF HEREFORD - SURRENDER AND DISSOLUTION OF THE MONASTERY.

Abbot Bromleigh resigned his functions in 1473, probably on account of age and growing infirmities, as he had now held office for over forty years. He was succeeded by John de Marlow, who appears to have enjoyed the dignity for about half a century. We cannot help contrasting the rapidity with which many of the foreign Priors disappeared from the scene of existence with the tenacity of life exhibited by the English Abbots.

The new Abbot was apparently a persona grata at Court, for we find him brought into closer communication even than his predecessors with the royal houses, both of Plantagenet and Tudor. In 1483 he is at Windsor, officiating as "Dekyn" (deacon) amongst the prelates who solemnized the obsequies of Edward the Fourth. Next he appears as the host of that monarch's widow, Queen Elizabeth Woodville.

The usual confusion prevails with reference to the circumstances under which this Queen became an inmate of St. Saviour's Abbey. The course of her life had subjected her to terrible and tragic vicissitudes - now radiant with the splendour of a Queen-Consort, sharing the wealth of the Sovereign of England; then humbled and reduced to penury; again exalted, invested with manors, palaces, and pensions; yet once more dispossessed, and dependent on the bounty of her royal son-in-law. Everyone is familiar with the causes of her earlier alternations of fortune, but great obscurity surrounds her relations with Henry the Seventh. In the first instance, we are told that,

A month after the marriage of her daughter to Henry the Seventh, the Queen-Dowager received possession of some of the dower-palaces, among which Waltham, Farnham, 'Masshebury,' and Baddow may be noted. Henry likewise adds a pension of £102 per annum from his revenues. If she were deprived of her rights and property once more, no evidence exists of the fact excepting mere assertion.

Thus far Miss Strickland. The Queen, nevertheless, is said to have intrigued against her son-in-law, and to have "fallen into disgrace with him for encouraging the rebellions of the Earl of Lincoln and Lambert Simnel." Professor Gairdner says:

> The King had held a Great Council at Sheen, the chief result of which was a very mysterious decision taken about the Queen-Dowager. That Elizabeth Woodville, when her daughter was actually Queen of England, could have knowingly joined in an intrigue to dethrone her husband is hardly credible in itself, and there is no reason to think it true. But she was a most unsteady woman, and her indiscretions may have been such as to serve the enemy's purpose almost as well as any active support she could have given them. Whatever may have been the case, the King thought fit, on due consideration, to deprive her of her jointure-lands, which he had only a year before restored to her, leaving her to find a retreat in the Abbey of Bermondsey, where she had a right to claim apartments as King Edward's widow, with a pension of 400 marks, which the King soon after augmented to £400.

The grounds for this "mysterious decision" remain as obscure as ever, and with regard to the "disgrace" of the Queen-Dowager, we find Henry endeavouring to promote a marriage between her and James the Third, King of Scotland, which was only frustrated by the death of the Scottish monarch.

Referring to the annuity of £400 granted by Henry in 1490, Miss Strickland says:

> No surrender of lands of equal value has yet been discovered; yet, strange to say, historians declare that she was stripped of everything, because about this time she retired into the Convent of Bermondsey. Here she had every right to be, not as a prisoner, but as a cherished and highly-honoured inmate; for the Prior and monks of Bermondsey were solemnly bound by the deeds of their charter to find hospitality for the representative of their great founder, Clare, Earl of Gloucester, in the state-rooms of the convent. Now, Edward the Fourth was heir to the

Clares, and Elizabeth, Queen-Dowager, had every right, as his widow, to appropriate the apartments expressly reserved for the use of the founder. She had a right of property there; and as it was the custom in the Middle Ages for royal persons to seek monastic seclusion when health declined, where could Elizabeth better retire than to a convent bound by its charter to receive her?
- *Lives of the Queens of England.*

It may, however, be that, with the view of spending the remainder of her days in retirement, the Queen effected an amicable arrangement with Henry the Seventh, by virtue of which she surrendered her estates to the King for the consideration of the annuity. Four hundred pounds at that period would represent between seven and eight thousand at the present time, and we can hardly conceive the parsimonious King disbursing such considerable sums without a very substantial equivalent. Such an agreement would have suited both; the Queen would be relieved from all the trouble and expense of administration, and the King would gain what he most desired - a valuable addition to the Crown property.

Certain passages in the Queen's will, dated April 10, 1492, indicate that she no longer retained possession of her estates:

Item. Whereas I have no worldly goods to do the Queen's Grace, my dearest daughter, a pleasure with, neither to reward any of my children according to my heart and mind, I beseech God Almighty to bless her Grace, with all her noble issue; and, with as good a heart and mind as may be, I give her Grace my blessing, and all the aforesaid my children.

Item. I will that such small stuff and goods that I have be disposed truly in the contentation of my debts, and for the health of my soul, as far as they will extend.

This testament is witnessed by "John, Abbot of the Monastery of St. Saviour of Bermondsey."

We cannot refrain from lamenting that there should have been no monastic scribe who might have left an account of the sojourn of the two Queens in Bermondsey Abbey. With what intense interest should we now read the story of Katherine of Valois' mournful end, and the manner in which John de Marlow fulfilled his trust in the case of Elizabeth Woodville! But, for aught we know, such records may have existed, and perished in the general havoc of the Dissolution.

Towards the close of the fifteenth century a remarkable rebellion took place in Cornwall, stated to have arisen from some oppressive imposts, and which was originally headed by a lawyer and a blacksmith. The rebels, gathering force, advanced into Somersetshire, and called upon James, Lord Audley, to become their leader. This nobleman consented, and marched at their head towards London; but they were defeated by the King's forces and their leaders captured. Lord Audley was executed on Tower Hill.

When enumerating the illustrious persons buried in the abbey church, Mr. Phillips tells us:

> Dame Anne Audley bequeathed her body to be laid here by her will dated in November, 1497, and would have a priest to pray for the souls of John, Lord Audley, her husband, and James, late Lord Audley, her son.

Queen Elizabeth Woodville died in the abbey in 1492, and was buried at Windsor, though without any great pomp; but we find Abbot Marlow figuring in the imposing funeral of her daughter, Elizabeth of York, Queen of Henry the Seventh, in February, 1503:

> On the twelfth day after the Queen's death Mass was said in the (Tower) chapel early in the morning.
>
> Then the corpse was put in a carriage covered with black velvet, with a cross of white cloth of gold, very well fringed. And an image exactly representing the Queen was placed in a chair above in her rich robes of state, her very rich crown on her head, her hair about her shoulders, her sceptre in her right hand, her fingers well garnished with rings and precious stones, and on every end of the funeral car was a kneeling gentlewoman leaning on the coffin, which was in this manner drawn by six horses, trapped with black velvet, from the Tower to Westminster. On the fore-horses rode two chariot-men, and on the four others four henchmen in black gowns. On the horses were lozenges with the Queen's escutcheons; by every horse walked a person in a mourning-hood. At each corner of the car was a banner of Our Lady of the Assumption, of the Salutation, and of the Nativity, to show the Queen died in childbed; next, eight palfreys saddled with black velvet, bearing eight ladies of honour, who rode singly after the corpse in slops and mantles; every horse led by a man on foot, bare-headed, but in a

mourning-gown, followed by many lords. The Lord Mayor and citizens, all in mourning, brought up the rear, and at every door in the City a person stood bearing a torch. In Fenchurch and Cheapside were stationed groups of thirty-seven virgins, the number corresponding with the Queen's age, all dressed in white, wearing chaplets of white and green, the Tudor colours, and bearing lighted tapers.

From Mark Lane to Temple Bar alone were 5,000 torches, besides lights burning before all the parish churches, while processions of religious persons, singing anthems and bearing crosses, met the royal corpse from every fraternity in the City. The Earl of Derby, the Queen's old friend, led a procession of nobles, who met the funeral at Temple Bar. The Abbots of Westminster and Bermondsey, in black copes and bearing censers, met and censed the corpse, and then preceded it to the churchyard of St. Margaret, Westminster. Here the body was removed from the car and carried into the abbey. It was placed on a grand hearse, streaming with banners and banneroles, and covered with a 'cloth of majesty,' the valance fringed and wrought with the Queen's motto, 'Humble and Reverent,' and garnished with her arms. All the ladies and lords in attendance retired to the Queens great chamber in Westminster Palace to supper. In the night, ladies, squires, and heralds watched the body in the abbey.

- *Lives of the Queens of England.*

Subsequently a deed called an "indenture" was executed between "The King, the Mayor and commonalty of the City of London, the Abbot and Convent of St. Peter, Westminster, and the Abbot and Convent of St. Saviour's, Bermondsey, for holding an anniversary in the Abbey Church of Bermondsey, on the 6th of February, to pray for the good estate of the King during his life, and the prosperity of his realm; also for the souls of his wife, late Queen, and their children; for the souls of his father and mother, on payment of the annual sum of £3 6s. 8d., and if it remained unpaid for twenty-one days, the Abbot and Convent of Westminster were to forfeit £5 6s. 8d., exclusive of the above sum of £3 6s. 8d. The deed also contains directions in what manner it is to be solemnized, of which the following is an extract:

> The Abbot and Convent of St. Saviour of Bermondsey shall provide at every such anniversary an hearse, to be set in the midst of the high chancel of the same monastery before the High Altar, covered and apparelled with the best and most honourable stuff in the said monastery convenient for the same. And also, four tapers of wax, every

one of them weighing viii. lb., to be set about the same hearse - that is to say, on either side thereof one taper, and at either end of the said hearse another taper. And all the same four tapers to be light and burning continually, during all the time of every such Placebo, Dirige, with nine lessons, lauds, and mass of Requiem, with the prayers and observances above rehearsed.

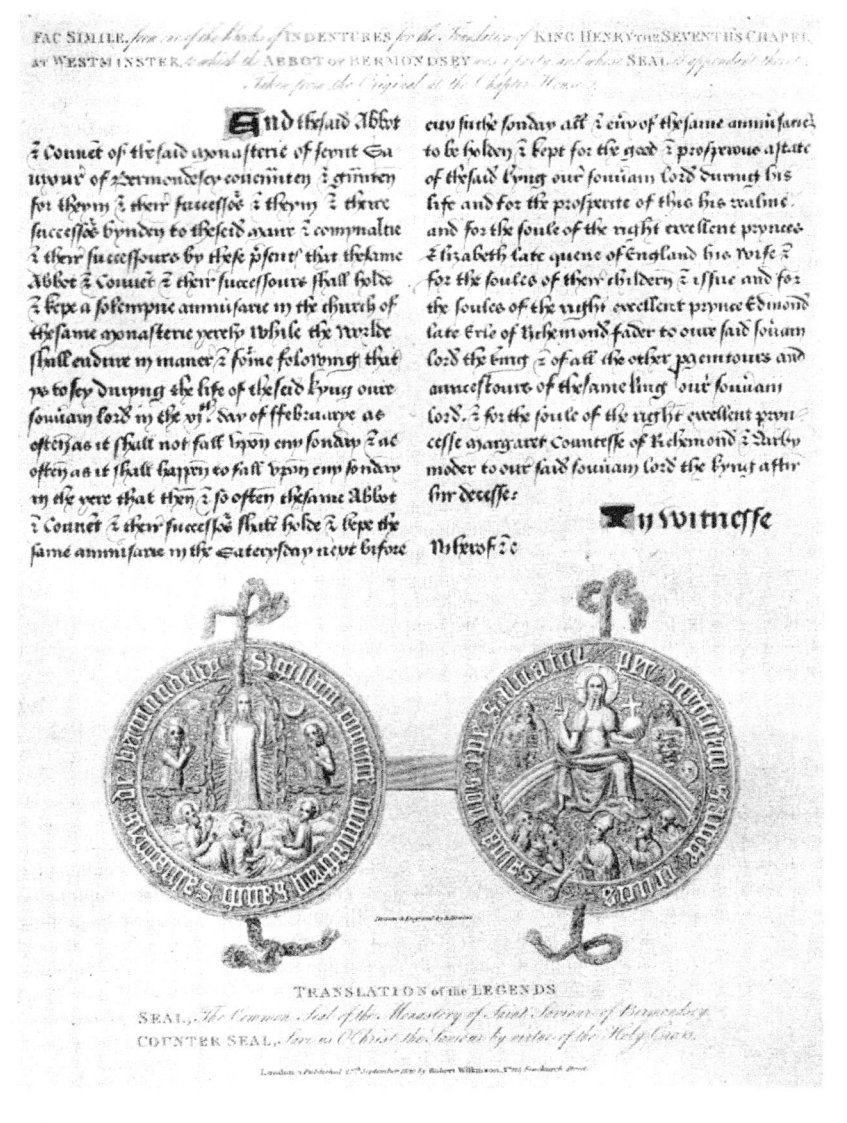

Facsimile of Indenture, bearing the Great Seal of Bermondsey Abbey

The Lord Abbot, or in his absence the Prior, and all the monks not "letted by sickness, or bounden to perform other masses on the same day," were required to be present and assist in the performance of this solemn function.

The seal of Bermondsey Abbey affixed to this document represents on the obverse the Transfiguration scene, and on the counter-seal Christ in the act of blessing, with the legend: "Sigillum Commune Monasterii Sancti Salvatoris de Bermondsey."

When Abbot Marlow died or resigned his office, we are not informed, nor at what period he was succeeded by the sixth and last incumbent, "Robert Wharton or Parfew, S.T.B. of the University of Cambridge," although it would probably have been between 1520 and 1530. All that we can learn of this last Abbot of Bermondsey is that

> He was Prior, according to Manning, as early as 1520. He was consecrated Bishop of St. Asaph July 2, 1536. He surrendered the abbey to the King, January 1, 1537-38, and obtained a pension of £333 6s. 8d. per year. In April, 1554, he was translated to Hereford by Queen Mary, of which see he died Bishop, September 22, 1557, and was buried there in his cathedral.
> - Phillips' *History of Bermondsey*.

Dugdale has no more to tell us. Yet we feel more curiosity with reference to the character of this Abbot than that of most of his predecessors, and are led to speculate on the influences which must have operated on his mind. He was Prior, we are told, as early as 1520, and could not have been destitute of feelings of attachment for the institution with which he had so long been connected. He may have been a shrewd and acute man of the world, with sufficient sagacity and penetration to discern that the days of monasticism were numbered, and that the contemplated change could not be averted, being merely the result of causes that had been long in operation. Evidences reached him on all hands of the growing irreverence of the laity; the violent attacks made upon the church would have impressed him with a belief that it was necessary to conform to the spirit of the age, that it was better to bend than to break, and that stubborn resistance to the movement that was in progress was sheer folly. He was not of the stuff of an Abbot of Woburn or of Glastonbury, and had no desire to win the crown of martyrdom.

We are now approaching the last scene in the history of monastic Bermondsey. Four centuries and a half of historic grandeur, of sovereign dominion over the souls and bodies of men, had now ended, and the great Abbey of St. Saviour was destined to become a vague and ever-fading tradition, an indistinct memory, like that of the palace which it had absorbed.

A violent rupture with the past had taken place; a mighty institution that had once, like a huge oak, struck its roots deep into the soil, and overshadowed the land with its branches, had decayed, and was about to be destroyed, that it might no longer cumber the ground. Monasticism, once so abounding in vitality, performing so many functions of utility, had now become an anachronism and an anomaly, opposed to the spirit of the age, in conflict with all the aspirations and yearnings which filled the minds of Englishmen. The sixteenth century was a period of political, social, and religious transition.

Feudalism had fallen, and monasticism was doomed. When the nobles were deprived of their special jurisdiction, and rendered amenable to the general law of the realm, it was no longer possible for a privileged class of spiritual magnates to claim exemption from lay authority and to maintain that influence which they had hitherto exercised. The clergy no longer enjoyed a monopoly of learning; men had now begun to think for themselves, they had broken loose from the leading-strings of ecclesiastical control; the saintly legends were dismissed as childish fables with which the infancy of the human intellect might be amused; the sacred emblems, the services and processions, all which had hitherto seemed so venerable, had lost their power over the imaginations of the people. They were now coming to be regarded as absurd mummeries, and even in some cases as impious mockeries. That in dark ages, when the majority were steeped in barbarism, monks should have preserved civilization from being overwhelmed, and learning from extinction, that they should have kept alive the sense of beauty, and preserved useful arts from being forgotten, are merits that will ever entitle them to the gratitude of mankind; but the cultivated intelligence and increasing skill of laymen had long deprived them of their superiority. The pupils had outgrown their teachers.

The strains of Leland, that enthusiastic panegyrist of monkish learning, who entered the library of a famous abbey with "awe and trembling," commemorating in his " Cantio Cygni"

> Barmsey's shrine,
> Where her priests labour in the work Divine,

appear to us like the last outpouring of antique devotion, the dying swan song of monastic glory.
With reference to the surrender of the monastery, Bishop Burnet tells us, under date of 1537:

> Two other surrenders are enrolled that year. The one was of Bermondsey in Surrey, the 1st of June, in the 28th of the King's reign. The preamble was, that they surrendered in hopes of greater benevolence from the King. But this was the effect of some secret practice, and not of the Act of Parliament, for it was valued at £548, and so fell not within the Act.
> - *History of the Reformation.*

The Bishop says the surrender took place on June 1, 1537; other authorities that it occurred on January 1. The Bishop estimates the income of the abbey at £548, whereas the official valuation represents it to have been £474 14s. 4d. This seems a very petty sum in the present day, but we must bear in mind that a pound in those days was equal to twelve in our own time, and that such a figure would now represent an income of nearly £6,000. We know not how large a portion of the original property was still retained by the community, as we find notices of sales, exchanges, and commutations recorded at different periods in the "Annals." Many causes had also operated to reduce the value of landed property, especially the conversion of arable land into pasture, which within the early part of the sixteenth century had been effected throughout a great part of the country. Monastic lands, moreover, were generally let at a low rental. The different payments, tithes, pensions, rent-charges, etc., pertaining to the monastery, though numerous, were often of very small amount. Moreover, we may regard the lesser estimate as representing the "net value" of the monastic property, and some important abbeys could be named with far less income, as, for instance, Wigmore, the Abbot of which was also a Suffragan Bishop, and the net value did not exceed £270 a year.

Bishop Burnet says: "They surrendered in hopes of greater benevolence from the King. But this was the effect of some secret practice, and not of the Act of Parliament."

The Act alluded to was that which had been passed some time previously, for the dissolution of the smaller monasteries, the income of which was less than £200 a year. The "secret practice," of which the Bishop speaks so confidently, still remains a secret, for it is impossible to discover the exact circumstances under which the abbey was surrendered.

The magnitude of the pension granted to Abbot Wharton constitutes a problem by no means easy of solution. That he should have received a retiring allowance of £333 6s. 8d. out of an income of only £474 14s. 4d. is incomprehensible when we reflect that many of his brethren were considered to be amply provided for with £100 a year, or even less, and that £200 was regarded as a most magnificent provision. The first mitred Abbot in England, he of St. Alban's, only received a pension of 400 marks, on the ground that his monastery was ill-governed, and he himself a man of loose character; but the Abbot of St. Edmund's Bury, who, though young, was of unblemished reputation, and strict in his administration, received on this account no more than 500 marks. The Abbot of Tewkesbury, he of the "hundred and forty-four liveried servants," was dismissed with 400 marks.

It has been suggested that Abbot Wharton was originally "put in with a view to surrender." But had he accepted office on these conditions, knowing that the surrender of his monastery was a foregone conclusion, he might surely have been contented with less compensation, especially as he had the preceding year been elevated to a bishopric.

We have hitherto dwelt, by preference, on the merits of monks, and the higher characteristics of monastic life, but we are neither indifferent to the darker features of that life nor blind to the inherent defects of the system.

Dr. Rendle, in his book on "Old Southwark and its People," says that Bermondsey Abbey ended "as a scandal to the neighbourhood"; but the only authority he gives for this remarkable statement is Taylor, the "Water Poet," who was not born until long after the Dissolution, and consequently could know nothing personally about the matter. It is not conceivable that a man of the eminence and high character of Leland, writing only a few years before the Dissolution, could have expressed the veneration he did for an institution that had become notorious. It would be too much to expect that the monks of Bermondsey should have been always exempt from the frailties of their brethren; but we should require stronger evidence than that of the "Water Poet" to induce belief in general corruption. The delinquencies of Superiors were fully exposed at the time of the visitation of the monasteries, but the utter absence of any imputation against the Lords of Bermondsey justifies the belief that the Abbots were men of regular and decorous lives.

There are other circumstances to be considered with reference to Abbot Wharton's pension. As he is reported to have made a voluntary surrender, we are to infer that he delivered the whole of the monastic property into the hands of the King's Commissioners, without reservation or deduction. It was generally asserted that in cases where the surrender was extorted the Abbots and Priors either concealed or disposed of the more valuable articles, leaving but a small residue to be taken possession of by the Commissioners. Now, the actual income of a monastery would represent but a portion of its wealth. The magnificent Church plate, the richly ornamented shrines, the costly reliquaries, the gorgeous vestments and profusion of rich materials of all kinds, made the spoil of the monasteries peculiarly coveted. It would be impossible to estimate the value of the gifts with which the devotion of centuries had enriched the Church of St. Saviour's. It may have been either with the object of removing any temptation to withhold portions of this wealth, or to reward his honest dealing, that so liberal a pension was conferred upon the retiring Abbot.

As the opinions of the reformers were now gathering force, many looked with stern satisfaction on the closure of Bermondsey Abbey, and the secularization of that property which, for so many centuries, had been administered by monks alone. In the eyes of these persons, the great abbey no longer possessed anything venerable or awe-inspiring; it was the abode of superstition, the seat of monkish imposture. The Abbot, the great "Lord of Barmsey," before whom, as he rode along Bermondsey Street, every head had bowed, whose name was pronounced with "bated breath and whispering humbleness," now, stripped of his feudal privileges and his high prerogatives, had sunk into an ordinary mortal, at whom they would scarcely turn their eyes to look. The monks had became objects of derision.

But, indifferent as the majority had grown, there were still some devout and tender individuals whose hearts clung with affectionate constancy to the fallen institution.

> "Perchance, e'en dearer in her day of woe
> Than when she was a boast, a marvel, and a show."

These persons had grown up in the shadow of the abbey; they were proud of it, and loved to dwell upon its grand traditions. To them the dissolution of the monastery meant the violent rending of old associations, the desecration of august memories, the destruction of all that they held most dear.

We can see them, when the monks had dispersed, and the last Abbot had ridden away from Bermondsey, gathering at night to gaze upon the huge dark mass of the monastic buildings, lying, in their desolation and abandonment, like the corpse of the defunct system, the sad emblem of fallen Monasticism. The dormitories were untenanted, the refectories deserted, the cloisters no longer paced by gliding, black-robed figures, the Abbot's quarters vacant, the guest-house empty, the House of Charity closed.

Their eyes turned to the abbey church, through whose windows for more than four centuries light had never ceased to gleam from tapers perpetually renewed and lamps incessantly replenished. All was now wrapped in darkness, the pealing organ mute, the voice of prayer hushed. The bells hung silent in the tower.

Their minds were dazed and bewildered, unable to comprehend the present or to penetrate the future. Retiring to their beds, and falling into uneasy slumbers, they awoke at a time when they had been accustomed to hear the chant of the monks. They listened in vain for the familiar sounds, and the conviction gradually sank into their minds that all was over - over for evermore.

But what were these feelings compared with those which must have been aroused when the end really came, when the despoilers and demolishers arrived to ply their implements and pursue their unholy task? The stained windows were shivered to atoms, the tombs of the illustrious dead defaced, the recumbent effigies of Knights and noble ladies dashed to fragments, their banners and escutcheons torn from the walls. The roof was stripped of its lead, the altars of their gilding and ornaments, the shrines of their votive offerings, and that fane, where Kings and Queens had knelt in prayer, where Princes and Prelates, Dukes and Earls, Templars and Crusaders, had worshipped, reduced to a shapeless ruin.

And the Rood - the once famed and venerated "Rood of Grace" - looked sadly down on the scene of desolation. No taper supplied by reverent hands now burnt upon its altar, no lamp cast its gleam upon the Cross, but the fitful moonbeams, penetrating through broken roof and shattered windows, illumined it with a wan and ghastly light. The fantastic effects which moonlight often produces, playing upon broken column and ruined tomb, seemed to evoke strange phantoms, as though the spirits of the mighty dead were rising to protest against the desecration of their sanctuary.

The genius of Scott alone could worthily depict such desolation. His noble lines on Melrose would have been equally applicable to Bermondsey:

> If thou wouldst view St. Saviour's aright.
> Go visit it by the pale moonlight:
> For the gay beams of lightsome day
> Gild, but to flout, its ruins gray;
> When the broken arches are black in night,
> And each shafted oriel glimmers white.

And thus the Night of Time closed in around St. Saviour's Abbey.

Saxon Cross fixed in the Wall adjoining the North Gate.

CHAPTER IX

THE "NEW MEN" OF THE TUDOR REGIME - SIR THOMAS POPE A TYPE OF THESE - HIS EARLY SUCCESS - FAVOUR OF HENRY THE EIGHTH AND SIR THOMAS MORE - CLERK OF THE BRIEFS IN THE STAR CHAMBER - CLERK OF THE CROWN - WARDEN OF THE MINT - KNIGHTED, AND MADE PRIVY COUNCILLOR - TREASURER OF THE COURT OF AUGMENTATION - HIS SHARE OF THE MONASTIC SPOILS - HE BUILDS BERMONDSEY HOUSE, AND FOUNDS TRINITY COLLEGE, OXFORD - GUARDIAN OF THE PRINCESS ELIZABETH AT HATFIELD HOUSE - HIS DEATH.

The decay of feudalism had given rise to a complete change in the political and social relations of England. The power of the great Barons, the authority of the dignitaries of the Church, were alike broken, and on the ruins of their influence had arisen the supremacy of the King. That element of personal government, which became gradually stronger and stronger under the Princes of the House of Tudor, was essentially different to the despotism of the ancient English monarchs, tempered by the resistance of their great feudatories. The change was in many respects a wholesome one. It was no longer possible for a great lord, entrenched in his moated fastness and surrounded by his armed vassals, to defy the authority of the Sovereign. All men, noble and Churchman, burgher and peasant, were alike subject to the law of the realm, and the King was no longer compelled to weigh the chances of rebellion, or to modify his policy in deference to the wishes or prejudices of powerful subjects. He was now emphatically the Head of the State, the Chief Magistrate, invested with unquestioned power to protect the loyal and punish the disaffected.

The former Kings had occasionally delegated their authority to favourites, who oppressed Barons and people alike, and whose career generally ended in a tragedy, disastrous both to their masters and themselves. But the new Sovereigns began to use their power of selection, and to choose, regardless of birth or connections, men whom they conceived to be best fitted to serve them with ability and to be useful to the State. These men were selected, not for physical qualities that were pleasing to the eye of the Sovereign, for conformity of tastes and inclinations, but for mental endowments and capacities which specially fitted them for the work of administration. Henry the Seventh was the first Sovereign who was his own Prime Minister, but though he chose to discharge those functions, he had no desire to surround himself with ciphers. It was of essential importance to him that he should secure the aid of sagacious and experienced Councillors, and trusty subordinates, performing with intelligent assiduity the functions assigned to them. In the system fostered by the first Tudor Kings we see the germ of a Civil Service, the rise of a new "bureaucracy."

Sir Thomas Pope

A very conspicuous example of the character of those men who arose under the new regime is furnished by the career of Sir Thomas Pope, the first lay "Lord of Barmsey," the outlines of which are to be found in the biography written by the Rev. Thomas Warton, Professor of Poetry at Oxford during the second half of the last century. Warton was a conspicuous figure in the literary history of the period, a member of the "Literary Club," a cherished associate of the Immortals who have rendered that fraternity illustrious; but in this case the work is singularly unworthy of his reputation. As a Trinity College man he undertook to write the life of the founder, and produced a dry, official biography, destitute of aught that could enliven or embellish a narrative. It is amazing that the historian of English poetry, and himself not devoid of poetic faculty, should have produced so dull and lifeless an account. His work might be cited as a conspicuous example of the "art of sinking" in biography. Nor is this all. Many of the most important circumstances of Sir Thomas Pope's career are passed over in silence, his connection with Bermondsey is never mentioned, his dealings with the monasteries are very briefly described. Those details which would now possess absorbing interest are altogether omitted, and their place is usurped by copious extracts from deeds and documents, possessing, as such matters usually do, certain special applications and defined importance, but with little bearing on the life and character of the man. It is possible that the task may have been an uncongenial one, undertaken solely at the instance of others; but it is to be lamented that Warton did not take a more exalted view of his subject, and endeavour to produce a work that would have been worthy alike of the theme and of himself.

A real biography of so remarkable a man as Sir Thomas Pope appears to have been, who enjoyed the favour of successive Sovereigns and the friendship of illustrious persons, and who played an important part in some of the most memorable events of that memorable age, would now possess singular historic interest.

Thomas John Pope, we are told, was born at Dedington, Oxfordshire, about the year 1508, when the reign of Henry the Seventh was drawing to a close. His parents were William and Margaret Pope, who lived at Dedington, but the family, "which seems, at least, to have been that of a gentleman, was originally seated in Kent."

Their son Thomas received the first rudiments of grammatical learning at the public school of Banbury, at that time a celebrated seminary, and kept by Thomas Stanbridge, of Magdalen College, Oxford, "an eminent instructor of youth."

Young Thomas Pope was subsequently sent to Eton, and finally to London to study law. After being called to the Bar, Pope would appear to have devoted himself to the cultivation of influential friends, for we learn,

> he was not much more than twenty-seven years of age when he had sufficient address or interest to procure his appointment to offices which seem to have been alternately bestowed upon Henry's most eminent favourites and the most popular characters of those times.

Pope practised in the Court of Chancery, and there gained the favour and friendship of the great Sir Thomas More.

> Having been early initiated into the business of Chancery, on the 5th day of October, 1533, he was constituted, by letters patent of Henry the Eighth, Clerk of the Briefs in the Star Chamber at Westminster.

Although this famous court was not stainless at that period, it had not then acquired the sinister reputation it was destined to attain in the seventeenth century. It is commonly stated to have commenced in the early part of Henry the Seventh's reign, and in its inception was designed to strengthen the authority of the King and to curb the power and insolence of the nobles. Sir Thomas Smith, in his "Commonwealth of England" (1609), says:

> There is yet in England another Court, of the which, that I can understand, there is not the like in any other country. In the Term time, every week, once at the least (which is commonly on Fridays and Wednesday's, and the next day after that the Term doth end), the Lord Chancellor and the Lords and other of the Privy Council, so many as will, and other Lords and Barons which be not of the Privy Council. and be in the Town, and the Judges of England, specially the two Chief Judges, from nine of the clock until it be eleven, do sit in a place which is called the Star Chamber, either because it is full of windows, or because, at the first, all the roof thereof was decked with images of stars gilded. There are plaints heard of riots, etc. And further, because such things are not commonly done by mean men, but such as be of power and force, and be not to be dealt withal of every man, nor of mean gentlemen; if the riot be found and certified to the King's Council, or if otherwise it be complained of, the party is sent for, and he must appear in the Star Chamber, seeing (except the presence of the King only) as it were the majesty of the whole realm before him, being never so stout, he will be abashed, and being called to answer (as he must come of what degree soever he be) he shall be so charged, with such gravity, with such reason and remonstrance, and of those chief

personages of England, one after another, handling him on that sort, that what courage soever he hath, his heart will fall to the ground, and so much the more, when if he make not his answers the better, as seldom he can, so, in open violence, he shall be commanded to the Fleet, where he shall be kept in prison in such sort as these judges shall appoint him, lie there till he be weary, as well of the restraint of his liberty, as of the great expenses he must there sustain, and, for a time, be forgotten, while after long suit of his friends, he will be glad to be ordered by reason. Sometimes, as his deserts be, he payeth a great fine to the Prince, besides great costs and damages to the party, and yet the matter wherefore he attempted this riot and violence, is remitted to the Common Law. For that is the effect of this Court, to bridle such stout noblemen and gentlemen which would offer force by wrong to any manner men, and cannot be content to demand or defend the right by order of Law.

The praiseworthy objects, however, with which this court was originally established were soon supplemented by provisions tending to gratify the avarice of the King.

> The chief objects of the King, through the instrumentality of this Court, were the restraint of the nobles and the support of the prerogative, but connected with these were the replenishing of the royal purse with the fines and commutations, and the money paid for pardons, even of great offences against the commonweal.
> The King's most notorious agents in these matters were Sir Richard Empson, Knight, and Robert Dudley, Esq., both lawyers, who not only acted as promoters - that is, as common informers, filing accusations in the Star Chamber - but also served the King as collectors of the fines imposed by the Court and of moneys paid for the King's favour, and for his pardon for murders, felonies, and misdemeanours.

As everyone knows, Empson and Dudley were brought to trial, and executed in the beginning of Henry the Eighth's reign.

We do not, however, in those days, read of tortures and cruel punishments, the infliction of which, in later times, has rendered the memory of the Star Chamber for ever odious. We have no information as to Pope's proceedings in this court, but as many of the cases brought before it concerned Abbots, Priors, and religious houses, we may regard the experience he gained there as being a very fitting preparation for the functions he was ultimately destined to perform.

Having, as we see, been appointed Clerk of the Briefs on October 5, 1533, he further received on the 15th of the same month, by letters patent of the King, a reversionary grant of the office of Clerk of the Crown in Chancery. In 1535 Pope was appointed Warden of the Mint, Exchange, and Coinage. In the same year one of the most sorrowful circumstances of his life occurred, which evidently caused him sincere affliction - the death of his friend and patron, Sir Thomas More, who died a martyr to his own honesty and consistency. To Pope was assigned the melancholy task of conveying the intimation of his doom to Sir Thomas More.

> On the 5th day of July, 1535, he waited on Sir Thomas More, then under condemnation in the Tower, early in the morning, and acquainted him that he came by command of the King and Council, to bring his unfortunate friend the melancholy news that he must suffer before 9 of the clock the same morning, and that therefore he should immediately begin to prepare himself for death.

More replied cheerfully: "Master Pope, I most heartily thank you for your good tidings."

> Pope, on taking his leave, could not refrain from weeping. More comforted him; 'I trust that we shall once in heaven see each other full merrily, where we shall be sure to live and love together in joyful bliss.'

In 1536 Pope was knighted, and a privy-councillorship ultimately closed the list of his honours. In the same year Sir Thomas was appointed to the office which has rendered him most memorable, that of Treasurer of the Court of Augmentations. This new department of State was created to facilitate the surrender of the monasteries, and to arrange for the disposal of their property. The amount of business which devolved upon it is clearly indicated in the following extract. Sir James Mackintosh, in his "History of England," after saying very significantly that it was not for their vices that the monasteries fell, states:

> The number of monasteries which either had been dissolved, or had surrendered, or ransomed themselves by payments of large sums to the

King, amounted to 376. They were the legal owners of a large part of the landed property of the kingdom. The numbers of the religious were probably about 6,000 or 7,000; that of their servants, dependents, and retainers may be estimated moderately at an equal number. £100,000 (probably a million and a half of the present value) came immediately into the Exchequer; £30,000 (probably half a million according to our wages and prices) were added to the annual revenue of the Crown.

But although these immense sums were paid into the Exchequer, it does not appear that the King himself was greatly enriched thereby, as he was compelled to assign a large share of the spoil to many powerful individuals whom it was necessary to conciliate, and whose cupidity was excited by the spectacle before them. These, of course, were either courtiers or local magnates of influence in their respective counties; but the favour of the King, and the position in which he was now placed, also enabled Sir Thomas Pope to lay the foundation of a great fortune.

> That his prodigious property was accumulated in consequence of the destruction of the monasteries is not denied, and the lucky opportunity of raising an estate from the great harvest of riches which now lay open before him seems to have diverted his thoughts from making a fortune by the law.
> - Warton's *Life*.

Dr. Rendle says of Sir Thomas:

> He had a great deal to do with the suppression of abbeys, but he had nothing to do with the hanging of Abbots. He received the surrender of St. Alban's, but he saved the abbey church from being pulled down.

One would think that the merit of having saved that noble edifice from destruction would have afforded an opportunity to Warton, but he has comparatively little to say on the subject. With respect to Sir Thomas Pope's accumulations, he says that he could give,

> in minute detail, from the most authentic evidence, the grants of abbey lands which he received during the reign of Henry the Eighth. But it may suffice to note generally that before 1556 he appears to have actually possessed more than thirty manors in different counties,

besides other estates, and several advowsons, some given to him by Henry the Eighth, some acquired by purchase, while he was connected with the Court of Augmentations.

Dr. Rendle states:

> The earliest notice of Pope's connection with Bermondsey I find is this: 'That Edward Powell is licensed to alienate a messuage there to Thomas Pope, Knt.,' the same year the monastery was dissolved. Three years and more after the surrender [i.e., 1541] the site of the abbey was granted to the Master of the Rolls, Sir Robert Southwell, at a yearly reserved rent of ten shillings. This was the 8th of July, and on 30th August following, by deed of bargain and sale, he conveyed this estate to Sir Thomas Pope and Elizabeth, his wife, in fee. This sale was afterwards confirmed by letters patent. Sir Thomas now proceeded to build himself a house; he pulled down the old church with the adjacent buildings, most probably only in part, and with the materials made himself a mansion, which he called Bermondsey House. It had orchards, edifices, gardens, stables, barns, pasture, and ponds, about twenty acres in all.

On the demolition of the abbey church he caused the "Rood of Grace" to be removed and "set up on the common in Horselydown, at the end of the present "Crucifix Lane." We may here also mention the ultimate fate of the famous rood.

> In an ancient diary of a citizen, who lived in the reigns of Henry the Seventh and Eighth, we have the following notice of the taking down of the Rood of Bermondsey, in 1559, in the mayoralty of Sir Richard Gresham: 'M. Gresham, mayr. On Saint Mathies day thapostull the xxiiij. day of February Sonday, did the Bishop of Rochester preche at Polls Cross, and had standyng afore him all his sermon time, the pictor of the Rood of Grace in Kent, which was greatly sought with pilgrims, and when he had made an end of his sermon, the pictur was torn all to pieces; then was the pictur of Saynt Saviour that had stand in Barmsey Abbey many years in Southwarke, takyn down.'
> - Phillips' *History of Bermondsey*.

The word "picture" was applied in those days to images and statues as well as paintings. The Kentish "Rood of Grace" above mentioned was that of Boxley. In the instance of the Rood of Bermondsey, the "taking down" was synonymous with destruction.

We should infer that some inhabitants of the parish had been present at Paul's Cross, and, repeating some of the Bishop's utterances, and describing the scene which followed, had roused their neighbours to fanatical violence, who thereupon wreaked their fury on the luckless rood. It is stated to have been a wooden crucifix, and therefore was probably committed to the flames. However senseless the rage of the populace may seem to calm observers at this distance of time, it must be remembered that they were newly freed from the rule of Mary, and that the fires of Smithfield were fresh in their recollection. The quaint spelling in the citizens diary may be matched by that contained in an inventory,

> indentyd and made of all the plate, juells, ornaments, and bells, wythe in the pshe Cherche of Mary Mawdelyn of Barmondesey, in the sixth year of the reign of our Sovereign Lord, King Edward the Sixth.

Much of this wealth is commonly believed to have been bestowed upon the parish church by Sir Thomas Pope, after the dissolution of the monastery. Those who have written upon the subject imagine that the splendour of the Abbots shines in the

> many copes of white damask flowered with gold; many more of blue silk flowered with white; chasubles of red velvet with gold crosses, and chasubles of Bruges satin with crimson crosses; dalmatics, with 'orphreys,' or embroidered borders, of the most costly kind; pixes of gold, and golden censers, together with a quantity of silver plate.

We shall have something to say on this point when treating of the parish church in the next section. The greater part of these costly articles was sold by the churchwardens, together with some which may have possessed greater value. They disposed of the "Lattyn bokys of parchment" for ten shillings, which Dr. Rendle considers "were no doubt the missals and other books of service - most of these books, no doubt, exquisitely illuminated, and yet sold for so little."

Whatever the books may have been, the churchwardens would hardly seem to have been competent to estimate their value, if we judge from the fact that one of them, Harry Etyn, was unable to write his name.

Although, from want of knowledge of the facts, we should hesitate to speak severely of this proceeding, too many instances occurred in which stolid and barbarous ignorance led to the dispersion and destruction of priceless treasures. Father Gasquet says, with great justice:

> No other instance is needed to rouse in all feelings stronger than regret than the loss of the precious manuscripts and other contents of the monastic libraries, which disappeared in the general havoc. How little such things were cared for may be gathered by the contemptuous references which occur in the account of the sales which took place. 'Old books in the choir, 6d.;' 'old books in the vestry, sold to Robert Dorington, 8d.;' 'old books and a cofer in the library, 2s.;' 'a mass-book with its desk, 8d.;' 'fourteen great books in the choir, 14s.,' are samples of the sales of manuscripts which would now be of immense value.

Fuller says,

> The English monks were bookish themselves, and much inclined to horde up monuments of learning.
>
> John Bale has left on record his experience as to the way in which the treasures described by Leland disappeared upon the destruction of the monasteries. The purchasers of the houses used the manuscripts for every vile and common necessity. 'Grocers and soapsellers' bought them for their business purposes, and 'whole shipsfull' were sent over the sea to the bookbinders. While one merchant bought the 'contents of two noble libraries for forty shillings' price,' and 'this stuff hath he occupied instead of grey paper,' adds the author, 'by the space of more than ten years; and yet hath he store enough for as many years to come.'

This account leads to the consideration of a kindred subject, which, in a certain respect, had considerable weight with Sir Thomas Pope. We read in Warton's Life:

> Yet a great temporary check given to the progress of literature at this period was the dissolution of the monasteries.
>
> For although these seminaries were, in general, the nurseries of illiterate indolence (?), yet they still contained invitations and opportunities to studious leisure and literary pursuits. By the abolition of the religious houses many towns and their adjacent villages were

utterly deprived of their only means of instruction. Nor should we forget that several of the Abbots were persons of public spirit; by their connection with Parliament, they became acquainted with the world; and knowing where to choose proper objects, and having no other use for the superfluity of their vast revenues, encouraged, in their respective circles, many learned young men.

We have said that this state of things had considerable weight with Sir Thomas Pope, but the deprivation of public instruction sustained by Bermondsey owing to the closure of the House of Charity, that "nurse of many students," did not move him to supply the want. The Church of St. Mary Overies, in the Borough, had been menaced with the same fate as the Abbey Church of Bermondsey, but the public spirit of the inhabitants of Southwark led them to make an appeal to the King, who finally consented to spare the sacred edifice on certain conditions, one being that it should henceforth bear the name of "Saint Saviour's."

Nor did their efforts rest here. They revived our monastic school in their own parish, and the remodelled foundation has continued to flourish down to the present time. In the documents relating to the purchase of land and endowment, the founders employed the seal of Bermondsey Abbey, which they had adopted, representing the Transfiguration.

Let it never be forgotten, to the honour of the people of Southwark, that to their affectionate devotion and enlightened zeal is owing the preservation of one of the noblest churches in London and the restoration of a great public school.

Sir Thomas Pope, although sharing abundantly in the spoils of the monasteries, never ceased to be a Catholic. His attachment to the old religion may possibly have induced a desire to emulate those ancient benefactors whose munificent endowments have gained them lasting fame. He resolved to employ a great portion of his acquired wealth in founding a college at Oxford, which was called Trinity College, and became one of considerable reputation. The monastic spoils enabled him to supply it with abundance of "inside plenishing," with costly plate and valuable books. He is believed to have enriched the college library with many of the best works contained in those of the abbeys which had surrendered to him, and it is probable that some of the most important may have belonged to Bermondsey. He, at least, as a man of learning, was capable of appreciating the value of such works, and no doubt sought to secure a fitting repository for them.

Inside one of the rooms under the Hall, Bermondsey House

Notwithstanding his eager pursuit of riches, Sir Thomas Pope possessed personal qualities that endeared him to some of his most eminent contemporaries, and have left him with, on the whole, a fair reputation. Fuller, the Church historian, says:

> However, by all the printed books of that age, he [Pope] appeareth one of a candid carriage; and, in this respect, stands sole and single by himself. That, of the abbey-lands which he received, he refunded a considerable portion for the building and endowing Trinity College, Oxford.

Dr. Rendle, writing in the same strain, says:

> He aimed to do good, partly because he was of a kindly nature, and loved to do good; partly, I think, as an expiation for his participation in doubtful matters, troublesome to the conscience, and he evidently had a conscience. It was the custom of the time to balance the earlier ill-deeds of people by good deeds and riches bestowed at the last; it was not possible for a sinner to take his riches with him; accordingly, some of this man's possessions passed in kindly gifts to people, and much in

founding a college at Oxford.

This college, being opened and supplied with Fellows and students, was watched over by the founder with paternal care. Good cheer was not lacking, and his visitation was the signal for great rejoicing. High festival was held in the halls of Trinity on St. Swithin's Day, 1555, although the account does not state whether Sir Thomas himself furnished part of the materials for the banquet, or whether the whole entertainment was provided by the college authorities.

> Among other good things mentioned are four fat does and six gallons of muscadel, and twelve minstrels made it otherwise pleasant to the company.

Although Sir Thomas had built himself so stately a mansion in Bermondsey, and at intervals resided here for some time, he possessed other lordly abodes, also the former seats of Abbots and Priors. He had in Clerkenwell "a capital messuage and seyte of the late dissolved monastery." In the country, his chief residence was at Tyttenhanger, in Hertfordshire, which had been the seat of the Abbot of St. Alban's. With reference to that structure with which we are chiefly concerned, Dr. Rendle says:

> The Manor House, Bermondsey House, must have been a noble and costly edifice; the site of it is represented by the present Bermondsey Square and the adjacent land. We need indulge in no mere conjecture as to the grandeur of the mansion. In its previous condition, Queens and other not much less distinguished people could be lodged and entertained over and above the usual numerous inhabitants of a great abbey.

From this it may be inferred that Sir Thomas had not only utilized the materials derived from the demolition of conventual buildings in the construction of his mansion, but had also included within it a considerable portion of the abbey, even as the abbey itself had formerly absorbed the palace. Dr. Rendle goes on to say:

> As to the noble construction of Sir Thomas Pope's mansion, much of it remained even up to the last century;

portions, evidently of a great mansion, were still left to be investigated by skilled and enthusiastic men. Carter, second to none as both architect and antiquary; Buckler, architect and enthusiast as to his native parish; Wilkinson, in his 'Londina Illustrata'; and Manning and Bray - all these leave little to be desired.

Outside of the Hall

Portion of Hall, Bermondsey House

We do not know whether Sir Thomas was in residence at the time, but the most remarkable event during the period of his occupancy was the coming of Sir Thomas-Wyatt and the men of Kent to Bermondsey in February, 1554.

The men of Kent were headed by Sir Thomas Wyatt, and came the usual way of all rebellious - from Dartford to Greenwich, and from Greenwich to Deptford. Then came Queen Mary and her ladies, riding to the Guildhall to consult the Lord Mayor and Aldermen for the safety of the city; for, whatever were poor Mary's faults, she had the high spirit of the Tudors and was no coward. Watch and ward were kept by harnessed men, and 500 footmen harnessed were sent by water to Gravesend. The Duke of Norfolk, who was sent against Wyatt, met with a repulse, lost eight pieces of cannon, and himself hardly escaped. Wyatt and his Kentishmen, encouraged by this success, marched to London, and about 3 o'clock in the afternoon, on the 3rd of February, he, with five ancients (ensigns, officers), having by estimation 2,000 men, left Deptford, and came towards London. Six or eight shots were fired from the White Tower, but missed them, sometimes shooting over, sometimes short. Were they very bad marksmen in those days? Or may we not suppose that they were trying the effects of a little wholesome fright? Then was the drawbridge cut down and the bridge gates shut. The Mayor and Sheriffs, harnessed, commanded each man to shut in his shop and windows, and to be ready harnessed at their doors what chance soever might happen.
By this time was Wyatt entered into Kent Street, and so on to St. George's Church into Southwark. Himself and part of his company came in good array into Bermondsey Street, and they were suffered to enter Southwark without repulse or any stroke stricken, either by the inhabitants or by others; yet in the inns were many men brought thither to resist Wyatt, but instead of going against the Kentishmen, they joined themselves with them, and the inhabitants with their best cheer entertained them, whether from fear or sympathy does not appear, but probably the latter, for the Spanish match was disliked throughout the kingdom.
Immediately on Wyatt's coming, he made proclamation that no soldier should take anything, but that he should pay for it, and that his coming was to resist the Spanish King.
Notwithstanding, divers of his people, being gentlemen (as they said), went to Winchester Place, made havoc of the Bishop's goods, not only of his victuals, whereof there was plenty, but whatsoever else, not leaving so much as one lock of a door, but the same was taken off and carried away; not a book in his gallery or library uncut or rent into

pieces, so that men might have gone up to their knees in leaves of books, cut out and thrown under foot.

At the bridge foot he laid two pieces of ordnance, and began a great trench between the bridge and him. He laid one other piece of ordnance at St. George's Church, and another at Bermondsey Street, and another towards the Bishop of Winchester's house.

The killing of a waterman by some of Wyatt's men, whose dead body was rowed to the Tower, caused the Tower guns to be pointed against the foot of the bridge, against Southwark, the tower of St. Olave's, and St. Mary Overies, for so still old Howes, in his abridgment of Stow's Chronicle, calls it. All the pieces on the White Tower, on the Diveling Tower, falconets over the Water-Gate, culverins, demi-cannons - all were turned against the Borough. Well might the inhabitants tremble, for it must not be supposed that the marksmen always missed their aim. And so the inhabitants, men and women, came and entreated Wyatt to leave them.

'For the love of God, take pity on us!' was their cry; and Wyatt, who seems to have been too gentle and irresolute for a conspirator, 'in most speedie manner marched away.'

- *Southwark and its Story.*

Inside of a room adjoining those under the Hall,
Bermondsey House

It is easy to conceive the consternation into which Bermondsey must have been thrown during the progress of these events. Although the inhabitants of the Borough had always been familiar with scenes of tumult and disorder, the secluded situation of Bermondsey had hitherto preserved it from invasion by insurgent bands. The peaceful existence usually enjoyed by dwellers on monastic estates had been little disturbed by the altered conditions, and the sudden irruption of an armed force would have caused as much dismay as if wolves had broken in upon a sheepfold. Terrified runners would come, bringing the news of the near approach of Wyatt's force, the numbers of which, probably not exceeding a few hundred, would be magnified to many thousands. Sir Thomas Pope's domestics, gathering in the western wing of Bermondsey House, and gazing down the darkened vista of Long Lane, would quake with fear as the tramp of marching men drew nearer, and the shouts with which they acclaimed their leader, "A Wyatt! A Wyatt!" no doubt seemed the prelude to pillage and destruction. The rubicund faces of the innkeepers in Bermondsey Street must have waxed pale as dim reminiscences of the tales they had heard of the doings of Wat Tyler and Jack Cade arose in their minds, with dread forebodings of the fate that might await them should they fail to satisfy these unbidden guests. The houses in the street would have been hastily closed, and doors bolted and barred, whilst pale faces peering from windows on the upper floors watched the progress of the rebel force. As the cumbrous ordnance then in vogue trundled past, accompanied by the gunners with their lighted linstocks, stifled shrieks arose, and the terrified inhabitants cowered in the recesses of their dwellings.

    That February night must have been one never to be forgotten by the dwellers in Bermondsey. With cannon planted and a military post established in Bermondsey Street, with distant and ominous sounds breaking the stillness of the night, the roar of artillery, and the rattle of arquebuses at the bridge, sleep must have fled from all, even had they sought their beds. We may imagine some ascending to points of vantage, to the roof of Bermondsey House, possibly to the tower of St. Mary Magdalen's, and as the view on the north was not then impeded by the huge mass of buildings now interposed between that spot and the river, they could discern the outline of the White Tower, lit up by the flashes of its guns. After that fearful vigil what intense relief they must have experienced when the news of Wyatt's retreat reached them!

To return to Sir Thomas Pope, it is a remarkable fact that both the distinguished residents in Bermondsey House should have been brought into close relations with Queen Elizabeth. The singular tact possessed by Sir Thomas, which enabled him to enjoy the favour of successive monarchs of dissimilar character, yet without labouring under the imputation of sycophancy, was conspicuously displayed in his discharge of the functions he was now called upon to undertake. When the Princess Elizabeth, shortly after Wyatt's insurrection, had been confined in the Tower, we are told that, after her release and restoration to favour,

> The Queen finally gave her permission to reside once more in royal state at her own favourite abode, Hatfield House, in Hertfordshire. At parting, Mary placed a ring on the Princess's finger to the value of 700 crowns, as a pledge of amity. It was not, however, Mary's intention to restore Elizabeth so entirely to liberty as to leave her the unrestrained mistress of her own actions, and Sir Thomas Pope was entrusted with the responsible office of residing in her house for the purpose of restraining her from intriguing with suspected persons either abroad or at home. Veiling the intimation of her sovereign will under the semblance of a courteous recommendation, Mary presented this gentleman to Elizabeth as an officer who was henceforth to reside in her family, and who would do his best to render her and her household comfortable. Elizabeth, to whom Sir Thomas Pope was already well known, had the tact to take this in good part. She had, indeed, reason to rejoice that her keeper, while she remained as a State prisoner at large, was a person of such honourable and friendly conditions as this learned and worthy gentleman. The fetters in which he held her were more like flowery wreaths flung lightly round her, to attach her to a bower of royal pleasaunce, than aught which might remind her of the stern restraints by which she was surrounded during her incarceration in the Tower, and her subsequent abode at Woodstock, in the summer and autumn of 1554. There is reason to believe that she did not take her final departure from the Court till late in the autumn. It is certain that she came by water to meet the Queen, her sister, and Philip at Greenwich, for the purpose of taking a personal farewell of him at his embarkation for Flanders.
>
> The respectful and kind attention which Elizabeth received from Sir Thomas Pope during her residence under his friendly surveillance is testified by the following passage in a contemporary chronicle:
> 'At Shrovetide Sir Thomas Pope made for the Lady Elizabeth, all at his own cost, a grand and rich masquing in the great hall at Hatfield, where the pageants were marvellously furnished. There were there twelve

minstrels antiquely disguised, with forty-six or more gentlemen and ladies, many Knights, nobles, and ladies of honour, apparelled in crimson satin, embroidered with wreaths of gold, and garnished with borders of hanging pearls. There was the device of a castle of cloth of gold, set with pomegranates about the battlements, with shields of Knights hanging therefrom, and six Knights, in rich harness, tourneyed. At night the cupboard in the hall was of twelve stages, mainly furnished with garnish of gold and silver vessels, and a banquet of seventy dishes; and, after, a "voide" of spices and subtleties, with thirty spice-plates - all at the charge of Sir Thomas Pope, and the next day the play of Holofernes.'
- *Lives of the Queens of England.*

We see by this that Sir Thomas was no niggard of his wealth, but his profusion seemed too great in royal eyes. The chronicler adds: "But the Queen, percase, misliked these follies, as by her letters to Sir Thomas Pope did appear, and so these disguisings were ceased."

Sir Thomas was evidently a man of chivalric propensities, for Warton relates that on one occasion he figured as one of the champions in a tournament in the presence of Queen Mary. Ordinary knighthood was not then the purely civil distinction it has since become; even a "City" Knight, which term, in later times, was almost an opprobrium, as denoting a most unwarlike individual, usually possessed some skill in arms. In City churches some evidences of this are to be seen in the shape of swords and portions of armour belonging to ancient Mayors and Aldermen who had received the honour of knighthood. Anyone in the position of a gentleman was formerly expected to have some acquaintance with the use of weapons and a knowledge of military exercises. Although We do not find that Sir Thomas Pope ever "set squadrons in the field," he is stated on the occasion of a levy to have been required to furnish his quota of men-at-arms. His will contains full directions with regard to the disposal of his arms and martial panoply, using the expression then common, but which now seems so amusing, his "artillery." Miss Strickland goes on to say:

The Princess continued in the gentle keeping of Sir Thomas Pope. He appears to have been really fond of his royal charge, who, for her part, well knew how to please him by her learned and agreeable conversation, and more especially by frequently talking to him on the subject nearest to his heart, Trinity College, which he had just founded at Oxford for a President priest and twelve Fellows. He mentions in one of his letters, with peculiar satisfaction, the interest she manifested in his college:

'The Princess Elizabeth often asketh me about the course I have devised for my scholars, and that part of the statutes respecting study I have shown her, she likes well. She is not only gracious, but most learned, ye right well know.'

Two of the Fellows of this college were expelled by the President and the society for violating one of the statutes. They repaired in great tribulation to their founder, and, acknowledging their fault, implored most humbly for re-admittance to his college. Sir Thomas Pope, not liking, by his own relenting, to countenance the infringement of the laws he had made for the good government of his college, yet willing to extend the pardon that was solicited, kindly referred the matter to the decision of the Princess, who was pleased to intercede for the culprits that they might be restored to their Fellowships.

We have now seen our Knight in his most amiable and pleasing aspect, and may here fitly take leave of him.

Sir Thomas Pope died at Clerkenwell, January 22, 1559, having made a liberal disposition of his property, and evincing in his testamentary injunctions that "kindly nature and desire to do good" with which he is justly credited by Dr. Rendle.

Mr. Phillips, in his "History of Bermondsey," states that Sir Thomas

> reconveyed the mansion called Bermondsey House, March 4, 1554-55, first and second Philip and Mary, to Sir Robert Southwell, his heirs and assigns for ever (reserving the manor with its appurtenances, and such other of the abbey estates as he had purchased of Sir Robert before, to himself), and it is supposed to be the same that afterwards came into the hands of Thomas, Earl of Sussex."

There is, however, no need for supposition in this case, as the fact is indisputably proved.

CHAPTER X

THE RATCLIFFES, EARLS OF SUSSEX - EARL HENRY PROTECTS THE PRINCESS ELIZABETH - EARL THOMAS - HIS DEVOTION TO ELIZABETH - APPOINTED VICEROY OF IRELAND - HIS DIFFICULTIES AND CONTEST WITH SHANE O'NEILL - THE EARL URGES THE MARRIAGE OF THE QUEEN - DISPUTES WITH LEICESTER - EMBASSY TO VIENNA - LORD SUSSEX MAKES BERMONDSEY HOUSE HIS TOWN RESIDENCE - THE NORTHERN REBELLION - SUSSEX INVADES SCOTLAND - VISIT OF QUEEN ELIZABETH TO BERMONDSEY HOUSE - DEATH AND CHARACTER OF THE EARL.

In the third volume of his "Baronage of England," Sir William Dugdale tells us, concerning the House of Ratcliffe:

> Of this family, that which I have first observed to be most memorable is, that, in seventh Henry the Fifth, Sir John Ratcliffe, Knt., being Constable of the Castle of Frounsack (Fronsac) in Aquitaine, had a thousand marks per annum allowed him for the guard thereof.

This gallant Knight, who distinguished himself in the wars of the period, was subsequently advanced to higher dignities, but it was in the next century that the family attained the zenith of its greatness. Robert Ratcliffe was created by Henry the Eighth Earl of Sussex and Lord Fitzwalter, and received a grant of abbey lands in Somersetshire. He was also invested with the "Manor of the Rose," mentioned in Shakespeare's "Henry the Eighth," a City estate previously belonging to the unfortunate Duke of Buckingham. Robert, Earl of Sussex, figured as a great officer of State on the occasion of the coronation of Anne Boleyn, and was prominent among the Councillors of Henry, but bore himself warily during the protectorate of Somerset and the intrigues of Northumberland.

Thomas Ratcliffe, Earl of Sussex

His son and successor, Henry, was also a man of distinction and of sterling merit. As Lord Fitzwalter, he had commanded a force of cavalry in Somerset's expedition to Scotland. After the death of Edward the Sixth, and when Northumberland was striving to establish Lady Jane Grey on the throne, Henry Ratcliffe, now Earl of Sussex, rallied to the cause of Mary, and, with other faithful nobles, repaired to her at Framlingham, ready to support her by force of arms. After the defeat of Northumberland's conspiracy, Mary was willing to secure peace by forbearance and toleration, and began by showing favour to some who had recently been in opposition to her claims. We are told that she felt herself able to neglect Sussex, Rutland, Derby, and Oxford, because she knew that she could rely upon their loyalty. Does not this speak volumes for the character of such men?

"True as the dial to the sun,
Although it be not shone upon."

An incident that occurred some time afterwards showed that no shade of sycophancy, no courtierlike obsequiousness, tinged the loyalty of Sussex. After the outbreak of Sir Thomas Wyatt's insurrection, the suspicions of Queen Mary were directed towards her sister Elizabeth, to whom Wyatt was reported to have addressed a letter, although no evidence of complicity on the part of the Princess could be discovered. The Queen, in her anger and excitement, resolved to send Elizabeth to the Tower, and the Marquis of Winchester and the Earl of Sussex were ordered to inform the Princess of this determination. Elizabeth, in natural alarm, besought an interview with her sister, but this was refused, and she then penned an appeal, which she begged the lords to deliver to the Queen. The Marquis hesitated to brave the wrath of Mary, but Lord Sussex, dropping on one knee, swore that, should it cost him his head, he would place the letter in the Queen's hands.

Mary received him with a tempest of rage, telling him that he would not have dared to act so towards her father, and wishing that Henry were alive to punish Sussex and his friends for their audacity. Elizabeth's appeal remained fruitless, and she was commanded to prepare for removal to the Tower, whither the two lords accompanied her. Received by Sir John Gage, the Lieutenant of the Tower, and Lord Chandos, Elizabeth was conducted to her place of confinement, and

> as she approached the room intended for her the heavy doors along the corridor were locked and barred behind her. At the grating of the iron bolts the heart of Lord Sussex sank within him. Sussex knew the Queen's true feelings, and the efforts made to lash her into cruelty. 'What mean ye, my lords?' he said to Chandos and Gage. 'What will you do? She was a King's daughter, and is the Queen's sister: go no further than your commission, which I know what it is.'
> - Froude's *History of England*.

All the dread memories of the Tower, the shades of the many illustrious captives who had found death within its walls, rose before the perturbed imagination of the Earl. He feared lest the Lieutenant, in addition to his public instructions, might have received some secret orders to dispose of the hapless Princess. It was with a heavy heart and evil forebodings that the Earl re-entered his barge, and many a sad and desponding look he cast back at the fortress in which the Hope of England was now immured. We are told, however, that he and other lords, who had

> so reluctantly allowed Elizabeth to be imprisoned, would not permit her to be openly sacrificed, or, indeed, permit the Queen to continue in the career of vengeance on which she had entered.

The Queen, however, had no intention of depriving her sister of life, and steadfastly resisted the promptings of Simon Renard, the Flemish envoy of Charles the Fifth, who was constantly urging the destruction of Elizabeth, and assuring the Queen that she would never be safe while the Princess lived. This consummate villain took credit to himself for this conduct in despatches to his imperial master, of whom he was a worthy instrument.

The noble Earl, whose manly and chivalrous feeling does him so much honour, died in 1556. He had been twice married: first to Elizabeth, daughter of Thomas Howard, Duke of Norfolk, by whom he had issue three sons, Thomas, Henry, and Francis; second to Anne, daughter of Sir Philip Calthorpe, Knt., by whom he had a son, afterwards Sir Egremont Ratcliffe, and a daughter.

Thomas Ratcliffe, the new Earl, whose career belongs both to romance and history, "a goodly gentleman, of a brave, noble nature," to use the words of Sir Robert Naunton, inherited the loyal virtues, the chivalrous feeling, and the martial qualities of his father. In the atmosphere of intrigue and treachery, of corruption and moral perversity, which surrounded him, the Earl ever maintained one guiding principle, solicitude for the honour of his Sovereign and the welfare of his country. His efforts to secure these objects were continual and unwearied; his constancy to these ideas enabled him to thread the mazes of contemporary politics, and to leave behind him a fame which, though not unsullied, is yet brighter than that of most other courtiers of the Maiden Queen. From first to last, Elizabeth was the object of his zealous and respectful devotion. He appeared to regard her with a sort of paternal affection. He never sought to promote his interest, like so many of the time-serving intriguers who surrounded the Queen, by pandering to her vanity; he did not court her favour with gross and fulsome flatteries, but scrupled not to tell her unwelcome truths. He bore with her caprices, but, though at times weary of her irresolution and grieved by her perversity and preference of tortuous methods, he never ceased to afford her the benefit of his counsel and experience, and, whilst chafing under the humiliations to which her fickle policy subjected him, yet remained to the last resolved to serve her in spite of all, to defend her from all peril, and to protect her from the consequences of her own errors. The Queen was not insensible to such unselfish devotion; she recognised the transparent honesty of the Earl, she respected his unswerving fidelity, she inwardly approved his sage counsels. This singular woman, whose character is an enigma, and who combined within herself so many conflicting and contradictory qualities, masculine energy, sagacity and penetration; feminine coquetry, caprice, and inordinate vanity, was most fortunate in her Councillors and in the possession of Ministers of rare ability. She who, living in the midst of dangers, in a realm teeming with conspiracies, and with hands, even in her own palace, armed against her life, displayed a fearlessness, a contempt for encircling perils, that would have been remarkable in a man, yet shrank pusillanimously from remote and impalpable dangers, from phantoms of her own creation. In many points her conduct still remains as incomprehensible as ever, and we are still ignorant of the causes of her extraordinary hesitation, when the bold and straightforward course seemed the path of safety. But when entangled in the meshes of her own intrigues, endangered by the presumption and the incapacity of those "handsome favourites," whom Macaulay says "she never trusted," she looked, to extricate herself from difficulties, to those "wise old statesmen whom she never dismissed."

    The words spoken by his father in the Tower seem to have been ever present to the mind of Sussex: "She was a King's daughter, and is the Queen's sister." It is very easy to conceive how the feelings of such a man were influenced by the circumstances of the time and the desire to avert very real and pressing dangers. The House of Tudor, so firmly seated on the throne of England in the person of Henry the Eighth, had yet, by that monarch's perversity, been exposed to imminent risk of deposition. The repeated dissolution of his marriages, and the branding of the offspring of these unions with illegitimacy, had confused the succession, and not only paved the way for the imposition of Northumberland, but opened the floodgates of pretension, and enabled many nobles, who claimed descent from scions of the race of Plantagenet, to aspire to the Crown. Like all patriotic Englishmen, Lord Sussex looked back with horror on the frightful period of the Wars of the Roses, and shrank from the prospect of a renewal of such calamities. The times in which he lived were so critical that the circumstances of the Royal Family and the state of the nation made even worse disasters possible than those which had marked the course of the former struggle. The question between the White and the Red Rose was clear and distinct: the issue was purely dynastic; the triumph of either side would have made little difference, as far as the internal government of the country or the national policy was concerned. But in the meantime the religious element had been introduced; the nation had been distracted by a

> moral war which raged in every family, which set the father against the son and the son against the father, the mother against the daughter and the daughter against the mother.

The course of the Reformation in England had been marked by vacillation and inconsistency, by a see-sawing between opposite principles. Men's minds had been perplexed by controversies which to the mass were unintelligible; their traditional beliefs were shaken, they were required to conform to opinions varying according to the views of the reigning Sovereign - one day commanded to adore the Mass, the next to repudiate it as idolatrous; now, the reading of the Bible inculcated as a duty; again, the possession of a Bible denounced as a crime; the faith of one day was proclaimed the heresy of another. Those whose convictions were strong and understandings enlightened were enabled, notwithstanding all this, to pursue their course unswervingly, assured that order would eventually be evolved from chaos; but we may imagine the consternation and bewilderment with which the multitude beheld the shipwreck of character amongst public men, the successive recantations of those whom they had been taught to venerate.

In such a state of things as this, one paramount necessity was felt - that of a settled government, which, while firmly maintaining the authority of the Crown, would not be guided by intrigue and self-seeking, but administered by men studious of the welfare of the State and desirous of the peaceful progress of the nation. Those who were imbued with this conviction, of whom Lord Sussex was one, considered that the religious question should be left to settle itself; that the attention both of rulers and subjects should be directed to more practical objects; that the fierce passions stirred by the conflict of rival sects and embittered by persecution should be lulled by the influence of a tolerant policy.

Queen Marys health was known to be precarious, and the prospect of her speedy dissolution was ever present to the minds of the statesmen who were watching the progress of events. Their eyes began to fix upon Elizabeth, not merely as the Queens natural successor, but as the prospective Sovereign, who would be likely to heal the wounds from which the nation was suffering and to lead it into a path of safety. The Princess, radiant with health and endowed with the physical qualities that appeared to promise a long life, had also given evidence of mental powers which fitted her for the position of a ruler, and of a prudent and forecasting spirit. Her religious convictions were not known to be strong; she at any rate appeared to be free from bigotry, and rather disposed to regulate her professions according to political circumstances and observation of the current of popular feeling.

The knowledge that the hearts of her subjects, alienated from herself, were turning to her sister added bitterness to the mental and physical sufferings of Mary. It may have been that, fearing lest an attempt might be made to place Elizabeth on the throne without waiting for the decease of her sister, the following resolution was adopted by the Queen's Council:

> It was agreed that, on one pretence or another, Derby, Shrewsbury, Sussex, and Huntingdon should be sent out of London to their counties.

Possibly with a view to get him still further out of the way, the Earl of Sussex was some time afterwards appointed Lord-Deputy of Ireland. We may be sure that the Earl did not solicit this appointment, and it was in an evil hour for his fame that he accepted it. It will be impossible to understand the position in which he was now placed without reference to the state of the country that he was commissioned to rule. For many generations the Lord-Lieutenant or Viceroy of Ireland has been, in the main, an ornamental personage, holding a minor Court, and representing with more or less dignity the majesty of the Crown. The government of Ireland is conducted by the Chief Secretary, aided by the staff of permanent officials at Dublin Castle: but in the sixteenth century the Lord-Deputy, as the Viceroy was then called, was of necessity a soldier, compelled to uphold the royal authority by force of arms. Even judges were sometimes compelled to buckle on their armour and take the field against lawless depredators. When for a time Ireland was divided into presidencies, Sir Edward Fitton, a judge in Dublin, on being appointed President of Connaught, exchanged his wig and gown for helmet and cuirass, and entered the field against the O'Briens of Thomond. Although Ireland had been for nearly five centuries under the nominal sway of England, the authority of the English monarch really existed only in the towns held by his garrisons and the districts occupied by his adherents.

The "English Pale," embracing some of the counties nearest to Dublin, was the chief - indeed, almost the only - seat of English dominion, the rest of the island being more or less under the control of native chieftains. Of these there were three supreme lords, two of whom claimed to represent ancient Kings of Ireland, and the third was descended from one of the most distinguished successors of Strongbow. O'Neill, created Earl of Tyrone, claimed to rule Ulster; O'Brien, Earl of Thomond (comprising the present county Clare), descended from Brian Boru, the conqueror of the Danes, ruled in the West with semi-regal power; and in the South the Earl of Desmond, Prince Palatine of Kerry, exercised sovereignty over great part of Munster. In addition to these great clans there were innumerable "septs," or native tribes who, in general, acknowledged no rule but that of their own chiefs, or that of the overlords under whose leadership they were accustomed to rally. What made the government of the country still more difficult was that, in many cases, the descendants of the Anglo-Norman invaders, and later English settlers, established among the native tribes, and intermarrying with them, had adopted the practices and ideas of the Irish, even exaggerating them, as a mediaeval chronicler, bewailing this degeneracy, laments that his countrymen had become "Hiberniores ipsis Hibernicis" - more Irish than the Irish themselves.

The Earl of Desmond was a conspicuous example of this tendency. By family a "Geraldine,"' allied to the Fitzgeralds, Earls of Kildare, the ancestors of the present Duke of Leinster, the Earl of Desmond, holding an Anglo-Norman peerage of ancient date, had relapsed into semi-barbarism, and contracted the habits of an Irish chieftain. He was in a state of permanent hostility to the Earl of Ormond, an Anglo-Irish Lord of the "Pale." Men of English origin displayed the wild and fickle character, the ferocity, the aversion to order and method, which characterized the native inhabitants. Amongst the Irish septs, rapine and slaughter, pillage and devastation, were looked upon as glorious deeds, worthy to be sung by bards, and boasted of by their perpetrators as exploits of transcendent merit.

It should, however, be borne in mind that savage lawlessness did not characterize Ireland alone, but that it was exhibited in all its odious features amongst the Scottish Highlanders, and even continued to exist amongst them long after it had been suppressed in Ireland.

Such were the conditions into which the Earl of Sussex was suddenly transplanted. A loyal, faithful, law-abiding man, attached to English customs, fond of an orderly and regular life, found himself in a sphere in which disorder was the rule, in which law could often be enforced by the sword alone, in which bloodshed was rampant, and treachery rife on every hand. Wily and self-seeking men were, moreover, always ready to throw dust in the eyes of a ruler fresh from England, to make him see the country and the people only through the medium of their own passions and sordid interests, to render it impossible for the most just-minded man to hold the balance evenly between contending factions. If Ireland without the Pale was a scene of violence and disorder, the Pale itself was full of intrigue and treachery, of injustice and maladministration. The ear of the Lord-Deputy was beset by complaints from all quarters, of injuries to be redressed and outrages to be punished; his mind was bewildered by conflicting and contradictory statements from which it seemed impossible to disentangle the truth.

The first trouble of the Earl of Sussex, however, was not with the Irish, but the Scots. A large body of these had settled in the east of Ulster, where they fomented disorder, allying themselves, when it suited their purpose, with the turbulent chiefs, and at all times repudiating the authority of the English Viceroy.

> In 1557 they penetrated as far as Armagh, whose inhabitants joined them against the Lord-Deputy. On that occasion, the English army plundered Armagh twice in the course of a month. The Scots were defeated, having lost 200 of their best men. The remainder of their forces then moved westward to join in a feud of the Burkes; but the Earl of Clanricarde, whom they went to oppose, nearly annihilated them, and their two chiefs were slain.

After this the Earl of Sussex was called into the West.

> The O'Briens of Thomond were now in insurrection (A.D. 1558). The Earl of Sussex marched against them, took their castles at Ennis, Bunratty, and Clare, banished Donald O'Brien, and delivered the territory to Connor O'Brien, son of Donough, who succeeded to the earldom of Thomond.
> - *History of Ireland*.

Whilst the Earl was making these vigorous attempts to enforce the recognition of his authority, greater changes and even more stirring events were impending.

> On the 17th of November, 1558, died Queen Mary, and the day after, Cardinal Pole, and with them expired Papal ascendancy in England and Ireland. In the following spring Parliament solemnly declared the spiritual supremacy of the Princess Elizabeth, and Protestantism at once recovered all that it had lost during the reign of Mary, with the addition of a numerous list of illustrious martyrs in its calendar.

The immediate result of this was to increase the difficulties of the Earl of Sussex. He was required to enforce the re-establishment of the reformed worship. Now, the arguments which so strongly recommended Protestantism to many Englishmen had no weight with Irishmen. The Catholic Church had not been unduly oppressive to the latter; their imaginations were still under the spell of its mysteries. The ease with which absolution was obtained made it, in their wild lives, especially precious to them, while they shrank with repugnance from the rigidity of Protestantism, its scrutiny of actions, its stern refusal to absolve the perpetrators of heinous offences. The attempt to dispossess the Romish hierarchy and to introduce Anglican clergy met, as may be imagined, with stubborn resistance in some quarters, and with indignant submission in those where the power of the Government made it possible to enforce the change.

The Earl of Sussex, studying the conditions around him, became convinced of the unwisdom of attempting, at this conjuncture, to interfere with the national religion. The Spanish Ambassador, De Feria, writing to Philip the Second on April 11, 1559, said: "Lord Sussex, heretic as he is, has warned the Council that Ireland will rebel if they enforce the alteration of religion there."

It was to Philip that the Irish chieftains were looking, not merely to aid them in maintaining the Romish Church, but to support them in efforts to expel the English from the island. Amongst those who aspired to bring about this consummation were O'Neill, Chieftain of Tyrone, and the young Earl of Desmond. Shane O'Neill, who now held sway over the greater part of the North of Ireland, was the natural son of that O'Neill who had been created Earl of Tyrone. This man, fierce and lawless, alternating between predatory adventures and wild debauchery, yet possessed some commanding qualities and inordinate ambition. Proud of his descent from the ancient Hy-Nials, Kings of Ireland, of whom the most renowned was Malachy the Great, he dreamt of reviving the glories of his ancestors, of acquiring the sovereignty of the whole island, and of consolidating his power by the expulsion of the Saxons. The religious conflict came powerfully to aid the furtherance of his schemes, and procured him allies in all parts amongst the disaffected chiefs, many of whom would not have been led by any other inducement to co-operate with him. He constituted himself the champion of the Church, taking the expelled Archbishop of Armagh under his special protection. Lord Sussex felt that, at all hazards, the power of this chieftain must be broken. He therefore assembled forces, made an incursion into

O'Neill's territory, seized Armagh, and fortified the cathedral. Not meeting with O'Neill, the Earl fell. back into Meath; but during his absence the garrison he had left in Armagh had a hard matter to keep their footing. Shane O'Neill, at the head of several thousand men, appeared on a height near the town; monks went through the ranks stimulating the zeal of his troops, whilst the Catholic Archbishop, in full canonicals, passed along the lines exhorting them to fight for Holy Church, and to expel the invaders from his see. The Irish, each bearing a faggot, with the purpose of firing the cathedral, advanced furiously, headed by the monks; but the English, though vastly outnumbered, met them with equal intrepidity, and although the Ulstermen penetrated into the town, and a fierce conflict ensued in the streets, they were finally expelled, and Shane retreated to his fastnesses. This temporary success, however, was speedily followed by a reverse. A detachment of Sussex's forces advancing into the country were suddenly fallen upon by Shane, and defeated with great slaughter.

The Earl of Sussex was now in the highest degree perplexed and exasperated. At the head of a disorderly and ill-disciplined force, with corruption rife amongst his officers, surrounded by spies, and unable to obtain any but the most scanty supplies, he appears to have lost heart, and felt that he was confronted with a problem beyond his capacity to solve. Expressions of despair occur in his letters and despatches, together with desperate yearnings to close with O'Neill. Right gladly would he have measured his broadsword against the chieftain's axe in open conflict, but the wily Shane, who on his part would have been nothing loath, yet knew that his surest game was to harass the English army and cause it to melt away.

We now approach a most painful episode, which constitutes the one great blot on the fair fame of Sussex. A demand came to him from Shane O'Neill to withdraw the garrison from Armagh. This demand was brought by O'Neill's seneschal, and one of his followers named Neil Grey. This man professed abhorrence of rebellion to the Lord-Deputy, and, we grieve to say, Lord Sussex incited him to assassinate his master. The Earl, in his letter to the Queen, says: "In fine, I brake with him to kill Shane!"

We should not attempt to palliate this crime, but may conceive how terrible must have been the condition of affairs, which induced a great English nobleman, usually upright and honourable in his dealings, and who in England would have shrunk with horror from the suggestion of murder, to suborn assassination. It furnishes one of the saddest of many instances in which a frank and generous nature has been warped by the evil conditions existing in the sister-island. In the history of English rule in Ireland during the later years of Elizabeth, we shall find instances in which men who were generally humane and distinguished for their virtues, such as Sir Humphrey Gilbert, guilty of deeds of ferocious cruelty. Fortunately, however, Neil Grey forbore to commit the murder.

It would appear that others besides Lord Sussex were anxious to remove this powerful chief by nefarious means, for a present of wine was sent to O'Neill from Dublin, in which he freely indulged, and, the wine having been poisoned, was brought nearly to the point of death in consequence. However, he survived all these attempts, and lived to plague other Viceroys, to oppress the North of Ireland, and to be ultimately slain by his quondam allies, the Scots.

The Earl of Sussex was recalled in 1564, and we shall henceforth see him acting in a sphere and in a manner more conformable to his nature and more creditable to himself.

We have already spoken of the anxiety which he and other statesmen felt to secure the stability of their mistress's throne, and to prevent the dangers to which the country would be exposed by a disputed succession. The next in line of inheritance was unquestionably the Queen of Scots, but the character and foreign connections of that Princess made her very undesirable as a Sovereign of England. Then there were the sisters of Lady Jane Grey and the Countess of Lennox, mother-in-law of Mary Stuart. The Earls of Rutland and Huntingdon, the Duke of Norfolk, and others still, were supposed to have claims founded on ancient alliances. The only way of averting the conflict that might be expected to arise on the death of Elizabeth was by persuading the Queen to marry, in order that a successor might be provided whose claims no one would presume to dispute.

On this point Sussex was peculiarly emphatic, and behaved with equal generosity and loyal devotion. He and many other leading men were in favour of the Queen's marriage with the Archduke Charles of Austria, an alliance which would secure

England from Spain. But the Queen, who coquetted with many, only appeared to feel real attachment for one, viz., Lord Robert Dudley, whom she afterwards created Earl of Leicester. Sussex had no love for Dudley, of whom he subsequently became the most determined opponent; but in this case he waived all personal feeling, and on being consulted by Secretary Cecil, afterwards better known as Lord Burleigh, wrote as follows:

> I wish not her Majesty to linger this matter of so great importance, but to choose speedily, and therein to follow so much her own affection as by the looking upon him whom she should choose, omnes ejus sensus titillarentur, which shall be the readiest way, with the help of God, to bring us a blessed Prince, which shall redeem us out of thraldom.
> If I knew that England had other rightful inheritors, I would then advise otherwise, and seek to serve the time by a husband's choice. But seeing that she is ultimum refugium, and that no riches, friendship, foreign alliance, or any other present commodity that might come by a husband, can serve our turn without issue of her body, if the Queen will love anybody, let her love where and whom she will, so much thirst I to see her love; and whomsoever she shall love and choose, him will I love, and whomsoever she shall love and choose, him will I love, honour, and serve to the uttermost.
> (October 24, 1560).

In this the true nobility of Sussex's nature is manifest, and with even greater generosity,

> on the 23rd April, 1561, at the annual meeting of the Knights of the Garter, Sussex proposed an address to the Queen, recommending Dudley to her as a husband.

This was demurred to by the other lords, and an address was presented,

> in the place of that proposed by Sussex, recommending marriage generally, but without Dudley's name, and the Queen replied in a passion that, when she married, 'she would consult her own pleasure, and not that of her nobles.'

With regard to every matrimonial project submitted to her, Elizabeth showed extreme perversity and capriciousness, now favouring the pretensions of some suitor, and even expressing impatience for the union; again, declaring with energy that her highest ambition was to die the Virgin Queen. Nor could her most trusted statesmen ever prevail upon her to name a successor. This reluctance did not appear to arise altogether from caprice, but - at any rate, in the earlier part of her reign - from knowledge of the perils which encircled her. The Queen thought that her days would be numbered if she consented formally to proclaim a successor.

The anxiety of Lord Sussex to save his country from perils, vexation at the Queen's perversity, and possibly greater insight into the character of Dudley, now Earl of Leicester, gave rise to the following:

> This summer (1566) the feuds between Sussex and Leicester ran so high on the subject of her Majesty's marriage that neither of them ventured abroad without a retinue of armed followers. Sussex, whose mother was a Howard, was the kinsman of the Queen, and his high sense of honour rendered him jealous of the construction that was placed on her intimacy with her Master of the Horse (Leicester), combined with her reluctance to marry. He was urgent with her to espouse the Archduke Charles, and with him were banded all the Howard lineage, and Lord Hunsdon, her maternal relatives. Cecil, her Premier, went with them as far as his cautious nature would permit. He has noted the following incident in his diary: 'June 16th, 1566. - A discord between the Earls of Leicester and Sussex at Greenwich, there appeased by her Majesty.'

It was probably this incident of which Sir Walter Scott availed himself in "Kenilworth" to depict the rival Earls in presence of the Queen. Who will not call to mind, "Sussex, I entreat; Leicester, I command you"?

However, in May, 1567, the Queen was brought to entertain the proposals of the Archduke Charles, and Lord Sussex was chosen as special Ambassador to carry the Garter to the Emperor at Vienna, and to see and report upon the Archduke.

> Very reluctantly Elizabeth had been brought so far upon the way. A month elapsed before she could resolve upon the form of Sussex's instructions, and almost a second before she could allow him to set out. At last, in the middle of July, she permitted him to go, and on the 9th of August he was at Vienna.

The Archduke Charles of Austria was brother of Maximilian the Second, the most tolerant of the Emperors of Germany, "the excellent Maximilian," as Schiller calls him. The Archduke himself was an accomplished Prince, of decorous life, amiable and kindly. Lord Sussex closely observed him, and was most favourably impressed. In writing to Elizabeth, after describing the aspect and physical qualities of the Archduke, the Earl said:

> His dealings with me are very wise; his conversation such as much contents me, and, as I hear, not one returns discontented from his company. He is much beloved here of all men.

The Archduke, however, was a Catholic, and it was necessary to sound him in order to ascertain how far he would be willing to conform to English practices in the matter of worship.

> Sussex gave the Archduke a hint that some indecision had been attributed to him on the point of religion - in plain language, that he meant to act according to the fashion of the times, and adopt the creed that best suited his interest and aggrandizement. 'Surely,' the Archduke replied, 'whoever has said this of me to the Queen's Majesty, or to you, or to any other, hath said more than he knoweth. My ancestors have always holden the religion that I hold, and I never knew other; therefore, I never could have purpose to change. I trust that her Majesty shall consider my case well; my determination herein shall not hurt my cause. For how could the Queen like me in anything if I should prove so light in changing my conscience?'

This candid dealing commended itself highly to the mind of the Earl of Sussex, who deemed it of good augury for the future. With intense gratification he wrote to the Queen:

> Hereupon I gather that reputation rules him much in the case of religion, and that if God couple you together in liking, you shall find in him a true husband, a loving companion, a wise counsellor.

He continued to pour forth aspirations for the union, and prayed that God "might not for our sins deem us unworthy of so great a blessing."

The negotiation, however, was wrecked on the religious point. The Archduke pledged himself not to obtrude his religion, and agreed to attend the services of the Anglican Church with the Queen, but insisted on having Mass privately celebrated by a private priest of his own. This seemed to Lord Sussex and others reasonable enough, but it was made the pretext for breaking off negotiations, and, as both the Archduke and the Emperor had reached the limit of their concessions, the Earl left Vienna vexed, humbled, and exasperated.

His indignation was mainly directed against Leicester, to whose intrigues he attributed this failure, and whom he threatened publicly to denounce. From this period reconciliation between the two Earls was impossible, Sussex continuing to regard Leicester as a crafty traitor, prepared to sacrifice his Queen and country for the sake of his own aggrandizement.

It was after this that the Earl of Sussex fixed his town residence in Bermondsey House, where he maintained an establishment that threw the state of Sir Thomas Pope and Sir Robert Southwell into the shade. The Earl was one of the greatest nobles of the time, eminent not merely for his rank and the high offices he had filled, but for his personal qualities. He was what would now be considered a great party leader, of commanding political influence, with a numerous body of adherents, and his credit was maintained by the unfailing respect and confidence of the Queen. The patronage and protection of such a man were eagerly sought; men of birth and fortune were proud of the distinction of serving him. In Bermondsey House his retinue of Knights and gentlemen, the officers of his household, the multitude of his domestics, formed an establishment greater than that of some Sovereigns in the present day, while the state and ceremony that surrounded him were equal to those of a Court. Here he received a visit from Queen Elizabeth in 1570.

In the meantime, however, the Earl was again called upon to abandon the pursuits of civil life for warlike operations. He was appointed to the high office of President of the North, with his headquarters at York. Mary Stuart was at this time a prisoner in England, and formed the centre of intrigues and conspiracies on the part of the Catholics. A plot was formed to rescue her from captivity, to depose Elizabeth and place Mary on the throne, and marry the latter to the Duke of Norfolk. The North had been ever since the time of Henry the Eighth the abode of disaffection and the theatre of intrigues amongst the adherents of the old faith.

> Lord Sussex was anxiously watching the condition of the Northern districts. As a friend of Norfolk, Sussex had been counted on by the Confederates as likely to be favourable to them. In their altered position, they were less able to tell what to expect from him. At the beginning of October, he invited the Earls of Northumberland and Westmoreland to York, to give him the benefit of their advice. Wishing to feel his temper, they immediately complied; and they found at once that he had not the slightest disposition towards disloyalty . . .
> They both assured him 'that they would never stand to any matters that should be to her Majesty's displeasure or against her surety,' and Sussex believed them, and allowed them to return to their houses. Reports reached him afterwards that they had taken arms, and that the country was up; but he ascertained that their stables were more than usually empty, that there were no signs of preparation in their establishments, and that, at least for the present, no danger was to be apprehended. He had a narrow escape of falling a victim to his confidence. Assured of the popular feeling on their side, the Earls believed that if they could seize York, and meke themselves masters of the local government, Lord Derby and the other waverers would no longer hesitate to join them. It was proposed that Northumberland, with a few hundred horse, should make a sudden dart upon the city some Sunday morning, lie concealed in the woods until the bell 'left knolling for sermon,' and then ride in, stop the doors of the cathedral, and take President and Council prisoners. 'Treason,' however, had a terrible sound to an English nobleman; they reflected that the thing might cause bloodshed, and so 'passed it over,' waiting till circumstances came to their assistance, and decided their course for them.
> - Froude's *History of England*.

The Queen, hearing of these proceedings, commanded the two Earls to come to London; but they refused to obey, and finally rose in arms, causing a wave of insurrection to spread over the Northern counties. Lord Sussex, surrounded by traitors, had but a handful of men at York, and the other royal commanders were compelled to shut themselves up with their scanty forces, in any available stronghold, leaving the rebels free to scour the country. Elizabeth was unable to comprehend the inaction of her officers, and was at first even inclined to doubt the loyalty of Sussex. She sent Lord Hunsdon and Sir Ralph Sadler to examine the position of affairs, and report to her.

When Hunsdon and Sadler arrived, they found that he (Sussex) had done as much as he could in prudence have ventured. He had collected within the walls almost three thousand men. He had not led them against the rebels because 'they wished better to the enemy's cause than to the Queen's.' But as Elizabeth believed that he had been wilfully inactive, Sadler ventured to tell her 'that there were not ten gentlemen in Yorkshire that did allow her proceedings in the cause of religion.' 'When one member of a family was with Sussex, another was with the Earls.' 'The cause was great and dangerous,' and Sussex had done loyally and wisely in refusing to risk a battle. If only their own lives were at stake, both he himself and Hunsdon and Sussex would try their fortunes, even 'with the untrusty soldiers they had,' but, 'should they receive one overthrow, the sequel would be so dangerous as it were better for the Queen to spend a great deal of treasure than that they give that adventure.' Hunsdon was able to say 'that if Sussex's diligence and carefulness had not been great, her Majesty had neither had York nor Yorkshire any longer at her devotion; he wished to God her Majesty knew all his doings. She would know how good a subject she had.'
- Froude's *History of England*.

The rebellion, which had at first seemed so formidable, and which, in the event of success, was to have been supported by Spanish troops from Flanders, after some desultory fighting, collapsed, through the incapacity and irresolution of the leaders. The Earls escaped into Scotland.

The Scottish Borders, as everyone knows, had been for centuries the theatre of predatory warfare, inhabited by a population who lived more or less by plunder, and affording a refuge for outlaws and desperadoes. As many of the insurgent leaders who had crossed the Border were still conspiring with the Scottish partisans of Mary Stuart, it was resolved to send an English army to ravage the Scottish counties nearest to England, under pretext of punishing the habitual depredations of marauding bands, as well as chastising the Scots for aiding the rebels against Elizabeth.

Lord Sussex wrote to Cecil that "before the light of the coming moon was passed," he proposed to leave a memory in Scotland, whereby they and their children should be afraid to offer war to England.

The Earl divided his force into three bodies, which were to

invade Scotland from three separate points. In many cases the people fled before the advance of the English, and only some strongholds of the robber chieftains held out; but these were subdued, and the Scottish Government was powerless to resist the invasion. Branxholme or Branksome, so famed in the "Lay of the Last Minstrel," the seat of Scott of Buccleuch, one of the most powerful of the Border chiefs, partially destroyed by Buccleuch himself, in anticipation of the visit, was blown up by Sussex on his arrival.

> There remained Hume Castle, which had been specially fortified, and was held by a garrison. This stronghold at least the Scots expected would be safe, and they had carried such property as they could move within its walls. The beginning of the following week, Sussex brought heavy guns from Berwick, and took it after four hours' bombardment. Fastcastle, the "Wolf's Crag" of the 'Bride of Lammermoor,' followed the next day, and both there and at Hume parties of English were posted, to hold them from the Scots. In the whole foray, 'ninety strong castles, houses and dwelling-places, with three hundred towns and villages, had been utterly destroyed.' Peels, towers, forts, every thieves' nest within twenty miles of the Border, were laid in ruins, and Sussex, whatever else might be the effect, had provided for some time to come for the quiet of the English marches.
> - Froude's *History of England*.

Such devastation seems appalling to modern readers, and the very fact that such a tremendous lesson was deemed necessary throws a lurid light on the conditions of Border life. The genius of Scott has cast a halo of romance around that region, and invested its freebooters with the lustre of paladins; but Sussex viewed the Border in its stern and hideous reality, and in the destruction of Branksome Tower was unmoved by any reminiscence of the "Lady of Buccleuch" or "Sir William of Deloraine."

After these exploits, we chiefly read of the Earl in civil life, constant in opposition to Leicester, ever the trusty counsellor of the Queen.

A man of liberal hospitality, of free and generous nature, his residence at Bermondsey House would have been marked by splendid entertainments. We may imagine a banquet preparing for the grandees of Elizabeth's Court. The Earl's retainers are marshalled in the hall, arrayed in their gayest liveries; the gentlemen and officers of his household, richly apparelled and wearing their chains of office, are ready to receive the distinguished guests; while My Lord himself, splendidly attired and with his insignia of the Garter, appears at the head of the grand staircase to welcome those men whose names are inscribed in ineffaceable characters on the page of history. Burleigh and Walsingham, Sidney and Bacon, pass through the portals of Bermondsey House. We see them descending into the garden, where Lord Sussex shows them his plantations, and the Lord Treasurer descants upon the grafting of fruit-trees in a manner worthy of Evelyn and Sir William Temple. They feed the carp in the fish ponds, and compare notes upon the size and weight of various specimens. The strains of musicians enliven the banquet, healths are drunk, the grave Lord Treasurer unbends, and gives utterance to some of those "merry jests" which his biographer ofttimes heard him tell; yet none overpass the limits of decorum. The dwellers in Bermondsey Street gather with eager and curious looks, to watch the departure of the noble company, whilst the poor of the neighbourhood look forward, with watering mouths, to their share of the broken meats and relics of the feast.

The rural surroundings of Bermondsey House are pleasantly exemplified in Gerarde's "Herbal." That old botanist says that

> bittersweet grows by a ditch-side against the garden wall of the Right Honourable the Earl of Sussex his house in Bermondsey Street by London, as you go from the court, which is full of trees, unto a farmhouse near thereunto. And melons are in very great plenty, near to the same house in Bermondsey, especially if the weather be anything temperate.

The question of the Queen's marriage still continued to occupy the minds of statesmen. Elizabeth, now in middle life, had the gratification of seeing youthful suitors contending for the possession of her hand. Before Lord Sussex's embassy to Vienna, overtures had been made to Elizabeth on the part of Catherine de Medici for the conclusion of a match between the English Queen and the youthful Charles the Ninth. The Queen on this occasion declined to make herself ridiculous by receiving the addresses of one so much her junior. But as time passed on she manifested no such scruples with reference to his younger brothers, both of whom were successively brought forward as candidates.

Anjou, afterwards Henry the Third, possibly having no belief in Elizabeth's sincerity, steadfastly refused to come to England, but Alençon, his junior, was persuaded to pay his court in person to the mature virgin. This Prince, though the youngest, was the most ill-favoured of the royal brethren. He appearance was grotesque. Deeply pitted with the smallpox, he would also appear to have exhibited that weazened, starveling aspect once commonly ascribed to Frenchmen in caricatures. It was a matter of astonishment to those who knew how strongly Elizabeth was impressed by personal advantages, and how great her aversion, in general, to physical defects, to see her fondle and caress this ugly stripling, kissing him in the presence of her courtiers, and lavishing marks of favour and attachment on him. The poor youth, completely overcome by her blandishments, was, or fancied himself to be, desperately in love with the Queen, and when Elizabeth became weary of the part which, for some secret reason, she had chosen to play, the awakening, to him, was rude indeed. It was with mingled feelings of humiliation and annoyance that the grave and experienced English statesmen watched the progress of this ridiculous drama. Sussex and his friends, although not approving of the match in itself, yet were willing to favour it on account of the important alliance it would bring to England, of inestimable value in view of the constant menace of a Spanish invasion. The Duke d'Alençon for some time refused to believe in the reality of his dismissal, and when at length he returned, dejected and humbled, a burst of indignation arose in France at the slight which had been put upon the Royal Family. The King expressed himself with justifiable severity, and warned Elizabeth of the dangers that might result from such trifling. The Queen, alarmed at the consequences she had brought upon herself, took to her bed, and sent for Sussex to advise her in this dilemma.

The matter was at length composed by the Queen's agreeing to support Alençon in the enterprise he had undertaken in the Netherlands.

Readers of "Kenilworth" are aware that Scott represents Sir Walter Raleigh as one of the gentlemen in attendance on the Earl of Sussex, but some obscurity prevails on this point. Whitehead, in his "Life and Times of Sir Walter Raleigh," says it has been asserted that Raleigh was originally introduced to Court by Lord Sussex, with the view of forming a counterpoise to the influence of Leicester; but neither this writer nor Mr. Fraser Tytler states that Raleigh was a member of the Earl's household. He was, no doubt, one of those whom the patronage and favour of Sussex aided in their upward course. Mr. Tytler, after describing Leicester, thus speaks of the Earl of Sussex:

> At this time another great man at Court was Ratcliffe, Earl of Sussex and Lord Chamberlain, whose blunt, open, and martial character comes out in striking relief beside the polished and brilliant personages amongst whom he moved. His abilities in war were of the highest order, as was repeatedly shown in Ireland; and although the rust of the camp and the smoke of battle had rather besmirched and unfitted him for the office of Chamberlain to a Virgin Queen, there was an affability and simplicity in his manners which attracted all honest men to his party, and enabled him, infinitely inferior as he was to Leicester in Court policy, to raise a party against him which had nearly ruined his great enemy, when Sussex showed the nobleness of mind to plead for a fallen foe ...
> Leicester, from his lordly state and influence, had acquired amongst the common people the title of the Heart of the Court, while Sussex, by his martial virtue, may be said to have been the soul of the camp.

We read also in Dugdale's "Baronage":

> It is reported of this Thomas, Earl of Sussex, by Sir Robert Naunton, in his 'Fragmenta Regalia,' that he was a goodly gentleman, of a brave noble nature, and constant to his friends and servants. Also that there was such an antipathy in his nature to that of the Earl of Leicester, that, being together at Court, and both in high employment, they grew to a direct forwardness, and were in continual opposition, the one setting the watch and the other the sentinel, upon the other's actions and motions.
> For this Earl of Sussex was of a great spirit, which, backed by the Queen's especial favour, and supported by a great and ancient inheritance, could not brook the other's empire, insomuch that the Queen, on sundry occasions, had somewhat to do to appease and restrain them, until death parted the competition, and left the place to Leicester.

The characters of these famous noblemen were not more strongly contrasted than the circumstances of their lives. Ratcliffe was born to his earldom and estates; Dudley owed his titles and possessions to the favour of the Queen. The high offices filled by Sussex were the meed of his deserts; those conferred on Leicester rather showed the measure of his incapacity than proved his fitness. Sussex possessed all the qualities of a soldier; Leicester was little more than a carpet-knight. Sussex furnished another example of the parsimony with which the Queen, who lavished her wealth on favourites, rewarded her loyal servants.

Another circumstance may be mentioned which redounds to the credit of Lord Sussex. When Sir Francis Drake returned from his glorious but really piratical expedition, as war had not then been declared by England against Spain, the Spanish Ambassador lodged formal complaints of his proceedings, and demanded the confiscation of his plunder. Drake, seeking protection from the Council, offered magnificent presents, which Leicester and some others took without scruple, but Burleigh and Sussex refused to accept the costly gifts.

In the beginning of June, 1583, Queen Elizabeth paid her final visit to Bermondsey House, where the Earl was then approaching his end. This must have been a solemn and affecting scene. Although not easily moved, it must have been with no common emotion that the Queen gazed, for the last time, on the face of that loyal and faithful adherent, whose life had been spent in her service, whose every thought had been solicitous for her honour and the prosperity of her realm.

Lord Sussex died on June 9, 1583. His apprehensions of Leicester, now about to be relieved from a formidable rival, were manifested in his dying moments. He said to the friends who surrounded his death-bed:

> I am now passing into another world, and must leave you to your own fortunes, and to the Queen's grace and goodness, but beware of the gipsy (as he was accustomed to call Leicester, on account of his dark complexion) - he will be too hard for you all; you know not the nature of the beast as well as I do.

Stow, in his *Chronicle*, gives the following account of the ceremonies attending the removal of the Earl's remains:

> On the 9th of June (1583) deceased Thomas Ratcliffe, Earl of Sussex, Lord Chamberlain to her Majesty, a Knight of the Garter, at Bermondsey beside London; and was, on the 8th of July following, conveyed through the same City of London toward Newhall in Essex, there to be buried. First went before him 45 poor men in black gowns, then on horseback 120 serving-men in black coats, then 25 in black gowns or cloaks, besides the Heralds-at-Arms; then the deceased Earl in a chariot covered with black velvet, drawn by four goodly geldings, next after was led the late Earl's steed covered with black velvet, then Sir Henry Ratcliffe, the succeeding Earl, chief mourner, and eight other Lords, all in black; then the Lord Mayor and Aldermen riding in murrey; and then on foot, the Gentlemen of Gray's Inn; and last of all, the Merchant Tailors in their livery, for that the said Earl was a brother of their Company, as many Noblemen, and famous Princes, Kings of this realm, before him had been.

The deceased Earl had been twice married: First, to Elizabeth, daughter of Thomas Wriothesley, Earl of Southampton, by whom he had issue two sons, Henry and Robert, both of whom died young. Second, to Frances, daughter of Sir William Sidney, and sister to Sir Henry Sidney, K.G., Lord Sussex' successor in the viceroyalty of Ireland.

This second Countess survived her husband several years, dying on March 9, 1589. She appears to have been a pious and benevolent lady, and it is interesting to learn that Sidney-Sussex College, Cambridge, the style of which commemorates her family name and her husband's title, was founded and endowed by this Countess Frances. This college became memorable in the next century as the place of Oliver Cromwell's education.

The Sir Henry Ratcliffe mentioned in Stow's account was the brother of the deceased Earl. He continued to occupy Bermondsey House, but there is no further record of the residence of the family after 1595. The title became extinct in the seventeenth century.

That we have not exaggerated the splendour of Lord Sussex' establishment is evidenced by the "120 serving-men" who rode in the funeral procession, and who probably represented the pick of his household.

One of the provisions of the Earl's will appears worthy of

note, as characteristic of the man. He directed that his executors should keep house at Bermondsey for twenty days after his interment. This shows sagacity and knowledge of human nature. Had the Earl enjoined that mourning should be kept up for him, his friends and retainers might have complied so far as to attend the funeral services, and exhibit the outward marks of affliction, but they would have been impatient to be relieved from this burden; and eager to forget, amidst more cheerful scenes, the gloom which had enveloped them.

But he chose the readiest method to keep his memory fresh. Those who still enjoyed the hospitality of Bermondsey House must of necessity have entertained kindly feelings towards the dead giver of the feast, and been disposed to expatiate upon his noble qualities, to commemorate his achievements, and to compare their mutual recollections. There is a large-heartedness, a broad-mindedness, in this which is pleasing to contemplate:

> I, Thomas Ratcliffe, have acted my part in life, and now pass away from the earth; but those who survive have still to bear their share in the universal effort. Let them, therefore, waste neither time nor strength in lamentation, but rather rejoice and strengthen themselves with food, that they also may perform the task allotted to them!

We may regard the death of the Earl of Sussex as closing the period of historic grandeur in relation to Bermondsey, because, although the later history contains much that is interesting, and much that is memorable, it is of a different character to the preceding.

One circumstance deserves to be noted, as rendering the early history peculiarly remarkable, viz., that the three great edifices which have made Bermondsey historical were not really separate and distinct structures, but one and the same, existing under altered conditions. First, in order of time, arose the Palace; next, the Monastery of St. Saviour; finally, the Manor-house. The priory, ultimately expanding into an abbey, absorbed the former royal residence, the Manor-house, built with the materials of the demolished conventual church and part of the monastery, yet was attached to and included within its precincts, the remaining portion of the Abbey; Bermondsey House was but Bermondsey Abbey transformed.

Similar modifications occurred throughout the country; many instances are to be observed in which abbeys and priories, falling into the hands of lay owners, were not absolutely demolished, but partially incorporated with newer structures; their noble halls and arched galleries - in some cases, even the cloisters - retained, and still testifying to the grandeur of their ancient lords. In Bermondsey the Abbey, the great central point of its history, was also the last to disappear. Long after the modern Manor-house had been demolished, the gates and ruined walls of the ancient Abbey still remained to remind the beholder of those princely monks who, for more than four centuries, were the Lords of Bermondsey.

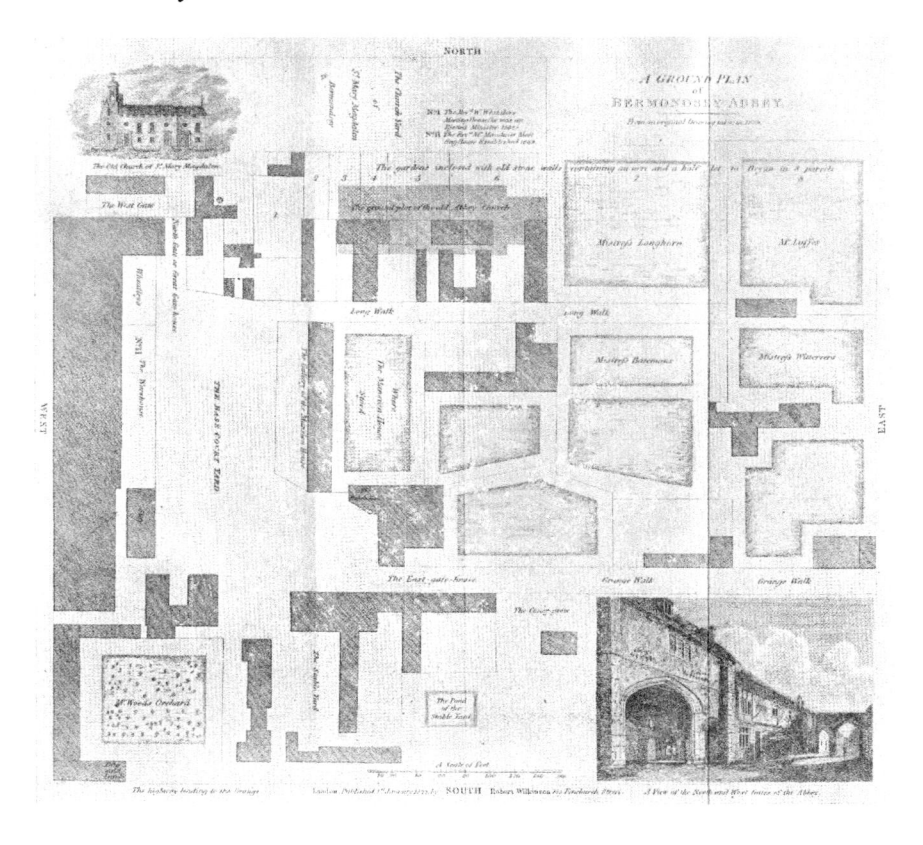

Ground plan of Bermondsey Abbey

CHAPTER XI

GROWTH OF BERMONDSEY - LEATHER INDUSTRY - THE SEVENTEENTH CENTURY - A CROMWELLIAN LEGEND - PEPYS - ST. MARY MAGDALEN'S CHURCH AND THE RECTORS OF BERMONDSEY - JAMAICA ROW CHAPEL AND JAMES JANEWAY - TOWNSEND, MASON, WATSON, AND THE DEAF AND DUMB SCHOOL - BACON'S FREE SCHOOL - BERMONDSEY SPA - CURTIS'S BOTANIC GARDEN - JOANNA SOUTHCOTT - LOYAL BERMONDSEY VOLUNTEERS - MR. G. W. PHILLIPS, THE HISTORIAN OF BERMONDSEY, AND MR. GARLAND PHILLIPS, THE MISSIONARY MARTYR OF TIERRA DEL FUEGO.

Having reviewed many of the most memorable scenes, and endeavoured to portray some of the principal characters associated with ancient Bermondsey, we shall now proceed to deal with changes that occurred in the district itself.

Antiquaries tell us that the "pastoral village, of character decidedly Flemish," as Miss Strickland describes it in the time of Henry the Second, had in the reign of Edward the Third become "extensive," yet still retaining its rural character. Its "well-cultivated gardens and wealthy velvet meads" - so pleasing to the eye - its meandering streams, its Woods and pastures, must have formed a prospect inexpressibly alluring, and, no doubt, many of the houses which, embosomed in trees, arose upon its expanse were retreats to which wealthy citizens gladly resorted, as an agreeable change from the murky atmosphere and narrow lanes of Old London.

Some eminent persons were, of course, actuated by motives of piety in seeking the retirement of monastic Bermondsey.

> Matilda, daughter of Guy de Beauchamp, Earl of Warwick, and wife of Geoffrey, Baron Say, after her husband's decease, which happened 26th June, 1359, 33rd Edward the Third, retired to a manse in this neighbourhood, called De La More, where she had license from the

Bishop, 18th October, 1363, to erect an oratory or chapel.

What the population of Bermondsey may have been in the monastic times, it is now impossible to ascertain; we have no statistics until after the Reformation, and then only the statement of the number of births and deaths inserted in the parish register. The population, however, must have been rapidly increasing, no doubt, from the development of industry, as we infer from a sinister detail in the early part of the seventeenth century. However picturesque in appearance, it would seem that Bermondsey, in those days, had little advantage over its populous neighbour on the northern bank, as it could not escape the ravages of the plague, that fearful scourge of former times, the visitations of which have happily become legendary. It is recorded that in 1625 no less than 1,117 inhabitants of this parish were carried off by that frightful malady.

All writers on the subject of Bermondsey declare their inability to assign any period for the commencement of the leather industry, for which the district has so long been famous, and a history of which would possess peculiar interest. The abundant water-supply, arising from the numerous tidal streams, is, of course, considered one chief reason for the establishment in Bermondsey of this manufacture. Charles Knight says:

> There was a mill at the riverside, at which the corn for the granary of the abbey was ground; and the mill was turned by the flux and reflux of the water along the channel. When the abbey was destroyed, and the ground passed into the possession of others, the houses which were built on the site still received a supply of water from this watercourse. In process of time tanneries were established on the spot, most probably on account of the valuable supply of fresh water obtainable, every twelve hours, from the river. This seems to be an opinion entertained by many of the principal manufacturers of the place.

Mrs. Boger, wife of the Rev. Canon Boger, for many years Headmaster of St. Saviour's Grammar School, has published an interesting work on "Bygone Southwark," and in the chapter entitled "The Industries of Southwark" says:

> Foremost among the industries of Southwark we must place tanning and the leather-trade, with the kindred art of saddlery. There seems no

record as to when the trade was started; but the oak-woods of Bermondsey were handy, and of water-power close to the Thames there was enough and to spare - literally, for was not the neighbourhood constantly flooded? Possibly, one of the ditches to drain the water off got filled with bark, and the discovery of tanning was made, as so many great discoveries have been, by what we call chance.
Is there such a thing?
It is probable, too, that among the oak-woods of Bermondsey pigs fed upon acorns, which is known to be their favourite food. So, given bark, water-ditches, and pigskins, there can be no reason to seek further for the origin of this industry.

Nevertheless, in a "Descriptive Account of Southwark and Bermondsey," published a few years ago, an attempt has been made to fix the period:

> The cause which led to Bermondsey originally becoming a centre for tanning and the leather manufacture is not generally known, and it is of singular historic interest. When the massacre of St. Bartholomew and the Revocation of the Edict of Nantes drove the Huguenots out of France, it occasioned the transference to England of capital and labour, the loss of which seriously weakened the French, and augmented the industrial prosperity of the British. No fewer than 1,300 refugees crossed over to the town of Rye, in Sussex, who were skilled in tanning, in leather manufacture, in silk-weaving, and in glassmaking. They were welcomed by religious sympathizers, but after their irate oppressors had made incursions across the water, and several times set fire to the town of Rye, the refugees decided on leaving, and came to London. Entering by the Kent Road, they observed that the district of Bermondsey was intersected by tidal streams, so favourable to leather manufacture, and those in the leather trade at once determined on remaining there and establishing themselves.
>
> This resulted in Bermondsey becoming the great centre for the tanning of skins and the manufacture of hides, which it has ever since continued to be.

The difficulty we are confronted with in this statement is that two historic events are mentioned together, which are separated by an interval of more than a century, and we are not informed at which period these refugees came to Bermondsey. If we take the earlier date, this statement could be reconciled with the undoubted fact that tanning was fully established here in the middle of the seventeenth century - consequently, long before the Revocation of the Edict of Nantes.

Although Bermondsey had suffered so severely from pestilence in 1625, we are told that "When the Great Plague raged in the City of London, many of the terror-stricken creatures fled to the Bermondsey tanpits, and found strong medicinal virtues in the nauseous smell."

One branch of the trade of which we have early mention in Bermondsey is woolstapling. The establishment of this may have been favoured by the originally pastoral character of the district; but, however that may be, we read of an eminent representative of this branch in the reign of Queen Mary, Master Henry Goodyere, Alderman of London, and "sometime merchant of the staple at Calais." The Alderman occupied a large and substantial house in Bermondsey Street, and was, "with two others, possessed of Horsey-down, as trustees for the parish of St. Olave's."

Machyn's "Diary" records the funeral of this personage on November 3, 1556:

> At St. Towly's (St. Olave's), in Southwark, in manner befitting his position - that is, with two white branches, twelve staff-torches, four great tapers, many mourners in black, both men and women, and the Company of Leathersellers in their livery.

The concentration of the woolstapling trade in and around Bermondsey Street is commemorated by the sign of an ancient tavern, called the Woolpack, formerly a place of great repute amongst the traders. Charles Knight says:

> The woolstaplers are wool-dealers, who purchase the commodity as taken from the skins, and sell it to the hatters, the woollen and worsted manufacturers, and others. They are scarcely to be denominated manufacturers, since the wool passes through their hands without undergoing any particular change or preparation; it is sorted into various qualities, and, like the foreign wool, packed in bags for the market.

The busy character which Bermondsey Street appeared to be acquiring in the seventeenth century is evidenced by the number of taverns which had arisen in that thoroughfare. The curious custom of issuing tradesmen's tokens had many examples in Bermondsey. Mr. Phillips says:

> The right of making these tokens was given by patent to individuals, who at times made a very great profit by them, the intrinsic value of them not being equal to their nominal value. The patentees, however, pledged themselves to take them back for something less than their nominal value; but it is supposed that they were never returned to them in any great numbers.

A selection from a list of tokens issued by tradesmen in this parish during the seventeenth century will afford some amusement, as showing how entirely the spelling of the name "Bermondsey Street" depended on the "taste and fancy of the speller":

1. Obverse: GEORGE CAVE, STONEBRIDG.
   Reverse: IN BARNEBY STREET. G. $^{C.}$ A.
2. Obverse: RICHARD GRAVES
            (two brewers supporting a cask).
   Reverse: IN BARNBY STREET. R. $^{G.}$ A.
3. Obverse: ELIZABETH HOPTON.
   Reverse: IN BARNIBY STREET. E. H.
4. Obverse: RICHARD MELTON IN (crosskeys in the centre)
   Reverse: BARNIBE STREET. R. $^{M.}$ A.
5. Obverse: JOHN STEVENS IN BARNABY'S J. $^{S.}$ A. 1666.
   Reverse: STREET, IN SOUTHWARKE, HIS HALFPENNY.
6. Obverse: W. T. A. AT THE WHITE SWAN
            (the swan in the centre)
   Reverse: IN BARNABEY STREET.

Even as the tradition of King John lingers in the minds of the inhabitants of Bermondsey, so a legend of Cromwell has arisen - it is impossible to say from what slight origin - and taken root in the popular imagination. In the north-eastern portion of the parish, at the end of Cherry Garden Street, leading from Jamaica Road to the river, there stood until late in the present century an old mansion, called Jamaica House.

> The house itself, which was named in compliment, no doubt, to the island which was the birthplace of rum, is traditionally said to have

been one of the many residences of Oliver Cromwell; but we cannot guarantee the tradition. It is thus mentioned in a work published in 1854:

'The building, of which only a moiety now remains, and that very ruinous, the other having been removed years ago, to make room for modern erections, presents almost the same features as when tenanted by the Protector. The carved quatrefoils and flowers upon the staircase-beams, the old-fashioned fastenings of the doors - bolts, locks, and bars - the huge single gable (which in a modern house would be double), even the divided section, like a monstrous amputated stump, imperfectly plastered over, patched here and there with planks, slates and tiles, to keep out the wind and weather, though it be very poorly, all are in keeping; and the glimmer of the gas, by which the old and ruinous kitchen is dimly lighted, seems to "pale its ineffectual fire" in striving to illuminate the old black settles and still older wainscot.'
- *Old and New London.*

Jamaica House, from Cherry Garden Street

But, however the story of Cromwell's residence arose, there is not a shadow of proof to substantiate it, and it has been said:

> There is scarce a village near London in which there is not one house appropriated to Cromwell, though there is no person to whom they might be appropriated with less probability. During the whole of the Civil Wars Cromwell was with the army. When he was Protector he divided his time between Whitehall and Hampton Court.

Still, it is easy to understand that the connection of the name of Cromwell with many houses must have arisen from his having temporarily occupied them during the frequent changes of his quarters.

Jamaica House, however, was not the only place in Bermondsey popularly associated with the name of Cromwell. Some premises in the rear of those old Plantagenet houses, so long a conspicuous feature of Bermondsey Street, but which have been recently demolished, were known as Oliver Cromwell's Stables, and tradition asserts that they were used as forage-stores during the Protectorate. We do not regard this as altogether apocryphal, for the following reasons:

> It is mentioned in the histories of England that shortly after the Battle of Edgehill the Common Council of London passed an act for fortifying the City, which was done with such dispatch that a rampart, with bastions, redoubts, and other bulwarks, was shortly erected round the cities of London and Westminster, and the borough of Southwark. It has been suggested that Fort Road, the thoroughfare running parallel with Blue Anchor Road, on the south side, from Upper Grange Road to St. James's Road, may mark the site of some of the fortifications here referred to.
> - *Old and New London.*

In pursuance of these vigorous defensive measures, troops would have been stationed in Bermondsey, and it is probable enough that the premises in Bermondsey Street were actually used as forage-stores for the Parliamentary army.

One more reference to Jamaica House, in connection with another historic personage. After the Restoration, this mansion was converted into a tavern, and being in the immediate vicinity of the Cherry Garden, which then formed a pleasant resort for the citizens from the opposite shore, must have thriven amain. Pepys, in his "Diary," records visits to both these places. On June 15, 1664: "To Greenwich, and to the Cherry Garden, and thence by water, singing finely, to the Bridge, and there landed."

It is not improbable that a modern Secretary to the Admiralty may have been in an equally genial condition after a whitebait dinner at Greenwich.

Again on Sunday, April 14, 1667: "Over the water to the

Jamaica House, where I never was before, and there the girls did run wagers on the bowling-green, and then, with much pleasure, spent little, and so home."

That ancient thoroughfare, Bermondsey Street, though no longer the scene of splendid pageants and stately processions, yet, as the centre of an industrial quarter, was beginning to acquire an importance undreamt of in the monastic times. It was a place of great resort, but instead of pilgrims wending to the "Rood of Grace," and magnates, with their train of attendants, passing to and fro, merchants and manufacturers, tradesmen and artificers, filled it with the hum of business. Since the last Abbot had been laid to rest in the Cathedral of Hereford, and the Earls of Sussex gathered to their fathers, new men had arisen, and new ideas claimed their sway. Yet, although the abbey now lay in ruins, Bermondsey Street still possessed a religious edifice, indissolubly linked with the traditions of the past, and illustrating in its history the changes and developments occurring in the Church of England.

Jamaica House, garden front

St. Mary Magdalen's, Bermondsey, West Front, 1841

In the description of Bermondsey contained in his "Survey of London," Stow says:

> Next unto this Abbey Church standeth a proper Church of Saint Mary Magdalen, builded by the Priors of Bermondsey, serving for the resort of the inhabitants (tenants to the Priors or Abbots near adjoining) there to have their Divine service: this Church remaineth, and serveth as afore, and is called a parish Church.

Even now, although it has undergone much rebuilding and many alterations, there is something peculiarly quaint and old-world about this church, befitting its character and appropriate to its remarkable history. It is commonly supposed to have been founded in the thirteenth century, but we think there can be no doubt that it is of far greater antiquity. The statement contained in the monastic annals, that in 1296 "the chapels of the Blessed Sepulchre and of St. Mary Magdalen are in the hands of the Prior and Convent of

Bermondsey," is usually regarded as fixing the date of the foundation of the church, but a very little consideration will show the fallacy of this. As the monastery was founded in 1082, and as only in some very rare instances conventual churches were used as parish churches, where did the cultivators of the manor worship prior to 1296? We cannot suppose that the monks left their "servants and tenants" in a state of spiritual destitution.

Another argument on which the theory of a thirteenth-century origin is founded is furnished by the fact that the central west window, and the two stone arches which support the roof of the vestibule are of thirteenth-century workmanship. But even this is not conclusive. We are told that this church, originally founded for the accommodation of tenants, etc., was subsequently declared parochial. Now, we have the record of an unbroken succession of Rectors of Bermondsey from A.D. 1291, and it is clear that a mere "chapel" could not have had a Rector. The church, therefore, had been "declared parochial" before 1296. The most rational supposition would be that a religious edifice of some sort had been established at an early period of the monastery's existence, and that, from the growing importance and increasing population of the district, it had been created the parish church of the manor, and its priest invested with the privileges of a Rector.

The first incumbent we find mentioned is "John de Ecclesia" - no doubt a real parson - "persona ecclesiæ." Among the successors of this reverend personage, we find names suggestive of high birth and distinguished connections, proving that the office must have been considered one of no small importance. John de Albini, whose name would indicate kinship to one of the greatest Norman Earls, Hugh de Babington, William de Montesfunte, John Fitz-Adam Cissoris, were evidently men of no common origin. Coming down the stream of time, we find, towards the close of the monastic period, University graduates, Bachelors of Laws and Masters of Arts, showing that no mere "Mass-priests" - men who possessed barely Latin enough to hurry through a service - were deemed worthy to officiate in St. Mary Magdalen's.

Bermondsey was a place where learning was cultivated, the abode of erudite Benedictines, the "nurse of many students." The Abbots felt that their honour and dignity were concerned in seeing that the parish church of their manor should be served by competent and learned men.

They were the patrons of the living, and, as we are told by Warton that many of these dignitaries exerted themselves to seek out youths of ability, and promote their advancement, it is probable enough that some of the Rectors may originally have been promising pupils in the monastic school, from whence they passed to the University, and, taking Orders, finally returned to officiate in the church of their former abode. It is natural to conceive them as having always occupied a high position amongst the secular clergy of South London. When we consider the importance of the Abbey, the dignity and influence of the Lords of the Manor, we feel that the parish church of Bermondsey, at the very gates of the monastery, must have been a place of no common resort and no small consequence.

The Church of St. Mary Magdalen was the St. Margaret's of the "Westminster of South London."

When the change came, the parish church remained untouched; the sacrilegious hands which laid the Abbey low were not uplifted against St. Mary Magdalen's. The latter, itself the offspring of the Abbey, survived and still survives, under altered form and changed conditions, with little of architectural splendour, or aught that is imposing in its aspect, but venerable from its antiquity, and memorable from its history and associations.

The inventory of effects sold by the churchwardens in the reign of Edward the Sixth exhibits the sumptuousness of its ancient furniture. Gorgeous vestments, embroidered copes and velvet chasubles, albs, dalmatics, crosses and crucifixes, silver paxes, golden censers, a "pair of organs," testify to the magnificence with which the services and ceremonies of the Church were conducted in St. Mary Magdalen's. But a great and salutary change had taken place. Those who now succeeded were resolved to discard external pomp and gorgeous accessories, and to mark the return to a purer faith by equal simplicity and sincerity of worship. God was to be adored "in spirit and in truth." They sold all these costly materials, retaining no more, even of the Church plate, than was necessary for the due performance of the services. One article they fortunately retained, which even then must have possessed considerable value. This was a richly-chased silver salver, representing a mediæval scene.

On the centre is a beautifully-chased representation of the gate of a castle or town, with two figures, a knight kneeling before a lady, who is about to place his helmet on his head. The long pointed solleretts of the feet, the ornaments of the armpits, and the form of the helmet, are supposed to mark the date of the salver as that of Edward the Second.

This valuable relic, still preserved in the parish church, is supposed to have belonged to the abbey, and to have been presented to St. Mary Magdalen's at the Dissolution. The plate has been an object of interest and curiosity to many, and is mentioned by every writer on the subject of Bermondsey. In 1831 Mr. Buckler, F.S.A., exhibited a drawing of this salver to the Society of Antiquaries.

A Communion-table took the place of the altar in the church. The doctrine of Transubstantiation, the very essence of the Romish teaching, was repudiated, the people were no longer required to kneel and adore the elevated Host, to kiss the pax, and to content themselves with the consecrated wafer, but were admitted to the Lord's Table, to partake of the Sacrament in both kinds. Although the bread and wine used were formally consecrated, there was no longer any mystery surrounding them; they were felt to be incapable of that strange operation, that subtle and pervading influence, they were once believed to exercise. Not the materials of the Sacrament, but the spirit in which they were received, the preparedness of the partaker, the devout frame of mind, were conducive to the sanctifying effect of the ceremony.

Of the residents in the adjacent Bermondsey House, Sir Thomas Pope remained to the last a Catholic; but the Earl of Sussex, although originally belonging to that communion, afterwards conformed to the Protestant faith, and was regular in his attendance on Divine worship. During the residence of this great personage, the parish church would have had no lack of noble company. We see the gates of Bermondsey House opening, when the bell was "knolling" for service, and the Earl issuing forth with his train of attendants, crossing the churchyard through a lane of bowing parishioners, reverently received by the officials of the church, and ushered into the state-pew. Not only my Lord, but noble and honourable guests who were partaking of his hospitality, would attend the local services. As few of the nobles of Elizabeth's

Court were devoid of some tincture of letters, the Rector of Bermondsey would feel himself on his mettle in addressing so distinguished an audience. Lord Sussex, although a man of the camp, had preserved much of his early acquisitions, was fond of quoting Latin, possessed some knowledge of casuistry, and, according to Froude, was disposed to pride himself on his logical faculty. Such men did not then feel the weariness which many of their rank would now be apt to experience in enduring a tedious discourse; they were accustomed to listen with critical appreciation; they closely followed the arguments of the preacher, and were prepared to discuss theological questions. The incumbent who filled the pulpit of St. Mary Magdalen's towards the close of Lord Sussex' life was one eminently fitted for such high companionship. The Rev. John Ryder was a scholar, author of a Latin Dictionary, no doubt one of those ponderous monuments of research and painstaking industry then in vogue. The hearers of Master Ryder's sermons would have found strong meat prepared for them. Arguments subtle and weighty, a discourse bristling with Latin and Greek quotations, discussing the knottiest points of casuistry, prophetic warnings, personal exhortations, would confirm the pious, gratify the learned, and bewilder the senses of ordinary laymen. It is to be presumed, however, that the later churchwardens were of a different stamp to the "Harry Etyn" before mentioned, and that such absolute illiteracy as his would have been considered a disqualification for office.

Master Ryder, subsequently translated to Ireland, ascended to high preferments - Archdeacon of Meath, Dean of St. Patrick's, and, in 1612, Bishop of Killaloe.

In the meantime, the Church of England had undergone some strange vicissitudes, to which we have adverted when treating of the Earl of Sussex. The system introduced by Henry the Eighth, which still retained many of the essential features of Catholicism, was further developed in the reign of Edward the Sixth into a Protestant establishment, in which most of the cardinal doctrines of Romanism were repudiated, a new Rubric, an altered discipline, and a Liturgy introduced, from which as much as possible savouring of superstition was eliminated. The favourers of the Protestant system - the Protector Somerset, Dudley, Duke of Northumberland, and Archbishop Cranmer - believed that, under the supremacy of the King, the new Church would be established on a firm basis, and would gradually draw to itself the majority of the nation. But all these hopes were shattered by the untimely death of Edward and the accession of Mary, whose Spanish blood, even more than the influence of her Spanish husband, made her uncompromising with reference to the restoration of the old faith. It is, therefore, not surprising that after all these violent changes and tragic episodes, the martyrdom of those who remained constant to their profession, the apostasy of so many more from whom consistency had been hoped and expected, a lukewarmness and indifference should have characterized many ministers of the Church as re-established by Elizabeth. In many cases the holders of benefices and ecclesiastical dignities, convinced, from the bitter experience of the past, of the instability and uncertainty of the whole existing system, anticipating that the death of Elizabeth might produce worse changes, and give rise to a renewed Marian persecution, evinced no ambition to win the crown of martyrdom, and concerned themselves far more with making provision for the evil days that might be in store, than in promulgating the doctrines of the Protestant faith. But although these worldly dispositions were very prevalent, the nation was not sunk in universal apathy. Two parties were inflamed with equal zeal for their respective creeds. Many of the fanatical Catholics braved imprisonment in loathsome dungeons, the rack, and the gibbet, with its frightful accessories, for the sake of their cherished doctrines and time-honoured ceremonies, as cheerfully as the Protestant martyrs had endured their fiery ordeal. So in the Church of England arose men imbued with all the fervour of the Apostles, and all the spiritual earnestness of the early ascetics. The Church they regarded but as a political compromise; the Royal supremacy they accepted as an unfortunate necessity; they were as desirous to be freed from "Erastian" control and regulation as the most advanced Ritualist of modern times. They desired that the Church of England, freed from the contaminations of Rome, possessing none of the old leaven in its doctrines or ceremonies; its pulpits filled with devout ministers, studious of the Word of God, earnest in reproof and exhortation, feeding their flocks, not with the vain traditions, the superstitious legends, of Rome, but with the true Bread of Life, the Gospel in all its purity, should become, as far as possible, the real Church of

Christ on earth. From their earnestness and solemnity, their practice of self-denial, their constant exhortations to purity of life, these devout men began to be termed "Puritans."

The pulpit of St. Mary Magdalen's was destined to be filled by some eminent members of this sect. In 1605 the Rev. Edward Elton was appointed Rector, and speedily signalized himself as a zealous preacher, and an upholder of those austere views of life peculiar to the stricter members of this body. The time-honoured institution of the Maypole, with its attendant games and diversions, was highly popular here, and had, no doubt, been favoured by the monks, who were not averse to the amusements of their tenantry. The earlier Rectors had troubled themselves little about the humours of the scene, having no desire to envelop their parishioners in gloom and austerity; but the fervent spirit of Elton saw dangers in this apparently harmless emblem. In his view it presented temptation, and no aspiration was more devout on the part of the Puritans than that of "Lead us not into temptation." The soul-searching divine knew how often a slight relaxation would prove the opening of the floodgates of tempestuous passion and unbridled indulgence. The May Day festivities involved drinking, and the merry-making often ended in fighting and general disorder. His exhortations to holiness would be forgotten amidst riot and drunkenness; his ears would be offended by oaths and ribaldry, and he saw no means of preventing a recurrence of such scenes save by the removal of the temptation - the destruction of the Maypole. In 1617 we learn that -

> Some of these parishioners, with friends of the Artillery Garden, intended sport, but Parson Elton would not have it so, and desired the constable to strike out the heads of their drums, and he preached against it many Sabbath days. Further, Elton and his people assaulted the said Maypole, and did, with hatchets, saws, or otherwise, cut down the same, divided it into several pieces, and carried it into Elton's yard.

Parson Elton would appear to have wielded the authority which a man of stern character and austere life is often enabled to exercise: his virtues, though uncompromising, commanded respect.

As most zealous divines in those days were authors as well, Elton published a volume of sermons in folio, "On St. Paul's

Epistle to the Romans," together with an "Exposition of the Epistle to the Colossians" and other works.

But the Puritans, although numerous and combative, had not yet gained the supremacy. The lukewarm divines of the early Elizabethan period had been succeeded by some who were as zealous in their way as the Catholics and their Puritan adversaries. The High Church movement, of which Laud had become the leader, and which grounded itself on the historical continuity of the Church of England, had waxed powerful under the patronage of the first Stuart Kings. On the death of Elton in 1624, Thomas Paske, D.D., who had previously been Master of Clare Hall, Cambridge, was appointed Rector. This clergyman, who, from the high academic position he had occupied, must have been a man of learning, appears to have belonged to the High Church party, for, although we have no record of his career as Rector of Bermondsey, we learn that in 1644, when the Puritans were in the ascendant, he was "ejected by the contagious breath of sectaries." It is suggested that this was in consequence of "ordinances this year for abolishing images and objects of superstition."

We may infer that under this incumbent the altar had been restored to its ancient position, that the church had once more reeked with incense, that prostrations, genuflections, and other "mummeries," favoured by Archbishop Laud, had offended the stern eyes of the Puritans. It was, therefore, to be expected that the next Rector would present a direct contrast to his ejected predecessor. The choice would seem to have been an excellent one.

Jeremiah Whitaker, a man of great learning and ability, succeeded, and gained golden opinions both from the members of his sect and the congregation to which he ministered. His importance is evidenced by the fact of his being elected member of the Puritan Convention, the great Assembly of Divines at Westminster. He is said to have been "remarkable for his skill in the Oriental languages."

Those whose souls had been vexed by the ceremonial observances of Dr. Paske looked back with affectionate veneration on the fervent earnestness and severe simplicity of Elton, revived, although in a milder form, by Whitaker, and, on the death of the latter in 1654, placed an inscription in the church to commemorate the virtues of both:

> Where once the famous Elton did entrust
> The preservation of his sacred dust,
> Lies pious Whitaker; both justly twined,
> Both dead, one grave, both living, had one mind,
> And by their dissolution, have supply'd
> The hungry grave, and Fame and Heaven beside.
> This stone protects their bones; while Fame enrols
> These deathless names, and Heaven embrace their souls.

The circumstances of the succeeding incumbency are not clear. We are told, on the one hand, that William Whitaker, the son of Jeremiah, was appointed to succeed his father in 1654; on the other, that the Rev. Dr. Parr, chaplain to Archbishop Usher, received the vacant benefice. Mr. Phillips, in his list of the Rectors of Bermondsey, does not include William Whitaker, but represents Dr. Parr as filling the office from 1654 till his resignation in 1682. He does, however, say elsewhere that William Whitaker was ejected at the Restoration.

Dr. Rendle's account of this divine is as follows:

> William, called in 1654 to succeed his father as Rector of Bermondsey, was a minister indeed; skilled in languages - Greek, Latin, and Oriental; fit to be a tutor at his college, i.e., Emmanuel, at Cambridge; a peacemaker, whose pride it was to settle disputes, and leave no rancour behind; just the man, making a conscience of his work, to be ejected. So in 1662 he was no longer Rector of Bermondsey.

The circumstances of the time would, no doubt, explain this seeming confusion. There must have been a de jure and a de facto Rector, even as, at the same time, a lawful King was supposed to be reigning, whilst a "usurper" held possession of the throne. Although the Independent party was now in the ascendant, the Puritans were still powerful in the Church, and no doubt had sufficient influence to maintain William Whitaker in his rectory. The patron of the living was a certain Rowland Trappes, by whom Dr. Parr was presented in 1654, but the latter was compelled to content himself with the title until after the Restoration. We know not whether it was as some compensation for this disappointment, that in the same year Dr. Parr was made Vicar of Camberwell, which living he held until his death in 1691.

We shall presently return to William Whitaker, but wish first to say a few words with reference to the clergyman who supplanted him.

Dr. Parr was no common man, for he is described as a "ready and good preacher, and is said to have broken up two conventicles by his attractive powers."

His sermon, preached at St. Saviour's, Southwark, in 1658, before the great Judge, Sir Matthew Hale, and his colleagues, is preserved, and has often been quoted. In this, after a solemn exhortation to judicial purity, he continues in a strain that would be echoed by many in the present day:

> Here is one grievance more you must help the country in, and rid the country of those innumerable pest-houses - we mean the tippling-houses that pester the whole nation, and ruin whole families. Sirs, you that are the standing magistrates of the country, will it be for your honour, think you, to give license to such - so many? Some you say must be, but why so many? . . .
> If you mean not to suppress them, let these mottoes be on the sign and over the door: 'Here you may buy beggary and disgrace at a dear rate; here you may learn the way to the stocks, to the gaol, the gallows, and to hell.'

William Whitaker was greatly beloved by his congregation, and in order that his sympathizers should not be deprived of the benefit of his ministrations, after his ejection from the rectory, he established a Presbyterian meeting-house in that part of Long Walk then called King John's Court. Dr. Rendle says:

> He, as well as many another ejected minister of great learning and worth, became a private teacher. So general was this practice that it helped most effectually to build up Dissent, and is, indeed, worth consideration as a great factor towards beneficial changes in fostering a much higher tone of religious thought in our country. His house full of candidates in divinity, he became a teacher of preachers and a father of divines. I have by me a picture of the wooden house, with one gallery, which was built for him in 1699, and which remained as a place of worship for about a hundred years. One of his successors at this meeting-house, Isaac Mauduit, is said to have preached at St. Mary Magdalen's, Bermondsey, a sermon on the death of King William the

Third, but whether the parish or the parish church is meant I do not know; but as he is said to have practised 'occasional conformity,' and the family monuments are noted in the church, it was probably there the sermon was preached. In the end, ministers far gone in Arianism preached from Whitaker's pulpit, and the thing died out; now Wesley's people took it, he himself preaching there from time to time. That there should have been two erratic meeting-houses on the very site of the old abbey, in Long Walk and King John's Court !

The Isaac Mauduit here mentioned, and who was buried in the parish church in 1718, is described as eminent for his learning and piety, but requires to be noted for another reason. All readers of Carlyle's "Frederick the Great" will remember his account of the famous "Mauduit pamphlet," which, appearing in the crisis of the Seven Years' War, produced almost as powerful an effect as Swift's "Conduct of the Allies" had done during the campaigns of Marlborough. Carlyle says that the author of this pamphlet is stated to have been "the son of a Dissenting minister in Bermondsey." This is true; Israel Mauduit, the author in question, was the son of Isaac Mauduit, of King John's Court.

A Rector who held this living for a few years in the time of George the First (1723 to 1726-7), the Rev. Dr. Taswell, deserves special mention. He was a distinguished scholar, and had been Classical Examiner at Oxford. This gentleman wrote a Latin autobiography, which, translated by his nephew, has since been published by the Camden Society. It contains chiefly personal details, with allusions to the theological controversies then raging, but the main point of historic interest is the statement that he was taken when about nine years old to witness the disinterment of the remains of the regicides, Cromwell, Ireton, Bradshaw, etc., and their exposure on gibbets. This affords a striking illustration of the callousness of feeling which prevailed in former times. Happily for ourselves, we are ignorant of the fierce passions aroused by civil war, but we could hardly conceive, under any circumstances, a boy of tender years being taken to view such a hideous spectacle. Of course, the object of his elders was to fill him with abhorrence of rebellion, and to impress his mind with the ignominy reserved for the "brave wicked man," as Lord Clarendon is said to have termed the once-dreaded Protector.

It would have been very interesting had Dr. Taswell inserted any description of Bermondsey in his memoir, or any facts connected with his incumbency; but the only local details we find are comprised in the statement that the parish of St. Mary, Newington, the rectory of which he held conjointly with that of Bermondsey, then contained 600 houses.

The custom of founding lectureships in connection with parish churches, which had grown up during the development of the Puritan movement, had an example in Bermondsey, although the first Lecturer does not appear to have been nominated until 1686. In 1741 we find the appointment of a Lecturer (Farmery Malthus), whom we note simply on account of his name, which, being so very uncommon and coupled with his clerical profession, would lead us to imagine that he must have been a connection of the famous (and reverend) writer on "Population." We shall have presently to speak of a far more memorable Lecturer and subsequent Rector of Bermondsey.

St. Mary Magdalen's, 1804.
(The school is seen over the porch)

Aubrey, in his "Antiquities of Surrey," devotes a considerable space to the parish church of Bermondsey, and gives engravings of some of the monuments. Many persons of high station, and some of distinction, are interred in St. Mary Magdalen's. Two High

Sheriffs of Surrey, Sir Thomas and Sir William Steavens, with several ladies of their family, here have their resting-place. An artist of some reputation, of whom a sketch is given in Horace Walpole's "Anecdotes of Painting" (Mr. Le Piper), was buried in the parish church.

Ancient wall on the East of St. Mary Magdalen's exhibiting Mason's and other marks

One inscription, to the memory of Dr. Joseph Watson, who died in 1829, and who also reposes in our church, should be for ever memorable. It states that this gentleman

> for more than thirty-seven years, held the important situation of teacher to the first public institution in this country for the education of the Deaf and Dumb, which was established in this Parish A.D. 1792. The institution commenced with only six pupils, and he was spared, by Divine Providence, to devote his talents to the instruction of more than one thousand. The difficulties which he had to encounter he overcame by a proportionate industry, and the success which attended his exertions was witnessed by the attainments of his pupils and the honourable and useful stations which many of them occupied in society.

The mention of the Deaf and Dumb School leads us to speak of another religious edifice, which possesses a history only second in interest to that of St. Mary Magdalen's. This is the Congregational Church in Jamaica Road, the precursor of which was known as Jamaica Row Chapel. This institution dates from the seventeenth century, having originated in a meeting-house established by the celebrated James Janeway in 1662. The place at first occupied by this pious and eloquent pastor appears to have been situated in Rotherhithe, near the boundary of the two parishes. It is said that the building in which the meetings were then held was Government property, and that when the authorities resolved to suppress them as illegal "conventicles," no less a person than Sir Christopher Wren, at that time Surveyor of Government Buildings, was appointed to superintend the execution of this odious task. We subjoin the biographical sketch of Janeway by the Rev. Dr. Cox:

> James Janeway was born at Lilley, Hertfordshire. He became a student at Christ Church, Oxford, in 1655, where he took the degrees in Arts in due time. At the close of his pursuits in the University, he went to reside at his mother's house at Windsor, and devoted himself to tuition. It is probable that he had no benefice, but as a Nonconformist was silenced by the Act of 1662. During the plague he was indefatigable in preaching the Gospel, but escaped the contagion. As soon as he supposed the persecuting spirit of the age allowed, a chapel or meeting-house, as it was then termed, was erected for him in Jamaica Row, Rotherhithe. It was, however, pulled down by the soldiers, but the people built another on the same spot upon a larger scale. He had numerous and respectable audiences, and was the honoured instrument of effecting a great reformation in the neighbourhood.
> The high party, being exceedingly exasperated at his popularity and success, made several attempts on his life. On one occasion, as he was walking along the Wall at Rotherhithe, he had a narrow escape from a shot. The bullet went through his hat, but inflicted no personal injury. At another time the soldiers broke into his meeting-house, exclaiming as they pressed through the crowd, 'Down with him! down with him!' They jumped upon a form or bench, with the view of pulling him out of the pulpit, but providentially the bench gave way. The confusion which ensued afforded an opportunity of escape, for some of his friends threw a coloured coat over him, and put a white hat on his head. The mob, however, probably misled as to his person by this clever deception, seized upon one of his people, Mr. Kentish, and carried him away to the Marshalsea prison, where he was confined for a considerable time. It is supposed that this was Mr. Richard Kentish, who had been ejected from St. Katherine's in the Tower. A further attempt was made to secure him (Janeway) when engaged in preaching at a gardener's house. The troopers, having dismounted, rushed into the premises; but

he had time to throw himself upon the ground, where his friends, intercepting the soldiers, concealed him so effectually from them, by covering him with cabbage leaves, that he again escaped. He died in the prime of life, on March 16, 1674, in the thirty-eighth year of his age, and was buried in St. Mary's Church, Aldermanbury, near his father.

And what manner of man was the object of this unremitting persecution? The enumeration of his distinguishing qualities in the funeral sermon preached by the Rev. Nathanael Vincent, entitled "The Saint's Triumph over the Last Enemy," furnishes an answer, and is supported by abundant evidence. We give the headings.

1. Great was the sweetness of his natural temper and disposition.
2. He made it his business to be religious.
3. He was a serious mourner for the decays of godliness in this backsliding age.
4. His heart was inflamed with love to Christ.
5. His bowels of compassion yearned towards immortal souls.
6. He laboured abundantly, spending himself in his Master's work.
7. He was a man mighty in prayer.
8. He was much for unity and love.
9. He abounded in works of charity.
10. He was exceeding humble.

The sermon concludes:

The loss of him is not only his relations' loss, but Redriff's [Rotherhithe's] loss, London's loss, England's loss, the Church's loss, for he was of such a public spirit that all are like to miss him.

The portrait of Janeway exhibits a countenance of singular sweetness and amiability. Dr. Cox's sketch and "Essay on the Family and Times of the Janeways" are prefixed to a work written by James, entitled "Heaven upon Earth; or, Jesus the Best Friend of Man," an admirable production, which in the earnestness of its exhortations, and the affectionate fervour of its personal appeals, recalls the "Saint's Rest" of his great contemporary Baxter. A copy of this work is deposited in the Bermondsey Public Library, and is one of the many books possessing local interest, the collection of which we owe to the zeal and industry of Mr. Frowde, the librarian.

Janeway's work affords an additional proof that many of the Puritans, although shunning all occasions to sin, and endeavouring to "avoid the appearance of evil," yet were not of forbidding austerity, but rather sought to win the hearts of their hearers by loving solicitation.

We heartily congratulate our neighbours of Rotherhithe on the possession of such a memory as this, enshrined amongst their other traditions. But although James Janeway himself is identified with Rotherhithe, the chapel in which his successors ministered was situated in Bermondsey, on the north side of the present Jamaica Road. The immediate successor of James Janeway was Thomas Rosewell, who is described as having been a man of some eminence, and remarkable for having been "tried by Judge Jeffreys, and escaped harmless." We are told that this congregation, being Presbyterian, gradually declined during many years, till scarcely any hearers were left. This induced the new pastor, Dr. Flexman, to resign in 1783, when the people dispersed. The chapel was then taken by the Independents, or, as they are now called, Congregationalists, and their first pastor was a man who is memorable in the annals of philanthropy.

St. Mary Magdalen's, from the East, 1810

John Townsend was born in London in 1757. He settled as minister to an Independent congregation at Kingston, whence, in 1784, he removed to Bermondsey, where he continued to reside during the remainder of his life. The compassionate nature of this truly Christian minister, which led him to commiserate all who were suffering and afflicted, specially induced him to relieve the condition of those unhappy beings whose physical defects disqualified them for the pursuits of active life, and who remained subject to the mockery of the heartless, and the useless pity of the benevolent. To the shame of England, no attempt had hitherto been made to ameliorate the condition of the deaf and dumb, although the subject had engaged the attention of some eminent men in the seventeenth century. Scotland, so inferior in wealth, had set a noble example in this respect, and the school at Edinburgh formed a model which Mr. Townsend earnestly desired to imitate. It is most gratifying to learn that at a period when much intolerance prevailed, and the Church was most unwilling to shake hands with Dissent, a Lecturer and subsequent Rector of Bermondsey should have come forward to co-operate with the Independent minister in this praiseworthy undertaking. Discarding all sacerdotal prejudices and sectarian distinctions, these pious men were drawn together by the benign influence of sympathy for helpless suffering. In 1792, by the united efforts of the Rev. Henry Cox Mason and Mr. Townsend, an asylum was opened in Fort Place, Grange Road,

> for the reception and instruction of those born deaf and dumb. This institution commenced with six pupils, and in a short space of time rapidly increased in number, many of them becoming useful members of society. The calamity, if not wholly removed, is at least mitigated, as far as human assistance can go. They were taught to write, to read articulately, and to cipher. Their first teacher was Joseph Watson, LL.D., a man who appears to have been eminently qualified for such a situation.
> - Phillips' *History of Bermondsey*.

A remarkable testimony to the eminence of Dr. Watson is contained in Miss Martineau's "History of England during the Peace." When enumerating the persons of distinction who died in the reign of George the Fourth, that lady says:

Another educator died during this period, whose name should not be ungratefully passed over - Dr. Watson, of the Deaf and Dumb Institution in the Kent Road, London. Without going into any general account of the education of the deaf and dumb, we may note, in explanation of Dr. Watson's services, that the most fatal oversight in that branch of education has been that of supposing that a full communication of mind, and reception of ideas, can be obtained by written language and gesture. Written words and gesture are but the sign of language, after all, and without oral communication, the mind cannot possibly be fully exercised and cultivated. This difficulty is, to all appearance, insuperable; but men have risen up from time to time who saw that, though the deaf and dumb can never be brought to an equality of cultivation with those who have the full use of speech, much is gained by giving them spoken as well as written language; and Dr. Watson was the man who gave the deaf and dumb more power in this direction than any preceding teacher. Bulwer, the chirosophist, opened up the track in England in the seventeenth century, and his work, dated 1648, plainly shows that he taught articulate speech, as well as the written and hand language. Wallis followed, being a contemporary of Bulwer, and anxious to engross the merit which belonged truly to him. Dr. Wallis had great merit, but he is proved not to have been a discoverer. Articulate speech had been found attainable for the born deaf previously in Spain, and subsequently in Holland, where Dr. Amman published his method in full; and during the eighteenth century Germany and France followed. Henry Baker taught various deaf and dumb persons to speak, but he bound them over not to reveal his method; and though he half promised Dr. Johnson to make it known, he never did so. Thomas Braidwood began his career in 1760 at Edinburgh, and carried to some extent the practice of articulate speech among his pupils. When he removed to London in 1783, Dr. Watson studied and worked at his institution, and made up his mind to devote himself to the education of that unfortunate class, of whom there are not fewer than 13,000 in our islands; and, in his eyes, the practice of articulate speech was indispensable to the attainment of such cultivation as could be afforded. For five-and-forty years he laboured at his benevolent task, and he carried the capability of speech much higher than any predecessor. In regard to the general run of his pupils, an authority declares: 'Some of the pupils articulate not unpleasantly; their reading is monotonous, but their animation in ordinary conversations, especially on subjects of interest to them, gives a species of natural tone and emphasis to what they say.' This, great as it is, is not all. A few days before Dr. Watson's death, one of his private pupils was called to the Bar by the Honourable Society of the Middle Temple. Here were tidings for a good man to receive on his death-bed! The days of miracles will never be over while human benevolence is unexhausted; and here we have, for a sign of our own times, a good man soothed to his rest by the blessings of the dumb. Dr. Watson died on the 23rd of November, 1829, in the sixty-fifth year of his age.

Messrs. Mason and Townsend's benevolent undertaking appealed so powerfully to the sympathies of charitable and wealthy individuals, that the surviving founder was enabled to erect the spacious building in the Old Kent Road so well known for many years as the Deaf and Dumb Asylum. A bust of the Rev. Mr. Townsend was placed in the committee-room, and the adjacent streets still commemorate the names of himself and his zealous coadjutor, the one on the right of the asylum being called Townsend Street, and that on the left Mason Street.

This effort did not exhaust the active benevolence of Mr. Townsend. Although the foundation of the Deaf and Dumb Asylum is the work with which his name will ever be associated, he also assisted in founding the London Missionary Society, the Female Penitent Society, and other charitable and Christian associations. He also established a school for the gratuitous education of the children of Dissenting ministers. Mr. Townsend died in 1826, Mr. Mason having predeceased him in 1804.

It is with pride that we record the three names of Mason, Townsend, and Watson, more illustrious than those of conquerors, and we trust that their association with Bermondsey will never be forgotten.

Although, since the closure of the Monastic School, Bermondsey had possessed no eminent successor - for St. Olave's Grammar School, though at one time established within the precincts of this parish, was not a Bermondsey institution - the principal seminary, for nearly a century and a half, was Bacon's Free School, situated in the Grange Road, opposite Bermondsey Square. It is thus described in Phillips' "History of Bermondsey":

> In the Grange Road, on the south side, is a free school built of brick. In the front is a niche, with a statue representing a boy, and underneath an inscription, dated 1752, and setting forth that the said building was erected in 1718, by Thomas Bacon, Esq., executor of Mr. Josiah Bacon, of London, merchant, a native of the parish, who, by his will, charged his real and personal estates with the raising of such a sum of money as

should be requisite for building of a free school in this parish wherein he was born, and also for a dwelling-house to adjoin the same for the master of the said school to dwell in, such building, with the ground to be purchased for the same, not exceeding £700. And his trustees were to settle not more than £150 per annum for the maintenance of the school and the payment of the master and usher. And the scholars and children that were to be admitted into the said school were to be poor children of such persons as should inhabit the parish, whose parents or friends were not able to pay for their learning, and should be there taught gratis to read English, and also writing and arithmetic, to fit them for trades, or to keep merchants' books, and that there should always be forty, and never more than sixty, scholars belonging to this school at the one time, etc.

The testator further 'desired and appointed that the Minister, Churchwardens, and other chief officers for the time being, for ever, should be the governors of the said school, and should, once or oftener, yearly visit the same, and make such rules and orders for the better government thereof, as they, or the major part of them, should think fit.'

The original school, with its old-fashioned Masters House, was pulled down a few years ago, and a handsome modern structure erected. This institution has always enjoyed good repute, and many of the most respectable inhabitants of Bermondsey have, since its foundation, been educated in it.

The Bermondsey United Charity Schools, founded the Boys' school in 1712 and the Girls' in 1722, and liberally supported by the inhabitants, long provided efficient means of instruction to many children of the labouring class.

In spite of its ancient Royal and Monastic glories and the greatness of its former residents, Bermondsey would hardly have been considered in modern times likely to become a fashionable Spa. We feel peculiarly interested in the efforts to invest it with that character made by Mr. Keyse, whom we regard as a man of singular merit, and of whom we should be glad to know more. This gentleman is described as a self-taught artist, and some time prior to 1770 he took a tavern which had recently become vacant, and there established tea-gardens, with a "picture-gallery," containing the productions of his pencil. The discovery of a chalybeate spring in the neighbourhood of this tavern gave rise to the Bermondsey Spa, the name of which is still preserved by the well-known Spa

Road.

> About 1780 Mr. Keyse procured a license for musical entertainments after the manner of Vauxhall, and for several years his gardens were open every evening during the summer season. Fireworks were occasionally exhibited, and at certain times in the course of the year was exhibited an excellent representation of the Siege of Gibraltar, consisting of fireworks and transparencies, the whole contrived by the proprietor of the gardens, who possessed considerable mechanical abilities. The height of the rock was about 50 feet, the length 200, and the whole apparatus covered about four acres.
> Mr. Keyse died in 1800, when his pictures were sold by auction. The gardens were shut up about the year 1805, and the site has since been built upon.
> - Phillips' *History of Bermondsey*.

That these efforts to amuse the public were not unappreciated is proved by an extract from a newspaper of June 5, 1800:

> SPA GARDENS, BERMONDSEY
> In celebration of his Majesty's birthday, this evening will be a grand loyal and military gala, with a most superb display of fireworks emblematical to the occasion, by Signors Rossi and Tessier. The concert (under the direction of Mr. Smethergill) will receive considerable addition, and consist entirely of loyal songs and choruses, and will be relieved by a military band in full uniform. The painting gallery will be opened as usual, and the gardens will be illuminated with additional splendour. Admission two shillings. The concert will begin at seven o'clock. On so glorious an occasion every exertion will be made to render the amusements superior to any ever known at these gardens. Several members of the volunteer corps to be reviewed by his Majesty this day, having expressed a wish to dine at the gardens after the review, a cold collation will be provided for parties of any extent. The doors will be open for that purpose at three o'clock, when the admission for the evening will be received, except of gentlemen in uniform, of whom none will be taken during the evening.

The Spa Gardens must have been a great acquisition to the neighbourhood in those days. As most of the master tanners and leather-manufacturers then resided on or near their business premises, it must have been a source of delight to their families to quit the dull streets of the ancient quarter for these gay and festive scenes, enlivened with the strains of martial music and the trills of professional vocalists. To an inhabitant of present-day Bermondsey, the notion of the Spa possesses a piquancy that is inexpressibly delightful. It was appropriate that the conductor of the enterprise should be an artist; we should be disposed to regard him as an idealist, and as possessing no small portion of that "dumb poetry" which Carlyle was fond of ascribing to many unlikely subjects. Such a man would have gazed with no common interest on the ruins of the ancient Abbey, and might have associated the spring so happily discovered during his occupancy with those "holy wells" so often found in the neighbourhood of monasteries. It is very amusing to read the description of Mr. Keyse given by Mr. J. T. Smith, the artist and antiquary: the Hogarth-like appearance, the whimsical expressions, the justifiable pride with which he recounted the two visits of Sir Joshua Reynolds, when that great painter examined his productions. Some of these were certainly of a very realistic character, being representations of a butcher's shop and a "green-stall," executed with the most painstaking accuracy, his "Bagshot mutton" in particular being depicted with Paul-Potter-like fidelity. But we see that he did not limit himself to the representation of peaceful scenes and still life, but was equally at home amidst the smoke of battle. He was capable of realizing the grandeur of one of the most heroic incidents of modern times - the glorious defence of Gibraltar against the combined fleets of France and Spain.

But, although Mr. Keyse received a certain amount of patronage, he would appear to have shared the fate of most entertainers of the public, as, at times, his success did not appear to be commensurate with his efforts. We feel peculiarly interested in Mr. Smith's account, which represents Keyse as superior to Fortune, and as preserving a delightful cheerfulness and serenity in the midst of disappointment, and in the presence of his "solitary visitor." The ringing of a bell being heard, Mr. Keyse said: "The bell rings, not for dinner or for prayers, but for the song," which was accordingly sung by a fashionably attired female to the proprietor and his guest. He then hospitably invited Mr. Smith to partake of a bottle of Lisbon wine.

We feel that such a man ought to have had a better fate, and wish to pay honour to his memory.

Some time towards the close of the last century a remarkable effort was made in the interests of botanical science by a man of eminence in his vocation.

William Curtis was born at Alton, Hampshire, in 1746, and apprenticed to an apothecary. But his love of botanical pursuits induced him to relinquish his profession, in order to establish a botanic garden and become a lecturer on that science. Besides his lectures, which were published with illustrative plates, he wrote "Practical Observations on British Grasses," "Flora Londinensis," and edited a botanical magazine. We do not know that Mr. Curtis was actuated by a desire to diffuse botanical knowledge amongst the inhabitants of Bermondsey, as it is supposed to have been the fact that the soil of certain parts of this parish was favourable to the cultivation of rare plants, which induced him to establish the "first scientific botanic garden in London," in Crimscott Street, Grange Road.

A movement initiated at the close of the last century affords gratifying evidence of the public spirit of the inhabitants. The tremendous struggle in which England was then engaged, the imminent danger of a French invasion, and the insufficiency of the regular army and ordinary militia for the defence of the country, caused the formation of volunteer corps in many quarters, and Bermondsey was one of the first to respond to the patriotic call.

On two separate occasions a force was raised and equipped in this parish. First, in 1793, two companies of seventy men each were enrolled under Major-Commandant Gaitskell; but it would seem that, when the crisis that caused the issue of the Royal proclamation had passed, this corps was either disbanded or merged in that which, a few years later, was established on a permanent footing. Mr. Phillips tells us that -

> Whilst the French Revolution was in progress, the inhabitants of this parish formed themselves into a Military Association for the defence of their families and country against invasion, rebellion, or riot, under the following engagement:
> 'We, the undersigned, do agree to form a Military Association, under the name of the Loyal Bermondsey Volunteers, as soon as commissions can be procured for officers (to be chosen from among ourselves for that purpose), by whom only we are to be commanded, unless in case of actual Invasion, Rebellion, or Riot, when it is in the power of his

Majesty to place the corps under the command of any superior or commanding officer of any other corps, to whom it may be attached, to do duty in this parish, or in the adjoining parishes of Rotherhithe and Newington, the Borough of Southwark and its Liberties, and in no case to march further; that we will furnish ourselves with an uniform-dress, arms, and accoutrements; and that we will abide by all such articles as a majority shall hereafter adopt, provided that they do not alter the original engagement.'

The second enrolment took place in 1799.

A black marble tablet in St. Mary Magdalen's records the death of Robert Rich, Esq., "late of this parish, who died on the 6th April, 1829, in the 77th year of his age, and was interred in a family vault in this Churchyard"; and states that "he was honoured with the command of the Loyal Bermondsey Volunteers."

This gentleman was evidently a most important inhabitant, as he is described as being J. P. for both Surrey and Middlesex, and Deputy-Lieutenant for the former county.

A newspaper of 1801 gives some interesting details relative to this force:

> May 8th, 1801. - The Bermondsey Volunteers, commanded by Major Gaitskell, on Thursday last had their first grand field-day for the summer, and were reviewed at the parade at the Spa by Lord Onslow, Lord-Lieutenant of the County of Surrey. Notwithstanding the winter recess, the corps performed the various evolutions and firings with such accuracy and exactness, as was highly honourable to themselves, and gratifying to the commanding officer, and which produced the most flattering commendation from his Lordship. A numerous assemblage of spectators were admitted by tickets, to whom the gardens afforded the most delightful promenade. After the field exercise, the corps, with Lord Onslow, the High Sheriff, and a number of visitors, partook of an excellent dinner, given by the honorary members, for whose liberality and politeness the corps is much indebted.

The colours of this original Volunteer force were, for many years after its dissolution, preserved in the parish church, until the late Canon Tugwell, in 1879, presented them to the members of the existing corps, in whose Drill-Hall they now remain. Captain Henry Bevington, great-uncle of Colonel Bevington, who has for so many years held the command of the present Volunteer battalion, was an officer in the original corps.

Jacob's Island

We have now to refer to the circumstance of Bermondsey having been selected as one of the many temporary residences of a famous impostor, Joanna Southcott. This extraordinary person, an ignorant and fanatical old woman, appears to have possessed a marvellous power of imposing on the credulity of the public, and her history is one of the strangest in the grotesque record of religious impostures. The claim of this woman to be a second and more exalted Virgin Mary, to be the "Mother of the Shiloh" by miraculous conception, even more wonderful in her case on account of her age, was eagerly recognised, and caused her to be surrounded by thousands of admiring disciples. They went the length of providing a silver cradle for the expected offspring; and although she quarrelled with some of her most devoted adherents, and migrated from place to place in consequence, the belief of many was not shaken by the bursting of the bubble and the death of the prophetess, but, marvellous to relate! the delusion continues to the present day.

We find in the list of "Religious Denominations having Registered Places of Worship" - "Believers in Joanna Southcott"!

For some time this woman occupied a house still existing at

the corner of Jamaica Road, adjoining the Drill-Hall of the Bermondsey Volunteers, from one of the windows of which she is represented in an old print as addressing the crowd assembled in front of the building. It has been asserted that in this house Joanna was supposed to have actually "lain-in of the Shiloh," but accounts are conflicting, and we can only verify the fact of her residence.

From this notorious person, we pass to one whose zealous labours have gained him honourable fame, and feel much pleasure in recording the fact that Mr. John Timbs, the antiquary, biographer, and author of so many delightful books which have done much to popularize knowledge, spent some of his earlier years within the precincts of Bermondsey. In his autobiography Mr. Timbs says:

> The love of gardening and raising flowers has ever been with me a favourite pursuit. Even in that sooty suburb of Southwark, Snow's Fields, at a very early age, I had the range of a large garden, and a plot set apart for my special culture. But I had fancied failures.
>
> Oh, ever thus from childhood's hour
> I've seen my fondest hopes decay;
> I never loved a tree or flower,
> But 'twas the first to fade away.
>
> Still, what I attributed to Fate was, in most cases, traceable to the poisonous atmosphere of the manufacturing suburb.

Horticulture and poetry in Snow's Fields! Who will deny romance to Modern Bermondsey after this? A great part of the thoroughfare bearing this name has been demolished of late years, and the site of the destroyed dwellings is occupied by stately buildings of the Guinness' Trust. Courts and alleys are replaced by spacious quadrangles; but until recently Snow's Fields was one of the dingiest and most squalid streets in the district, and so idyllic a scene as that indicated by Timbs would have seemed more improbable than the existence of a Spa where we now see railway arches and jam factories.

The very peculiar and exceptional characteristics of Bermondsey, which until the second half of the present century rendered it unique among Metropolitan districts, no doubt commended it to the special attention of writers of fiction. In "Oliver Twist," Charles Dickens drew the most graphic picture of the waterside region, making Jacob's Island the scene of the pursuit and death of Sikes. Charles Kingsley, in one of the most powerful chapters of "Alton Locke," represents the same locality as the scene of some most ghastly incidents. Henry Cockton introduces a description of Bermondsey into "Valentine Vox." At a later period an accomplished lady, long resident in the parish, wrote a novel, entitled "From Bermondsey to Belgravia," in which she lends a sort of romantic interest to some familiar scenes in this district.

At the period commemorated by the novelists Bermondsey contained little more than a third of its present population, and extensive tracts of ground, now thickly covered with houses, then lay waste, or were under cultivation as market gardens. The riverside was densely populated, one part of it presenting clusters of the most squalid habitations, separated and insulated by tidal ditches, forming the once famous Jacob's Island. Other streets in the same neighbourhood contained houses of a better description, chiefly inhabited by lightermen and barge-owners, sea-captains, pilots, and other nautical personages. The neighbourhood of the Old Church, and the region lying between Bermondsey Street and the Borough, was the oldest inhabited part of the parish, and exhibited many quaint structures and specimens of a bygone style of architecture.

The eastern end of the parish presented a remarkable contrast to its northern and western counterparts. Rows of red brick houses, mostly dating from the early Georgian era, were inhabited by persons of substance and respectable position. Spacious mansions, shaded by trees and approached by avenues and carriage sweeps, stood in the midst of extensive grounds, and formed the residences of some leading manufacturers and other wealthy and important persons, for Bermondsey was still a "residential quarter."

In those days the people of Bermondsey were not compelled to traverse miles of streets before they could enjoy a rural walk. A long stretch of market-gardens and meadow-land extended between the Blue Anchor Road (now Southwark Park Road) and the Old Kent Road, and from the Upper Grange Road to Rotherhithe.

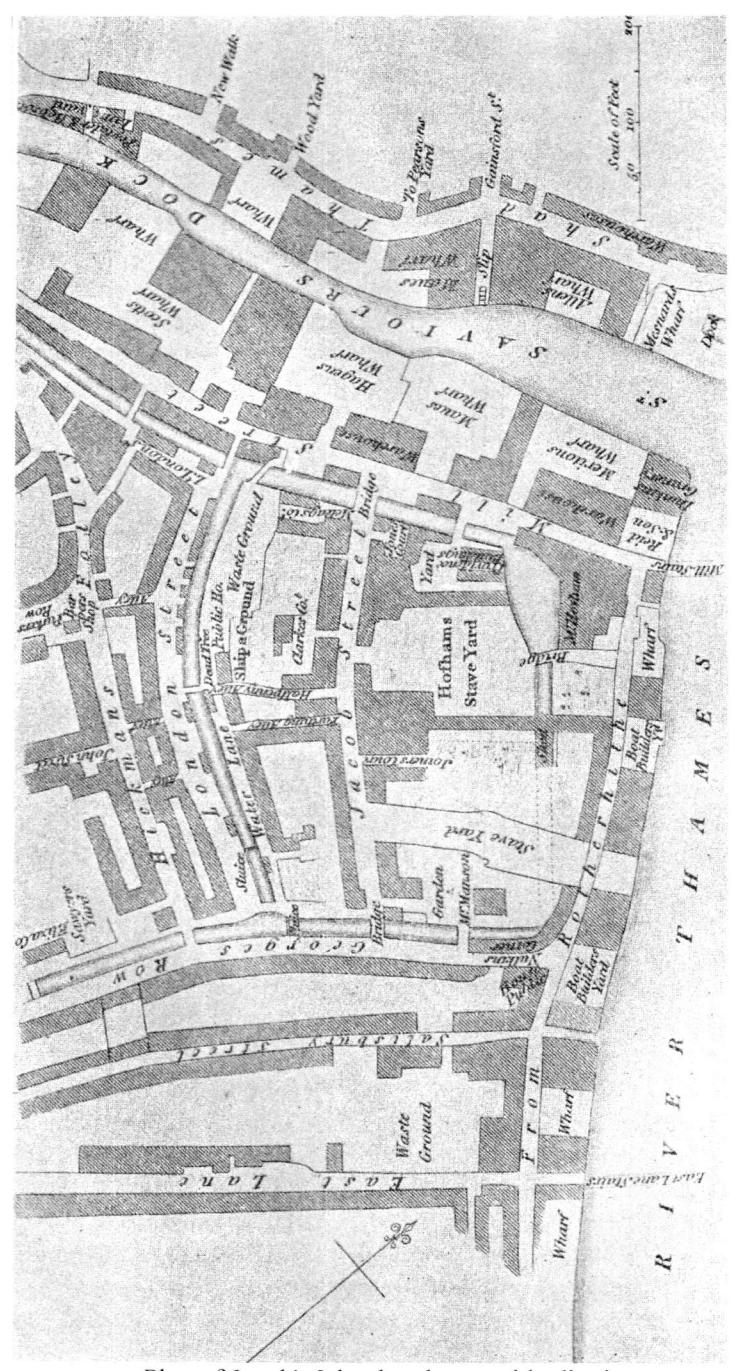

Plan of Jacob's Island and waterside district

The Blue Anchor Road, now a continuous line of houses, was then bordered by hedges and overshadowed by trees, exhibiting a few houses in gardens, inhabited by workmen of the better class, rustic taverns, windmills, and wooden shanties. In the neighbourhood of Rotherhithe a little cluster of islands had been formed, which, diversified by winding paths, furnished with rustic arbours, booths for the sale of fruit, cakes, and ginger-beer, and enlivened by the screaming of parrots and chattering of monkeys, formed a place of simple recreation for the youth of the district.

A Dutchman would have felt at home in Bermondsey. The ditches flowing through some of the streets, shaded here and there by trees, would have reminded him of "the slow canal, the willow-tufted bank," of his native Holland.

But all this rusticity has long disappeared. Like much else of a picturesque character, it was more pleasing to the eye of the artist than gratifying to the sanitary reformer. The ditches were filled up many years ago, greatly to the advantage of the health of the inhabitants. The market-gardens have long been converted into building plots, and the meadows drained and made the basis of new streets and roads. In the older quarters great demolitions have been carried into effect. In place of a congeries of small streets, huge warehouses or gigantic blocks of model dwellings are now to be seen.

Ancient houses in Long Walk

Old landmarks are rapidly disappearing. Those antique houses in Bermondsey Street, believed to have been built towards the close of the Plantagenet period, were demolished a few years ago, and their place is occupied by warehouses. King John's Court, with its ancient dwellings of a decidedly monastic character, has long disappeared; but Long Walk still exists in part, although the passenger who now enters it would find a difficulty in realizing its condition when the Lord Abbots pursued their meditations beneath the shadow of its trees. Bermondsey Square, once the great court of the monastery, is partially demolished, and most of its houses are doomed, in view of the formation of a new approach to the Tower Bridge. One relic of the monastic times is still preserved in Grange Walk, on the south-east of the square, where in the wall of an old house "the hooks are still to be seen" on which the east gate of the monastery hung, which was taken down in 1760.

Such changes as those we have described are, of course, inevitable; the whole Metropolis is a witness to the havoc that has been made within the last generation. Venerable structures and time-honoured localities have disappeared on all hands. But we cannot refrain from offering a protest against one form in which change has manifested itself here. A mania for altering the names of familiar places has long prevailed; the common names of many streets have been exchanged for singularly ambitious designations. Although not greatly moved by these vagaries with respect to places having no special associations, we must plead earnestly in favour of the retention of those names which are endeared to us by a thousand reminiscences. We trust that "Crucifix Lane," which still commemorates the "Rood of Grace"; "Abbey Street," which commences where the west gate of the monastery once stood; the "Neckinger," "The Grange," "Grange Walk," "Grange Road," even "Long Walk" - for in its later character has it not memories of Whitaker and Wesley? - will be allowed to retain their appellations.

We shall conclude the present chapter with a reference to two men of singular merit, yet whose names seem to be strangely forgotten in the place of their birth. These are Mr. G. W. Phillips, the historian of Bermondsey, and his brother, Mr. J. Garland Phillips, the missionary martyr of Tierra del Fuego.

We deeply regret that we have been unable to obtain any

account of the first of these gentlemen, whose work we have so frequently quoted, and to whom we owe a debt of special gratitude. We can only form a conception of him as exhibited in his works. His book on the "History and Antiquities of Bermondsey" embodies the results of very laborious researches, pursued at a period when many sources of information were far less accessible than at present, and when the gathering of materials such as those which Mr. Phillips so industriously collected would have involved many journeys and applications to persons reported to be in possession of facts. His work, though small in compass, as he chiefly confines himself to the statement of ascertained facts and the citation of authorities, is invaluable to the student as well as to anyone who desires to write upon the subject. All the information relating to the ancient monastery is most minute and accurate; he deciphered the monkish Latin of the "Annals" in the original manuscript (as it was not until many years later that this was printed amongst the Rolls publications); he gives the quotation from Domesday in the original; he embodies all the facts enumerated by Dugdale; he exhausts every source of antiquarian information, and all the allusions contained in the numerous Metropolitan and county histories. And all this learning and research is displayed in the humblest and most unostentatious manner, as the work of a man imbued with the love of his subject, to whom the consciousness that he had been instrumental in rescuing the glories of the past from oblivion was in itself a sufficient recompense.

We owe to Mr. Phillips another work of peculiar interest, the touching and beautiful memoir of his brother, J. Garland Phillips, who perished under the hands of the Fuegian savages in November, 1859. In this narrative, which is charming in its simplicity, we see a pious duty well performed.

We have the picture of a devout and earnest man, affectionate and sincere, ever solicitous for the spiritual welfare and the material improvement of all around him. His love of Christ and intense appreciation of the blessings of Christianity led him to compassionate all who were without the sphere of its influence, and sent him to that remote and inhospitable region, where he was destined to meet his fate.

St. James's Church, Bermondsey, 1829

Old Toll-house and bridge in Upper Grange Road, Bermondsey, 1820

In Bermondsey Mr. Garland Phillips had signalized himself by the establishment of free evening schools, providing instruction for many who would otherwise have remained steeped in ignorance. He was a man of considerable mental culture, a very respectable poet, and his letters and journals, incorporated with the narrative, possess more than ordinary merit. Amidst his arduous labours in the Falklands and Tierra del Fuego, he devoted an hour daily to learning Spanish, which "to anyone acquainted with Latin and French is comparatively easy." He also exerted himself in the endeavour to systematize the Fuegian language. As the missionary party were acting under very primitive conditions, personal labours of the most strenuous character devolved on Mr. Phillips. He aided in building, carpentering, quarrying stone, digging and planting, dragging heavy burdens, cooking for the whole company. Yet, amidst all these overwhelming toils, together with his teaching and spiritual ministrations, the heart of Garland Phillips ever turned fondly to his native place; his letters express the joy with which he learnt that the good work in the evening schools was flourishing under his successors, and the pleasure he felt at the opening of a

Working Men's Institute in Bermondsey Street. Had he survived, his generous heart would have been gladdened by the success which for many years attended this Institute; it proved a means of elevating the minds and brightening the lives of many. The tragic death of Mr. Garland Phillips is thus described by his brother:

> On Sunday, November 6, 1859, the little missionary band, with one exception, left the vessel at half-past ten o'clock, intending to hold a service of prayer and praise in the half-finished house on the shore. Fearless of danger, these Christian men assembled to worship their God and Saviour in the presence of a heathen people. Scarcely had the service commenced, when the natives, who now numbered about 300, having first secured the oars, so as to cut off all hope of escape by the boat, rushed into the house, and furiously attacked the worshippers with their clubs. They attempted to get to the boat, but in vain. Captain Fell and his brother stood back to back, and were miserably beaten to death with clubs by the infuriated savages. Mr. Phillips reached the water's edge, but at the moment he had his hand on the boat he was struck on the head by a stone, and fell stunned into the water; but the natives dragged him out, and killed him on the spot.
>
> In one short hour from the time they had left the ship in health and strength, to join together in prayer with the Church militant on earth, they were called to join the eternal song of praise with the Church triumphant in heaven.

Monastic Bermondsey had its Saint; Protestant Bermondsey sent forth its Martyr.

Old stone-faced house in Grange Walk

CHAPTER XII

MANUFACTURING BERMONDSEY - EMINENT REPRESENTATIVES OF THE LEATHER TRADE - CHURCHES, SCHOOLS, AND PUBLIC INSTITUTIONS - THE NEW MUNICIPALITY - IMPORTANCE OF CULTIVATING LOCAL HISTORY

In the present day, Bermondsey is essentially an industrial quarter, and the trades carried on within its precincts are many and various. Workers in many metals, iron and brass founders, engine and boiler makers, makers of all kinds of machinery, manufacturers of dyes and chemicals, vinegar-makers, distillers, preparers of spices and condiments, makers of jams, pickles, and preserves, wholesale biscuit manufacturers (the immense factory of Messrs. Peek, Frean, and Co., in Drummond Road, is one of the largest and most remarkable in the Metropolis), millers, corn-factors, granary-keepers, lime, stone, slate, and coal merchants - such are but a few of the callings which flourish in Bermondsey, and afford employment to thousands of its population.

Hatting was formerly one of the principal industries of Bermondsey, which at one time was called the "Hatters' Paradise," and then numbered 3,000 of that fraternity among its inhabitants. When Mr. Phillips wrote his "History," this manufacture was in a most flourishing state, and he gives a description of the spacious factory in Bermondsey Street belonging to Messrs. Christy, then "supposed to be the largest manufacturers of hats in the world." These premises are still occupied by the same firm, but many causes have combined to deprive Bermondsey of its pre-eminence in this branch of trade.

But the great staple industry which dominates all the rest, and has become historical in relation to this quarter, is the leather trade in all its branches. As we have already said, it is known to have existed here for at least three centuries. There is something peculiarly interesting in the fact of a manufacture of this kind having been established here at a remote period, and steadily pursued from generation to generation and from century to century, rising from small beginnings, and attaining gigantic developments; at first, the minute subdivision of labour, then the gradual combination, and the final concentration, as we now, see in those vast establishments in which every step in the process of leather manufacture is conducted under the same auspices - a manufacture which the skill and ingenuity of generations of craftsmen have been employed in bringing to perfection. All this affords a spectacle of progress most gratifying to the intelligent and reflective observer.

One very interesting circumstance, testifying to the importance which this manufacture had attained in the beginning of the last century, is the fact that in the second year of Queen Anne a charter was granted to the tanners of Bermondsey constituting them a Corporation, with a Master and Wardens, as in the case of the City Companies, but this charter remained inoperative. No explanation of this is given; we know not whether that independence of feeling which formerly characterized Bermondsey people caused them to cherish the principle of individual enterprise, unhampered by restrictions, and untrammelled by the regulations of a guild. But although we may admit that in some cases more has been accomplished by individual than by corporate effort, still, it is an established axiom that the unit, as member of a fraternity, finds his individual force multiplied according to the number of the associates whose combined efforts are directed to the same end. We cannot, therefore, help indulging some feelings of regret that the provisions of this charter were not carried into effect.

The great Corporation of Tanners, embracing the representatives of every branch of the leather trade, would have been consolidated by an esprit de corps, and in itself proved a powerful incentive to local patriotism. The enormous amount of capital embarked in its industry, the wealth of its members, the vast extent of their business operations, the mass of their products, would have assumed a collective importance that must have been patent to all, and have greatly enhanced the fame of Bermondsey. Had the Guild been established, the great manufacturer might have been proud of being one of its rulers, the lesser of being a member of the fraternity, the workman of being employed by men of such consequence, the inhabitants that their home should be the seat of such a body. Many families would be proud to trace their connection with some eminent Master or Warden of the Corporation. Their personal history, the traditions connected with them, would have been public property, nor would this have been confined to the locality. Visitors from distant quarters would have become imbued with the same feeling; the name of Bermondsey would have awakened intelligent interest amongst dwellers in remote districts. The greatness of the Guild would have helped to keep alive the traditions of ancient glory. It would have been widely known that Bermondsey, so famous for the products of its industry, also possessed a history of peculiar interest and dignity.

However, we have not to deal with hypothetical conditions, but must apply ourselves to the consideration of existing circumstances, which are sufficiently important.

The following passages from the interesting description of Bermondsey contained in Mr. Charles Knight's "Illustrated London" are even now worth quoting:

> A circle of a mile in diameter, having its centre at the spot where the abbey once stood, will include within its limits most of the tanners, the curriers, the fellmongers, the woolstaplers, the leather-factors, the leather-dressers, the leather-dyers, the parchment-makers, and the glue-makers, for which this district is remarkable. There is scarcely a road, a street, or lane into which we can turn without seeing evidences of one or other of these occupations. One narrow road, leading from the Grange Road to the Kent Road, is particularly distinguishable for the number of leather factories which it exhibits on either side - some timeworn and mean, others newly and skilfully erected. Another street, known as Long Lane, and lying westward of the church, exhibits nearly twenty distinct establishments, where skins or hides undergo some of the many processes to which they are subjected. In Snow's Fields; in Bermondsey New Road; in Russell Street, Upper and Lower; in Willow Walk and Page's Walk and Grange Walk, and others whose names we cannot now remember - in all of these leather, skins, and wool seem to be the commodities out of which the wealth of the inhabitants has been created...
>
> If there is any district in London whose inhabitants might be excused for supporting the proposition that 'There is nothing like leather,' surely Bermondsey is that place.

This description requires some modification in the present day, because, although a vast quantity of leather continues to be manufactured here, and tanneries and leather factories still abound, this industry is now carried on in a variety of places. Alterations in the processes, facilitating more speedy production, the rapidity of conveyance, and other causes, have combined to make Bermondsey, in the present day, quite as much an emporium for the sale of goods manufactured elsewhere as of its own native products. Most of the leading manufacturers are now leather-factors as well, and many once-important tanneries have been within recent years disposed of for building purposes, or utilized for the benefit of alien industries. The site of a very extensive leather factory in Page's Walk is now occupied by some huge blocks of dwellings belonging to the Guinness Trust, and in the Spa Road a large tannery has been converted into a jam factory.

Connected with the leather trade are many men, the extent of whose business operations places them high amongst commercial magnates, and whose public spirit and cultivated intelligence would render them an honour to any community. It is impossible within the limits of this chapter to mention more than a few of these gentlemen, but some details may not be unacceptable.

Leather Exchange, Bermondsey

All persons having any connection with Bermondsey, and, indeed, most travellers by the London, Brighton, and South Coast Railway, are familiar with the great establishment known as the Neckinger Mills, belonging to the Messrs. Bevingtons and Sons. In this factory, originally built for a paper mill, a leather manufacture was established about the year 1800, by the brothers Samuel, Henry, and Timothy Bevington, who were succeeded in the business by their sons. Under the latter, the manufactory attained still further development, especially through the exertions of Mr. James Buckingham Bevington, the senior partner of that generation, who established the warehouse at Cannon Street, and subsequently in St. Thomas's Street, Southwark. This gentleman was a very energetic man of business, and remained an active partner in the firm until his eightieth year, dying at the advanced age of eighty-eight. The following description of the factory is worth quoting:

> Here Messrs. Bevingtons and Sons carry on the manufacture of moroccos, roans, skivers, seal, kid, chamois, calf, and glove leathers, on a scale of considerable magnitude. The whole processes are fully exemplified, from the dressing of the raw material to the most advanced stages of currying and enamelling; and the works, which cover an area of three and a half acres, give employment to upwards of 500 hands. It may be unnecessary to state that the several departments of work are under vigilant supervision, and the firm have an unsurpassed reputation for the superior quality of their light leathers, all kinds of which are produced. The situation of the works is most favourable, and they are intersected by the lines of the South-Eastern and London, Brighton, and South Coast Railways, the arches of which afford suitable accommodation for storage. Ample water is supplied by a special outlet from the Thames. Messrs. Bevingtons' speciality may be said to lie in the manufacture of all the principal classes of light leathers of the kinds above specified, and also those of a like nature. They are widely known as extensive importers of the very best grades of French calf, and have large dealings with wholesale houses all over the country, in every department of the leather trade and leather-working industries. Another important feature of the firm's work consists in their operations as wool merchants, a branch of the business that has assumed extensive proportions.
> From 1856 to 1874 the firm conducted an establishment in Cannon Street, City, for warehouse and sale-room purposes, and in the latter year they removed to the present warehouse in St. Thomas's Street, a

structure in which the fullest accommodation is afforded for the requirements of the large business there centred.
- *Southwark and Bermondsey.*

In Charles Knight's "Dictionary of Manufactures," published in 1851, one of the illustrations exhibits Messrs. Bevingtons' premises as a typical leather factory.

Colonel Bevington, J. P.

Colonel Samuel Bourne Bevington, the present head of this firm, son of the Mr. J. B. Bevington previously mentioned, may be considered, both from his personal qualities and from the prominent position he has so long and worthily occupied, as a representative of the manufacturing interest in Bermondsey. Well known as an active and energetic man of business, the Colonel is even more widely appreciated as one of the most distinguished Volunteer officers. His name is identified with the history of the Volunteer movement in Bermondsey.

When after the Italian campaign of 1859 the strained relations which had for some time existed between England and France, the vapouring of French military men, and the ambitious designs attributed to the Emperor, aroused feelings of serious apprehension, and awakened the memory of that remarkable association which in the beginning of the century had contributed to avert the danger of a far more formidable invasion, a wave of patriotic excitement swept over the country, thousands of men eagerly enrolled themselves as volunteers, and formed the nucleus of that citizen army which has now become one of the permanent forces of the kingdom.

Bermondsey, as on the former occasion, was one of the first districts to respond to the patriotic call, and amongst those who enthusiastically volunteered for this service none displayed greater ardour than Mr. Samuel Bevington. Having joined the 1st Surrey Rifles as a private in 1859, Mr. Bevington was gazetted Ensign in the 10th Surrey (Bermondsey Rifles) in 1861. Passing through the successive grades, he became in 1885 Commanding Officer of the 3rd Volunteer Battalion, Queen's Royal West Surrey Regiment. From first to last the Colonel has shown unflagging Zeal in promoting the efficiency of the service, and it has been well said of him that

> keen and strict disciplinarian as he is, Colonel Bevington has won the esteem and regard of all who serve under him, for, in addition to many other qualities, he has the advantage of an enthusiasm for his calling, and so found it an easy task to obtain the confidence and regard of his fellow-soldiers.

Colonel Bevington has recently retired from the command of the fine battalion, which now has a full strength of 621. His successor is Lieutenant-Colonel Walter C. Dixon, a member of the important firm of Dixon, Sons, and Taylor, leather manufacturers. As a testimony to Colonel Bevington's generosity and solicitude for those who have served under him, it was stated at the banquet in celebration of the Volunteer Centenary, held in July, 1899, by Colonel (then Major) Dixon, that Colonel Bevington

> had helped them out of many difficulties. When the corps was first formed, they had a room in the Leather Market, in which they kept their arms, and they drilled on the hard rough cobbles in the yard. That went on until Colonel Bevington said he could not and would not stand it any longer. Others said that many times, but they did not know how to

get out of it. But the Colonel knew a way out of it, and in 1876 he built the hall in which they were assembled entirely at his own cost. There was a time when the 23rd Surrey Rifles had headquarters at Rotherhithe. They, however, got into financial difficulties, and in order to put matters right the Colonel paid £500 of the £1,000 which they were in debt. Had they not possessed such a Colonel, the Volunteers would have fizzled out.

Colonel Bevington, in response, said

it was quite true that he built the hall, and he supposed that in all he had spent £10,000 first and last on the Volunteer service. Nor did he think the money could be spent much better. Money was not of any use unless it was laid out well. Those who commanded money were bound to spend it, and should do so in the interests of others. He could not take it with him into the future world, but was only too pleased to use it for the benefit of his fellows. He believed that good had been done by means of the Volunteer movement, for one who renders himself subservient to military discipline is a better citizen in consequence in many ways.

A sketch of this gentleman's career given in the "Southwark Annual" states:

Colonel Bevington was born in 1832, educated at a Quaker school in Croydon, and subsequently at King's College, London, where he spent two years in the school and three in the college, in the department of applied sciences. He entered the firm of Bevingtons and Sons, Neckinger Mills, Bermondsey, and St. Thomas's Street, Southwark, in 1851. As his father did, he takes an active part in the management of the concerns of this house, which enjoys a wide reputation in home and foreign markets, and of which he is now senior partner. In 1890 Colonel Bevington made a visit to the United States, largely for the purpose of gaining information with regard to the American markets, and as the result of this journey he obtained possession of much exceedingly useful knowledge in this connection, as the letters which he sent to the leather trade organs are evidence. In 1895 he also travelled to Ceylon, Madras, and Australia, visiting the principal cities in that colony. . .

We may add that Colonel Bevington is a J. P. for Surrey and the county of London, and is member of committee of various local Board Schools in Bermondsey; Chairman and Treasurer of Bacon's School; an Associate of King's College, London; Past Master of the Worshipful

Company of Leathersellers; Chairman of Herold's Institute School for Tanning; Chairman of the Bermondsey Free Library; member of the Council of the Borough Polytechnic; and for the year 1896 President of the Swedenborg Society, besides being associated with numerous other societies. In politics he is a Liberal Unionist and a member of the Reform Club.

The Colonel, in addition to many contributions on technical and trade subjects, has published "Journal of an Italian Tour" and "Journal of a Voyage to Australia." His eldest son, Mr. R. K. Bevington, is a Major in the 3rd Volunteer Battalion (Queen's).

Another firm, not so old as that of Messrs. Bevingtons, yet exhibits a conspicuous example of what may be achieved by industrial skill and business energy.

> Probably in South London, or, for that matter, in any part of the kingdom, it would be difficult to find a contemporary house whose status in the tanning industry is of a more conspicuous and firmly-established character than that of the well-known firm of Messrs. Samuel Barrow and Brother, Limited. Fifty-three years ago the founder, senior partner, and present chairman and director of the concern, viz., Mr. Samuel Barrow, J. P., came to London, and took service in the tanyard of Mr. Elias Tremlett. Here he worked side by side with his father, who was also one of Mr. Tremlett's employees up to the year 1848, acting for the greater part of this period as manager of the beam-working department. In the year named Mr. Tremlett's yard was closed, and for the moment Mr. Barrow's occupation was gone. With characteristic enterprise, however, he decided to open a yard of his own, and with this view acquired premises in Wild's Rents, where a business was started under the style of John Barrow and Sons, the partners being Mr. John Barrow, Mr. Samuel Barrow, and Mr. James Barrow.

From these small beginnings the firm, after many changes to be presently referred to again, ultimately rose to a most commanding position.

> Important developments had been effected, not the least momentous of which was the purchase of a supplemental yard at the Grange, and the erection of the present substantial warehouses in Weston Street by Mr. Samuel Barrow, who in 1864 purchased a large tannery at Redhill, where he has since resided, and in 1891 the entire enterprise was

registered under the Limited Liability Companies Act, with a capital of £300,000, privately subscribed by the partners. As it stands to-day, Messrs. Samuel Barrow and Brother's organization embraces four great tanneries, viz., the Grange, the Grange Road, the Spa Road, and the Redhill establishments, together with warehouses in Weston Street, Maze Pond, and St. Thomas's Street. . .

Over the commercial, technical, and general ramifications of this immense business, Mr. Samuel Barrow still continues to give that personal attention to which much of its past success has been due. He enjoys the respect and esteem of a wide circle of business friends and connections, and is equally well known as a public man and as a liberal supporter of various philanthropic movements.

- *Southwark and Bermondsey.*

R. V. Barrow, Esq., late M.P. for Bermondsey

The "Brother" of this firm is Mr. Reuben Vincent Barrow, late M.P. for Bermondsey. We have been enabled to gather some particulars of this gentleman's remarkable career from authentic sources. Mr. R. V. Barrow, born at Exeter in 1838, was brought to London in 1842, on the removal of his parents to the Metropolis. He received the rudiments of his education at the Church school in Star Corner, from which he was transferred, at the age of ten, to the Borough Road School, so famous as a training institution. Here he highly distinguished himself by his intellectual energy and eager pursuit of knowledge, and gained a first-class Queens Scholarship. He did not, however, pursue the scholastic vocation, but devoted himself to business, spending twelve months in a currier's shop, and twelve more in his father's tannery.

In December, 1855, Mr. Barrow competed for and obtained the appointment of schoolmaster on board an emigrant ship bound for Adelaide, after arriving in which port he procured a situation with a firm of tanners and curriers in that city. The hours of manual labour were from 6 a.m. to 6 p.m., and from 7 to 9 p.m. Mr. Barrow conducted an evening school for young men. After a service of three years, Messrs. Peacock, his employers, decided upon an effort to develop their trade by sending a representative throughout the settled districts of the colony, and appointed him their first traveller. As a pioneer of commercial enterprise, Mr. Barrow's journeys contrasted strangely with the experiences of those who traverse the same region in the present day. The colony was then in its infancy; very few roads existed, few rivers were bridged, all travelling had to be performed on horseback and under very primitive conditions. After pursuing this occupation for two years, Mr. Barrow resolved to comply with the urgent desire of his parents that he should return to England. His natural intelligence had been further developed by the strange and unfamiliar conditions under which he had lived; the difficulties he had been compelled to overcome had redoubled his energy and rendered him fertile in resource. The estimation of his business capacity was shown in the public dinner given to him before his departure. Returning to England in June, 1861, Mr. Reuben Barrow entered his father's firm, and on the death of the latter, in 1864, accepted the offer of partnership made by his elder brother Samuel. The joint undertaking has since developed into one of the largest tanning and leather-factoring businesses in the trade, having branches in Leicester, Kettering, Madras, Boston, and Sydney.

Mr. R. V. Barrow removed to Croydon in 1873, where he has since resided, and speedily gained popularity in his new sphere. On the town obtaining a charter of incorporation in 1883, he was returned to the Council at the head of the poll, and elected an Alderman, becoming Mayor 1885-86. But higher dignities were in store. Bermondsey, in the meantime, had been created a Metropolitan borough, and it was natural that Mr. Barrow should desire to represent the constituency with which he and his family had been so long and closely associated. At the General Election of 1892, therefore, Mr. Barrow stood for the borough, and, after a hard contest, was elected Member for Bermondsey by a majority of 653. Although he may have justly felt proud of having attained this position, it was not for the gratification of such feelings that Mr. Barrow sought the distinction. He was actuated by motives which reflect the highest credit upon him, and bear the most striking testimony to his public spirit.

The question of equalization of rating had long engaged the attention of politicians, but, like many other matters of great public importance, after being occasionally revived and made the subject of prolonged discussion, was again suffered to fall into abeyance. Mr. Barrow having, with his usual energy, applied himself to the mastery of the details, was resolved that this important question should be brought "within the range of practical politics," and within eight months of entering Parliament moved a resolution for "the greater equalization of the rates throughout London." Having carried his resolution, Mr. Barrow had the further satisfaction to find it adopted by the Government, and made the basis of a measure destined to relieve the pressure on the poorer parishes of London. An idea of the gross inequalities then prevailing will be gathered from the fact that some of the richest were rated at 3s. 10d. in the pound, whilst the poorest were rated as high as 7s. 10d. The effect of the Bill was to inflict an extra rate of 6d. in the pound upon all parishes paying less than 5s. 3d., and handing the proceeds over to the relief of districts paying more than that sum. This measure resulted in Bermondsey receiving about £8,000 the first year towards its rates, which amount has gone on increasing each successive year. As a consequence of the Act, the richer parishes of the Metropolis are extra-rated to the amount of £320,000 (the City itself contributing £140,000), all which is applied to the relief of the poorer districts. It is an achievement of which any private member might be proud, to have, shortly after entering Parliament, initiated a measure which has produced such prodigious results, and it should be a source of pride to the inhabitants of Bermondsey that this triumph was scored by one who was not merely their Parliamentary representative, but identified with the industry of their quarter.

It would have been natural to expect that, after rendering this important public service, Mr. Barrow would have had a long political career, but at the General Election of 1895 he was unseated.

The importance of Mr. Barrow's position, and the estimation of his merits in other quarters, are shown by the honours conferred upon him. In 1886 he was elected a Whitgift Governor and a Borough Justice of the Peace, in 1889 appointed a Justice of the Peace for the counties of London and Surrey, and in 1894 elected Chairman of the Croydon County Bench. In June, 1898, he was elected President of the Free Church Federation for Croydon and district, and re-elected in 1899.

It is needless to say that the present work is altogether independent of politics, and that, in speaking of eminent persons associated with Bermondsey, we are merely attempting to do justice to incontestable merit.

A. Lafone, Esq., M. P.

The sitting member, Mr. Alfred Lafone, Who now represents the constituency for the second time in the Conservative interest, is the head of one of the greatest firms of leather-factors, trading under the style of Boutcher, Mortimore, and Co. Mr. Lafone has been honourably associated with the Public Library movement; he was the first Chairman of the Bermondsey Library Commissioners, and we are informed that he is the only surviving member of the original Committee of the Liverpool Public Library. This gentleman has always maintained more than a business association with Bermondsey, having filled many local offices and taken an active part in parochial administration. At the present time the sympathies of all are with him in the melancholy bereavement he has sustained. His eldest son, Captain Lafone, of the Devonshire Regiment, was killed in the gallant defence of Ladysmith against the assault delivered by the Boers in January, 1900.

Mr. Henry Lafone, of Butler's Wharf, brother of the Member for Bermondsey, is also widely known and respected for his interest in local matters, and his benevolent exertions in promoting the settlement of serious trade disputes.

A notable politician and public man in Bermondsey is Mr. John Dumphreys, who presents a conspicuous example of that character which at one time was believed only to exist in the fertile imagination of Lord Beaconsfield, the "Conservative Working Man." Mr. Dumphreys, who is a leather-dresser, continued for many years to work as a journeyman, whilst leading a life of great political and general activity, addressing public meetings, and acting as member of the London School Board, County Councillor, and member of the Bermondsey Vestry. His political courage is evidenced by the fact that he on one occasion contested West Birmingham against Mr. Chamberlain.

Two gentlemen occupying high local positions deserve to be specially noted for their interest in antiquarian research, and their efforts to awaken public interest in the history of this quarter. These are the Rev. W. Lees Bell, Vicar of Christ Church, Bermondsey, and Rural Dean of Southwark, who wrote a "History of Bermondsey," published in 1883, and Dr. John Dixon, Medical Officer of Health for Bermondsey, who pursued extensive researches on this subject, the results of which he embodied in able and highly-appreciated lectures.

A native of Bermondsey who now occupies a distinguished position in another hemisphere is one of whom we may feel justly proud. Mr. W. J. Ashley, educated at St. Olave's Grammar School, gained a scholarship at Balliol College, Oxford, and, after graduating with high honours, became Fellow of Lincoln College. In 1883 he published "James and Philip Van Artevelde," a historical work greatly commended for the research and painstaking accuracy it displayed, and subsequently a treatise on political economy. Mr. Ashley's mastery of this science is demonstrated by the fact that he is at the present time Professor of Political Economy in Harvard University.

We must now say something about the religious and educational condition of Bermondsey.

In 1801, when the population was 17,169, the whole district comprised one vast parish, and, as in the monastic times, the only church for the accommodation of the orthodox was that of St. Mary Magdalen. For those not belonging to the Establishment, there were three or four Dissenting chapels, and a small Roman Catholic chapel existed near the river. Compared with this meagre provision, the ample means of religious instruction we now possess seems remarkable, for although the population has increased fivefold, spiritual organization has more than kept pace with it. The ancient parish church still continues to be the centre of Church work; it has been served during the past century by a succession of earnest and pious ministers, and the present Rector, the Rev. Henry Lewis, yields to none of his predecessors in fervent preaching of the Gospel, and efforts to promote the spiritual and moral welfare of his parishioners. But in addition to this venerable fane, we now have seven district churches, and at least a dozen churches and chapels for the accommodation of Dissenters and Roman Catholics, not to mention mission-halls in connection with the various religious bodies. Nor are Dissenting chapels any longer the cramped and inconvenient buildings once so familiar, and of which we still see some specimens. Many of those we now possess are lofty and spacious structures, displaying considerable elegance in their design, and affording ample accommodation for worshippers. Nor is improvement in the character of the buildings the only change observable. Earnest and faithful as ever, the pastors of the present day possess a learning and a range of mental cultivation to which many of their predecessors were strangers. No longer shrinking from "profane" studies, they draw lessons from history, from science, from general literature, to confirm their spiritual teaching.

The schools are numerous and ably conducted.

Bacon's Free School, the old foundation mentioned in the previous chapter, has long departed from the original scheme; its scope is enlarged, the number of scholars increased, and the curriculum adapted to modern educational requirements. It furnishes another example of the munificence of Colonel Bevington. We read in the "Southwark Annual":

> The funds of the school have always been inadequate to meet all the demands made upon them. The trustees recently secured the abolition of the payment of £50 per annum for scholarship, and partially in consideration of this relief Colonel Bevington has endowed the school to the extent of £1,000 as a memorial to his daughter, Miss Mary Elizabeth Bevington, who died March 10, 1899.

The most important foundation now appears to be the Boutcher Schools in Grange Road, of which we have the following account in the " Southwark Annual":

> The Boutcher Schools, erected by the late Mr. William Boutcher in 1871, have carried on a most useful work in the parish. In demonstration of the high-class education given by the staff, the reports of H.M. Inspector, Mr. A. P. Graves, who visits all the voluntary schools in Southwark, may be quoted. The report has reference to the year ending April 30, 1899, and states as follows:
> 'The Boys' School is a most thoughtfully governed school, and conducted on the soundest educational lines. The boys acquit themselves remarkably well, and are under the best discipline. The Girls' School is a quite unusually well-taught and well-governed school. The Infants' School is doing good work in every respect.'
> The school has secured the highest awards for the ordinary class subjects, for drawing and for French, chemistry, shorthand, bookkeeping, domestic economy, and cookery. At the London County Council scholarship examination three boys were successful. A boy secured one of the scholarships given by the City Companies, which is valued at £120, and three girls occupied the fourth, sixth, and twenty-first places on the list respectively. Four girls were successful in the London County Council examination, three of them occupying

respectively the eighth, seventeenth, and twenty-fourth places. When it is borne in mind there were 1,306 boys competing for 194 scholarships, and 921 girls for 135 scholarships, the significance of these results is apparent. Three boys also obtained St. Olave's Grammar School scholarships.

The commercial class for senior boys and girls is not only examined by the Government Inspector, but also supervised once a quarter by a gentleman connected with the firm of Messrs. Boutcher, Mortimore and Co. There is not any difficulty experienced in Boutcher scholars obtaining situations.

The governors of the school are Mr. A. Lafone, M.P., Mr. Ernest Boutcher, Mr. Foster Mortimore, Rev. J. Ainsworth (Vicar of St. Luke's).

St. Olave's Grammar School

The Board Schools of Bermondsey afford accommodation for more than 14,000 children. The largest of these schools, situated in Monnow Road, Southwark Park Road, in which a high training is given, will accommodate 1,819 scholars.

A training institution of peculiar importance in regard to Bermondsey is the Herold's Institute Technical School for Tanning in Drummond Road. Here courses of lectures are delivered, models exhibited, chemical experiments conducted, and the rationale of all the processes scientifically explained. Students are prepared for the

City and Guilds of London examinations, at which many have taken honours and gained medals. The intelligence of the artisan is developed, his emulation excited, and his practical skill increased by scientific training.

The Bermondsey Settlement, established in a large building in Farncombe Street, Jamaica Road, offers great advantages in the way of lectures and evening tuition, embracing a great variety of subjects. Any who possess artistic tastes or skill in manipulation may receive instruction in clay modelling, drawing and colouring, freehand and geometrical drawing, metal work, and wood-carving. Classes for English grammar and literature, French, German, Latin and Greek, mathematics, chemistry, natural philosophy, botany, vocal and instrumental music, theology, etc., are held, and technical instruction of a peculiarly useful character is imparted. University Extension lectures are also given. The Warden of the Settlement is the well-known Rev. J. Scott Lidgett, M.A. But in addition to its educational advantages the Bermondsey Settlement is also a philanthropic agency, by means of which much good has been effected and much meritorious work performed in the neighbourhood of this institution. The waterside district has always been one of the poorest quarters of Bermondsey, and those working in connection with the Settlement have done much to relieve distress, to alleviate suffering, and to brighten lives which have been hitherto spent in gloom. Some time ago an exhibition of a singularly interesting and touching character was held at the Settlement. It consisted of models, carvings, and other ingenious productions, by the execution of which crippled, maimed, and other afflicted persons had solaced their weary hours.

Amongst the public institutions of Bermondsey, the Town Hall in Spa Road is conspicuous, erected in 1880 at a cost of £60,000, the facade of which is imposing enough, although the rest of the exterior is only remarkable for its size. From the ample accommodation it affords, however, it has become one of the most well-known places in South London, and is devoted to the most miscellaneous uses. It contains offices for the accommodation of the different branches of the local administration, a Coroner's Court, etc.; but these are mere details. The Town Hall constitutes a feature of the Bermondsey life of to-day which has hitherto had no parallel. The Vestry of the period, when reproached with having incurred such heavy expense in the erection of a building, the necessity for which was then by no means apparent, replied that they were acting with a view to the future, and providing for the needs of the next generation. The event has justified their prescience. The Town Hall has become the centre of the political and social life of the district. Public meetings are there held on all questions agitating the community, and addressed by persons of exalted rank and distinguished reputation. Eminent statesmen, even Prime Ministers, do not disdain to appear on its platform and expound the principles of their policy. Lectures are delivered on all conceivable subjects, religious services held, concerts, balls, and dramatic representations given. The municipality recently created will probably invest it with even greater interest and importance.

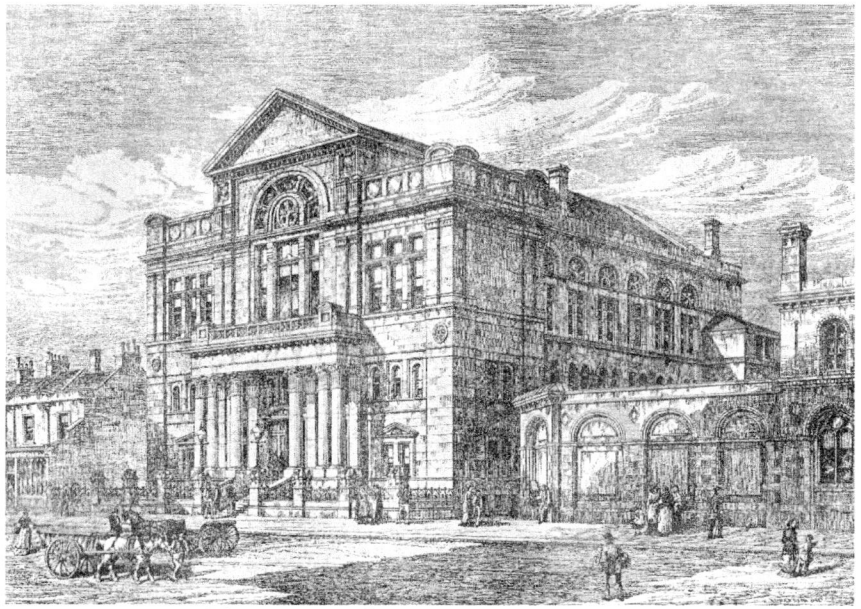

The Town Hall, Spa Road, Bermondsey

Adjoining the Town Hall is the excellent Free Library, the importance of which, like that of the former, will become more manifest in the future. We regard the Free Libraries in general as furnishing the most efficient means for the higher education of the people. The education given in the Board Schools appears in most instances to foster a taste for reading, if we may judge by the avidity with which newspapers and periodicals of all kinds are read by the youth of the working class. This is an excellent sign, and should be taken advantage of by those who are anxious to secure the elevation of the people. Not so many years have passed since a taste for reading amongst members of this class was the exception, and the boy who exhibited it was likely to incur the ridicule of his fellows. It is true that in those days the means of instruction were limited, and thousands grew up without having learnt to read or write. But the fact remains that the youth of the working class have now learnt to read and to enjoy reading, and therefore it is incumbent on those who are competent to advise to see that this taste is directed into a worthy channel. For this purpose the Free Libraries will, we believe, prove of inestimable value.

When opening one of these institutions a few years ago, Lord Rosebery uttered some observations that should be borne in mind. After speaking of the confusion likely to be experienced by one who strays into these libraries without any guide or principle of selection, and comparing the judicious choice of books to the operations of a tea-taster, Lord Rosebery went on to say: "It is essential that every Free Library should possess a taster in the shape of a librarian - that is, a man who not only knows the outsides of books, but is familiar with the insides as well."

The Commissioners of the Bermondsey Public Library have been fortunate in securing the services of a gentleman who eminently fulfils these requirements. Mr. John Frowde, who has held office since the foundation of the Library in 1892, is equally distinguished for his ardour in antiquarian research and his zeal for the propagation of good literature. He is at all times ready to place his knowledge and experience at the service of inquirers, and his advice and assistance are invaluable in dealing with the treasures contained in the Library. The collection, which now comprises about 16,200 volumes, and to which large additions are frequently being made, is peculiarly rich in historical literature. Not only the best standard histories, but numerous mediaeval chronicles, and annals of many abbeys and monasteries, are included. It is singularly appropriate that this should be so, and we indulge no vain hope by anticipating that Bermondsey, as of old, will be "the nurse of many students."

Bermondsey Free Library

    But a feature of peculiar interest to the inhabitants of Bermondsey is the Local Collection of works written by persons now residing in, or still retaining connection with, the parish, and by some long departed, but who deserve to be held in permanent remembrance. Amongst these we find histories, scientific treatises, novels, poems, experiences of travel. A volume of essays, written by a man famous in his generation, "Scott of Amwell," possesses more than ordinary interest from the fact that the author was a native of Bermondsey, having been born in Grange Walk in 1730.

    The life of Scott, prefixed to the essays, is written by Hoole, the translator of Tasso, who states that the task was to have been performed by Dr. Johnson, but was relinquished by him on account of failing health. In a letter to Mr. Hoole, the Doctor said: "I loved Mr. Scott, and would willingly have written his life."

    The formation of this interesting and valuable collection has been a labour of love on the part of Mr. Frowde, and the importance of the work he has performed has already become manifest.

    Since the commencement of this work the London

Government Act has been passed, and most important changes are imminent in the administration of Metropolitan districts. Considerable astonishment and dismay were at first caused by the rumour that it was intended to abolish the time-honoured name of Bermondsey, and to merge this historic quarter in a municipal borough, to be called East Southwark, which would also include Rotherhithe, Horsely-down, St. Olave's, and St. Thomas's. Subsequently it was understood that the designation of East Southwark had been abandoned, and that a proposition had been made, which received influential support, that the name of St. Olave's should be selected for the new borough, chiefly on the grounds that this term had been used for the last thirty years to designate a Poor-Law Union, including the above-mentioned parishes. It was natural that a vehement opposition should be aroused amongst the merchants and manufacturers of Bermondsey in view of the serious inconvenience they would sustain through the substitution of any other appellation for that familiar name. The great commercial importance which this district has acquired, the amount and variety of its products, have carried the name of Bermondsey to the most distant quarters of the globe. A petition on behalf of the manufacturing interest was therefore presented to the Privy Council. Nor were their efforts limited to such representations. When introducing the measure, Mr. Balfour had said that in selecting the names for the new boroughs "care should be taken not unnecessarily to break the continuity of historic tradition."

Those who valued the traditions of past grandeur and glory were powerfully moved by the prospect of their extinction, and resolved to make vigorous efforts to avert such a calamity. Their opportunity was afforded by the holding of an inquiry at the Bermondsey Town Hall by George Pemberton Leach, Esq., assistant Government Commissioner. The principal object of this was to collect information requisite for the settlement of boundaries, etc., but the Commissioner was also empowered to hear evidence that would enable his colleagues to decide on the name.

A mass of historic evidence was laid before him, and the cause of Bermondsey was powerfully advocated by Mr. Wheeler, Q.C., who in the course of his speech said:

I also desire to express acknowledgment of the great assistance I have received from the librarian of this Library, who is an antiquary - a class of learning and knowledge which largely obtains in Bermondsey - who has furnished me with a very clear and concise history of this ancient part of the town.

Colonel Bevington expounded the views of the manufacturers, and the Rector of Bermondsey dwelt with great force and cogency of argument on the necessity for the retention of the name. Mr. Lewis placed the matter in so clear a light that we cannot do better than quote his observations. The rev. gentleman said that he desired to refer to four points,

> which I think in adjudicating on the name of the new borough ought to be considered. First of all, the name should be identical with, and in some measure suggestive of, the past history of the area which the new borough is to cover; and then, further, we consider that the name should be a dignified one - a name calculated to inspire the respect of the citizens of the new borough. Further, the name should be an indication of the extent of the area which the new borough is to comprise, and if possible of the nature and character of the people of the borough; and the fourth point, that the name, whatever it is, should meet the needs of the future development and growth of the borough. The historical claims of Bermondsey as a name are stronger than any other name which can be suggested for the borough now under consideration. The time was when, as we have heard, Bermondsey was the only name of commanding importance in the neighbourhood, and, as we have already been told, it was a name equal to that of Westminster. It stood for the Abbey, which was situated within a stone's throw of where you are now sitting. It stood for the Abbey, with all its ecclesiastical life and government, and for a good deal of secular administration. There are Parliamentary associations, for Sir Walter Besant says in his book on South London: 'There are associations of two Queens, not to speak of many great lords, of State functions, and of Parliaments, connected with Bermondsey Abbey.' The name of St. Saviour's Cathedral is the same as that of St. Saviour's Abbey. <u>The seal of St. Olave's Grammar School is the old seal of Bermondsey Abbey</u>. Bermondsey possesses two out of the three local railway-stations, South Bermondsey and Spa Road. The local Volunteers, although their proper style is the 3rd Volunteer Battalion (Queens) West Surrey Regiment, are more familiarly known as the Bermondsey Volunteers. Sir Walter Besant declares that Bermondsey, with Horselydown and St. Olave's, forms the industrial centre of South London.

In reference to the fourth point, the Rector said:

> The answer will be gathered from a consideration of how the borough is likely to shape itself with regard to making new roads, the grouping of commercial and social interests. This is shown by the importance of the southern approach to the Tower Bridge, and the new road is likely to become as important, as much used, and as widely known, as High Street, Borough. If so, the fact that it passes through Bermondsey for the most part of its length leaves us to feel that the name is as appropriate for the future purposes of the new borough as any name could possibly be.

It will be observed that the Rector founds his principal claim for the retention of the name of Bermondsey on the distinction of the ancient Abbey. This is a remarkable fact. In Bermondsey we are always coming back to the Abbey. It is the tradition to which we specially cling, and which we shall never again willingly suffer to "drop out of history." The incidents connected with the recent inquiry furnish the most striking proof of the force of historic evidence as enabling the imagination "to body forth the forms of things unseen." The "Forgotten Monastery," the memory of which Sir Walter Besant sought to revive, "not one stone of which now remains upon another" - this extinct foundation, this "shadow of a shade, whose very name has been given to another," to quote the words of Mrs. Boger, in "Bygone Southwark," is emerging from oblivion; this "airy nothing" is once more claiming for itself "a local habitation and a name." The name of Bermondsey Abbey is becoming familiar to many who had not previously heard of its existence.

The local authorities have now been officially informed not merely that this ancient quarter is to retain its designation, but that the new borough will be known as Bermondsey. Here, again, the decision is historically justified. Bermondsey Abbey furnishes the connecting link which binds the associated parishes together; it is the common tradition, the heritage in which all participate.

Rotherhithe once formed part of the great ecclesiastical manor; St. Thomas's possessed the famous hospital governed for centuries by the Priors and Abbots of Bermondsey; St. Olave's is rich in memories of spiritual magnates, friends and neighbours of the "Lords of Barmsey." The glory of Bermondsey Abbey, the

"Westminster of South London," is reflected upon all.

All - Rotherhithe, Horselydown, St. Olave's, St. Thomas's - have their ancient traditions, their legends, their memories of eminent persons, which they should sedulously cherish and regard as precious possessions. All these local histories are valuable; they are so many little rills, tributaries of the great stream of general history. It is the habit of certain "superior persons" to regard attachment to a particular locality as an indication of narrowness of mind. But no one need be ashamed of local patriotism. Attachment to the place in which we were born, or which has become endeared to us through long association, is perfectly compatible with pride in being citizens of this great Metropolis, in being Englishmen, in being subjects of that great Empire on which the sun never sets.

In concluding this humble and imperfect work, undertaken solely from love of the subject, we may be permitted to [hope that the creation of the new Borough of Bermondsey](#) will mark the commencement of a new era of prosperity and progress, and that all may learn to be proud of that venerable name.

St. Mary's Church, Rotherhithe

NOTES TO TEXT

Chapter V
This, be it observed, was not the famous "Horn Fair.": FamLoc note: See Records of the Woolwich District, vol. II, also published by FamLoc, for much information on this fair at Charlton.

Chapter XII
The seal of St. Olave's Grammar School is the old seal of Bermondsey Abbey: In consequence of the recent amalgamation of St. Saviour's Grammar School with St. Olave's.

Hope that the creation of the new Borough of Bermondsey: FamLoc note: Bermondsey did indeed retain its name in the new borough; it became the Metropolitan Borough of Bermondsey in 1900. That borough was abolished in 1965 when it became part of the London Borough of Southwark.

Printed in Great Britain
by Amazon